South Africa in Question

**EDITED BY
JOHN LONSDALE**

Director of Studies in History
Trinity College, Cambridge

AFRICAN STUDIES CENTRE
UNIVERSITY OF CAMBRIDGE

IN ASSOCIATION WITH

JAMES CURREY
LONDON

HEINEMANN
PORTSMOUTH (N.H.)

Published by University of Cambridge African Studies Centre (CASC)
Free School Lane, Cambridge CB2 3RQ

In association with

James Currey Ltd
54 Thornhill Square, Islington, London N1 1BE

Heinemann Educational Books Inc
70 Court Street, Portsmouth, New Hampshire 03801

British Library Cataloguing in Publication Data

South Africa in question.
   1. Apartheid — South Africa — History
   2. South Africa — Race relations — History
   I. Lonsdale, John   II. University of
Cambridge.   *African Studies Centre*
   323.1'68   DT763

   ISBN 0-85255-325-0 (James Currey Cased)
   ISBN 0-85255-326-9 (James Currey Paper)

Library of Congress Cataloguing-in-Publication Data

South Africa in question.

   Bibliography: p.
   Includes index.
   1. Apartheid—South Africa.   2. South Africa—
Politics and government—1978-   .   I. Lonsdale,
John.
DT763.S6428   1988   305.8'00968   87-29396
ISBN 0-435-08023-7 (Heinemann Inc Paper)

The extract from the poem 'Sounds of a Cowhide Drum' by Mbuyiseni Oswald Mtshali c
229 comes from the book of that title published by Renoster Books, Johannesburg in 19
Oxford University Press, London in 1972. It is reproduced by kind permission of
University Press.

Keyed in 10/12 Times by Ludgard De Decker, Paula Munro and Janet Seeley at the Univer
Cambridge African Studies Centre
in association with the University of Cambridge Computer Laboratory
and printed in Great Britain by Villiers Publications, London N1

Contents

Guides to Further Reading will be found at the end of each chapter

Pages which raise the central issues of each major theme may be found by reference to the entries under 'Questions' in the Index

LIST OF MAPS

Foreword

The African Studies Centre of the University of Cambridge is concerned principally with the support of research and with the coordination of interdisciplinary teaching on Africa within the University; it also acts as a home for the many African students we welcome yearly to Cambridge. In its more than twenty-year history the Centre has always seen it as one of its main duties to organise an annual course of public lectures on a major theme of African interest, so as to bring the problems and excitements of Africa to a wider audience. In recent years courses of lectures have been given on such topics as Ecology and Conservation, Health and Nutrition, Agrarian Systems, and Migration and Ethnicity. In the academical year 1986/87, a course of 15 lectures was given under the title 'Southern Africa: behind the Crisis'; twelve of the lectures are presented in this collection. Pressures of time and events have unfortunately prevented the publication of the other three. Wally Serote, poet and politician, started us off by outlining how the African National Congress approached the future, and has been busy helping to create that future ever since. Ian Linden then talked on the theme of Christian liberation and vested ecclesiastical interest, taking some brief hours off from running the Catholic Institute of International Relations. John Battersby, of the South African Morning Newspaper group, spoke at first hand on the struggles by the media, black and white, against the government's increasing determination to appropriate the truth – just before he was recalled home from London. Those who were lucky enough to hear their lectures will know that this collection is the poorer for their absence.

While all the talks reproduced here have subsequently been revised, some of them substantially so, it must be remembered that **all references to recent events are made from the standpoint of the period October 1986 to March 1987.**

This is the first of the Centre's lecture series to be published; it will surely not be the last. Such rapid publication would have been unthinkable without a degree of efficiency from the contributors which is not usually associated with academics, or without the support of the Centre's Director, John Sender and its Chairman, Ray Abrahams. And it would have been quite impossible without the heroic efforts of Bobbie Coe and the Centre's staff, Ludgard De Decker, Paula Munro and Janet Seeley, to all of whom I give my grateful admiration.

John Lonsdale
Member, Management Committee, African Studies Centre

Glossary of Abbreviations

AHI	Afrikaanse Handelsinstituut
ANC	African National Congress
ASSOCOM	Associated Chambers of Commerce
BLS	Botswana, Lesotho and Swaziland: formerly British territories, linked to South Africa in a Customs Union
CIIR	Catholic Institute of International Affairs
COSAS	Congress of South African Students
COSATU	Congress of South African Trade Unions
CUSA	Council of Unions of South Africa
DET	Department of Education and Training
EDA	Environmental and Development Agency
FCI	Federated Chambers of Industry
FedTraw	Federation of Transvaal Women
FLS	Frontline States
FRELIMO	Mozambique Liberation Front
GDP	Gross Domestic Product
HNP	Herstigte ('Purified') Nationale Party
IDAF	International Defence and Aid Fund
IDP	Industrial Development Point
JMC	Joint Management Centre (of the security system)
MAWU	Metal and Allied Workers' Union
MK	Umkhonto we Sizwe (military wing of the ANC)
MNR	National Resistance Movement (of Mozambique)
MPLA	Popular Movement for the Liberation of Angola
NECC	National Education Crisis Committee
NOW	Natal Organisation of Women
NP	National Party
OFS	Orange Free State

PAWO	Port Alfred Women's Organisation
RENAMO	alternative name for MN...
RSA	Republic of South Afric...
RSC	Regional Services Coun...
SAAU	South African Agricultu... Union (of white farmers...
SADCC	Southern African Development Coordinati... Conference
SADF	South African Defence Force
SAIRR	South African Institute ... Race Relations
SAP	South African Police
SPP	Surplus People Project (... research into forced removals)
SRC	Student Representative Council
SSC	State Security Council
SWAPO	South West Africa Peop... Organisation
TB	Tuberculosis
TBVC	Transkei, Bophuthatswan... Venda and Ciskei: the f... 'independent' Bantustans...
TRAC	Transvaal Rural Action Committee
UDF	United Democratic Front...
UG	Union Government
UNITA	National Union for the Total Independence of Angola
UP	United Party
UWCO	United Women's Congre... (of Cape Province)
UWO	United Women's Organisation (now withi... UWCO)
VD	Venereal disease
VOW	*Voice of Women* (journa... of ANC women's sectio...

Notes on Contributors

Neil Andersson is director of the Centre of Tropical Disease Research at the University of Guerrero in Mexico. An epidemiologist, he is author of *Namibian Health Sector Policy Options* (UN Institute for Namibia, 1984) and, with Shula Marks, of *Apartheid and Health* (World Health Organisation, 1983).

William Beinart teaches history at Bristol University, is an editor of the *Journal of Southern African Studies* and the author of many studies of South African rural history including *The Political Economy of Pondoland 1860-1930* (Cambridge, 1982); with Peter Delius and Stanley Trapido: *Putting a Plough to the Ground* (Johannesburg, 1986); and, with Colin Bundy: *Hidden Struggles in Rural South Africa* (London, 1987).

Gavin Cawthra left South Africa in 1977 in order to avoid conscription into the armed defence of apartheid, and is active in the Committee on South African War Resistance. He has written a number of studies on the region's militarisation, including *Brutal Force: the Apartheid War Machine* (London, 1986).

Frene Ginwala has been active in the cause of the African National Congress since the 1960s, when she was forced to leave South Africa. She has published a number of works on the South African situation including, for the United Nations, a study of the press in 1972.

Elizabeth Gunner lectures in Commonwealth literature at the University of London. She has published a *Teachers' Guide to African Literature* and, with H.L.B. Moodie and E. Finnegan, *A Handbook for Teaching African Literature*. She has worked extensively on Zulu praise poetry in its cultural context both past and present, and is engaged on a biography of the Zulu prophet Isaiah Shembe.

Adam Kuper is Professor of Social Anthropology at Brunel University, after having taught at Universities in Uganda, Holland, Sweden and the USA. He is the author of a number of books, the most recent being *Wives for Cattle: Bridewealth and Marriage in southern Africa* (London, 1982) and *South Africa and the Anthropologist* (London, 1987).

Merle Lipton, Research Fellow of the Centre for International Studies at the London School of Economics, has previously been attached to Sussex, Johns Hopkins and Yale universities and to Chatham House. She is author of *Capitalism and Apartheid: South Africa 1910-1986* (paperback, 1986) and of the forthcoming Economist Intelligence Unit report, 'Sanctions against South Africa'.

John Lonsdale teaches history at the University of Cambridge and has written a number of studies on East African and African history. He is currently working on the history of the Mau Mau rising in colonial Kenya.

Shula Marks is Director of the Institute of Commonwealth Studies and Professor of Commonwealth history at the University of London. She has written widely and edited a number of studies of South African history, being herself the author of *Reluctant Rebellion* (Oxford, 1970) and *The Ambiguities of Dependence in South Africa* (Baltimore, 1986).

Colin Murray teaches in the field of Third World development at the University of Liverpool. Author of the study of migrant labour from Lesotho, *Families Divided* (Cambridge, 1981), he is currently writing a history of the Thaba 'Nchu district, Orange Free State, based on field and archival research.

Roger C. Riddell is a Research Fellow of the Overseas Development Institute, London. He was formerly Chief Economist of the Confederation of Zimbabwe Industries and Chairman of the Presidential Commission into Incomes, Prices and Conditions of Service in Zimbabwe. Author of many works on southern Africa's economic problems, his most recent book is *Foreign Aid Reconsidered* (London, 1987).

Christopher Saunders teaches history at the University of Cape Town. He has published widely on South African history and is author of the forthcoming book on South African historiography, *The Making of the South African Past*.

Elaine Unterhalter is a Senior Research Officer in the Department of Sociology at the University of Essex. She has written extensively on South African Women, edited the Anti-Apartheid Movement Women's Committee newsletter and is author of *Forced Removal: the segregation, division and control of the people of South Africa* (London, 1987).

Harold Wolpe is Reader in Sociology at the University of Essex and co-ordinator of the London Education Committee of the African National Congress. He has published widely on the contemporary political economy of South Africa, including the forthcoming *Race, Class and the Apartheid State*.

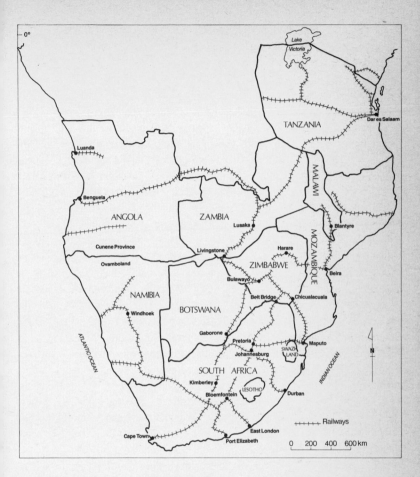

Map 1 *South Africa, with Bantustans*

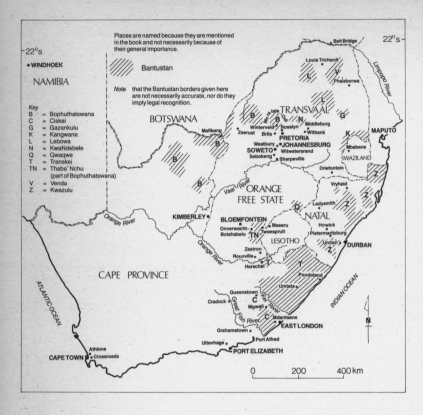

Map 2 *Southern Africa: South Africa and the SADCC countries*

Introduction: South Africa in Question

JOHN LONSDALE

Aim

South Africa is in crisis, perhaps in a revolutionary situation. The state has lost almost all its legitimacy, even amongst those one would imagine to be its most fervent supporters; its government has no clear vision of the future with which to invite a wider allegiance; and its power appears to be based increasingly upon force. More and more of South Africa's black population (and not a few among its whites) have withdrawn their support from the institutions by which their values and identities were previously moulded and their actions constrained. Events, in consequence, seem at times to be moving very fast indeed. Everybody who reads a newspaper knows that. The contributors to this book were asked **not** to recount these day-to-day events of the crisis, but to analyse the deeper structures of conflict which lie beneath its surface. For these have had a much longer history than the present political upheaval and are likely to have a more intractable future. South Africa's structures are not going to be easy to change, whatever the strength of political will which is applied either to their reform or to their revolution. At this very moment however, if in very contradictory ways, women, mothers, workers, peasants, capitalists, army conscripts, health-workers, students, poets and intellectuals – all of whom will be met in these pages – are themselves putting the future of their own particular South Africa in question. Even those who are oppressed by apartheid will disagree on their vision of the future, their definition of liberation; some of them may indeed find that their self-interest seems best tied to the social structures which apartheid has so painfully created. If many different futures are in question, we must ourselves then question the past which has brought into being so contested a present.

The public lecture series on which this book is based was designed to introduce academics and other experts on South Africa to an intelligent lay audience, so as to oblige them to present their most deeply considered thoughts in as plain as possible a form. Each of the chapters which follow represents a fifty-minute lecture, printed more or less as it was delivered, with a minimum of reference matter but with suggestions for further reading. Each is designed to be used as the starting point for group discussion, whether in class or in meeting-room. Equally, this book will introduce in brief compass – to readers who have not got time for more – the research findings of scholars who will have written, or who are about to write, a full-length study of the issues which they have compressed into a chapter here. The University's African Studies Centre invited as speakers people who are well known for their questioning role in the study of South Africa, a country whose future is very much in question. The title of the book is intended to convey this double meaning.

The opening lecture was given by Wally Serote, a poet who finds he must also be a politician, a relationship explored by our last contributor, Liz Gunner. Serote talked of the ANC's perspective on change in South Africa. But politicians have more urgent demands on their time than the writing of treatises, so the ANC's views on the future are not directly represented here. It is true that the majority of our contributors are South African exiles, whether black or white, who have distanced themselves from their native land for the sake of conscience and, some of them, from necessity. Their scholarship cannot be other than politically committed (indeed, it is difficult to think of any scholarship anywhere which is not), but even those chapters which are written by active members of the ANC are not political programmes; even Frene Ginwala's eloquence does not claim to unlock the mystery of the future. Nor is there any other political blueprint here, whether from the ruling party or from any of its other opponents: the overriding mood of the book is one of informed uncertainty. But politicians are, after all, in the business of making their views known to anybody who cares to listen; and people who are concerned with the future of South Africa will already know what they say. This book is designed, rather, to help those interested students and members of the public to listen more critically to the politicians, to question them more acutely, and to read tomorrow's newspapers with a sharper eye.

The book starts with the past, with the intellectual and ideological struggles which underpinned and questioned the building of white supremacy and industrial capitalism. For the past is never sufficient unto itself; its ideologies tend to outlive the political demands which gave them birth. Present-day South Africans are the victims not only of contemporary nightmares but also of those once dreamed by powerful yet haunted men who are long since dead. The past always constructs the future, but which past and which future is still very much in question, for the present always has the power to reconstruct the past. That is why the educationalists of black emancipation, discussed by Harold Wolpe towards the end of the book, have produced, as their first new school syllabus, a new history of South Africa. They understand, much better indeed than people who have never been consciously oppressed, how necessary it is to rediscover the past, to people it anew with men and women now silenced or demeaned by their rulers' self-regarding histories[1] – if the disregarded men and women of today, especially South Africa's literally and scandalously 'surplus people', are ever to dare to attempt to recover their future.

The middle chapters, by Gavin Cawthra, Roger Riddell and Frene Ginwala, detail the bitter course and consequences of the present crisis, both within South Africa and beyond, and call for the mitigation of its destructive effects by international action. In their accounts we can see the past come to angry fruition. They deal with much of the present agenda. But the remaining chapters, the bulk of the book, have as much to do with the questions which remain unanswered for the future. They are concerned with the forms of human life which the South African state has tried to impose, whether deliberately or by malign neglect and which South African men and women are struggling to endure or overcome and, in overcoming, to create new forms of political community, whether by private ingenuity or professional expertise, in mass organisation or in popular song.

The questions in South Africa

What South Africans now have the power to make of themselves is largely determined by what their previous generations made of the past. But that past is radically uncertain in character, as our first three contributors in particular show. In his survey of how successive historians have tried to explain the peculiarities of the successive South Africas in which they lived, **Christopher Saunders** reveals how fundamentally scholars could disagree, even when they only considered

---

[1] For a recent account of such self-regarding history see, Leonard Thompson, *The Political Mythology of Apartheid* (Yale University Press: New Haven and London, 1985).

3

the most obvious historical actors, the white communities as a whole and those small minorities in their midst who organised the country's economic exploitation. Has white supremacy always been fatally flawed, even on its own terms, founded on a contradiction between archaic minority control and a would-be modernising capitalist expansion? Or have the oppressions inherent in white domination guaranteed the only kind of capitalist growth which was historically possible in an economy based on mineral extraction, requiring vast amounts of cheap labour from out of a peasant population? Or, in the insurrectionary present in which South Africa now finds itself, are these, as Saunders concludes by suggesting, quite the wrong questions? How far, instead, did the early practices of racial segregation and migrant male black labour reflect not so much a white strategy of dominance as a black determination to resist proletarianisation? And how far are the more recent phases of apartheid an ideological disguise for an uncontrollable reality – an unacknowleged autonomy of black urban life in 'white' South Africa? It is difficult to square the cultural vibrance of Lewis Nkosi's 'Fabulous Decade' of the 1950s, discussed in Gunner's last chapter, with omnipresent white control. The social history of modern *black* South Africa has only begun to be written.

One can begin to see some of the inner uncertainties of white power in **Adam Kuper**'s chapter on anthropology and apartheid. Not only has the profession been divided between its Afrikaner and English-speaking scholars, between a stress on inherited culture and one on changing social function, but the Afrikaner ideologists, he shows, found it impossible to reconcile their respect for African cultures with either a belief in white superiority or with its material consequence, the black poverty with which they came face to face in their field work. And this, he implies, is of vital importance when one comes to the question of the future of apartheid. One of its chief architects, Prime Minister Verwoerd, had earlier been the professor of Sociology at the University of Stellenbosch. In his case, the organising power of his ideas clearly helped to organise his idea of power. But if power loses its central idea, how can it continue to be organised other than as a mere force – a theme which is later taken up by Gavin Cawthra?

It is not just at the ideological level that white power is riven with doubt, although that is perhaps the most vital weakness in any ruling regime. **Merle Lipton**'s chapter, a summary of the main argument in her recent book of the same title, is an eloquent restatement of the liberal historians' thesis analysed by Saunders, that there is a conflict between an expanding capitalist economy and the repressive politics of minority white supremacy. But it is important to be clear what Lipton is and is not saying. She does not say that some, an increasing number, of white capitalists are closet non-racial democrats. She argues, rather, that until very recently South African capitalism was internally divided with regard to black labour and the size of the domestic market. In the past decade, however, thanks to the increasing sophistication of South African capitalism as a whole and to the rising anger and determination of black workers, the interests of white employers have begun to converge. They are now more ready to accept progressive industrial relations and rising standards of consumption – and therefore real wages – among South Africa's blacks. But we must not expect that the political consequences of this economic interest will be actively pressed by capitalists; their overriding preoccupation lies in stability, and in trimming their sails to the prevailing political wind. It is up to blacks to change that wind by taking advantage of whatever greater room for manoeuvre the expanding needs of capitalism may have opened up for them. Wolpe's chapter on education justifies Lipton's argument that capitalist self-interest may have unintended consequences in sharpening black opposition; but the limits of purely capitalist-inspired reform are underlined in Ginwala's chapter and in our next, by Cawthra.

The South African regime is at war, both with its own people and with its neighbours. Appropriately enough, but to an extent which is not sufficiently realised by western public opinion, the government itself and the institutions of white society have been extensively militarised. That is the central message of **Gavin Cawthra**, a consciencious objector active in assisting fellow whites of military age who follow him into exile. His chapter here summarises his recent book, *Brutal Force*. His thesis expands on the argument of preceding chapters, that the South African state is beset with internal contradiction. The army's national security doctrine is coherent and sophisticated. It is based on the realisation that internal war cannot be won on the battlefield alone (especially when guerrilla opponents are so careful to avoid pitched battles) but must be fought on the field of political allegiance as well. This belief lay behind the recent extension of a communal franchise to South Africa's Indians and 'coloureds'. It is doubtless one of the calculations behind the policy of forcing 'independence' on the Bantustans. But where, as in Namibia or in the townships which sprawl around the white cities, the government has no worthwhile concessions to offer, the army and the police have no

5

instrument of control other than force. And that defeats its own object, as South Africa's generals very well know from their study of people's war elsewhere in the world.

Just how far, and how little, South Africa is prepared to go in prosecuting its external war with its black neighbours is explored by **Roger Riddell**. The theme of contradiction and doubt is nowhere more clearly visible than here. The black states of southern Africa have suffered enormous losses from South Africa's deliberate policy of destabilisation. But, Riddell suggests, the South African government is caught in the tension between its need for military security, which requires that its neighbours be forced to their knees, unable to act as secure external bases for guerrilla war, and the economic benefits it enjoys from the regional market. He concludes that we have to examine very cautiously the warnings from western leaders, that South Africa will merely export northwards the costs it will incur from any more comprehensive international campaign for economic sanctions.

Such a campaign is **Frene Ginwala**'s concluding demand. It has recently, in July 1987, been backed by the second annual conference of the Congress of South African Trades Unions, representing the people who will be hit most directly by any deepening of the existing economic recession. Ginwala's perspective reinforces Riddell's opening observation, that the South African crisis is clouded with misinformation, by which sectional propaganda is transmuted into conventional wisdom. She takes in turn the various western objections to sanctions and shows how they stem from the west's self-interest rather than from its professed concern with the interests of the blacks of South Africa. Above all, and this is the crucial and hardest point for a western (and white) readership to grasp, she demands clear thinking on whom we accept as the legitimate authors of political change. If we resist sanctions, she urges, then we must believe – however much we may protest that we mean no such thing – that the white minority government retains the right to prescribe what it thinks best for the future. Sanctions, on the other hand, are the most practical assistance that outsiders can give to blacks who have committed their own energies, and their lives, as historical actors in their own right, to the struggle for revolution. Reform offers no fence to sit on.

The rest of the book shows just how difficult either thoroughgoing reform or an even more thoroughgoing revolution must inevitably be. Our remaining contributors look into the underside of the crisis. The first six chapters were concerned principally with what one may call the high politics of the problem: the conflicts between different sections of capital, between businessmen and politicians, between politicans and generals, between the international strategies of revolution and reform. From now on we are more interested in deep politics, the experiences and struggles of ordinary people obliged by circumstance to organise themselves into their own complex, local constituencies of interest, which may or may not coincide with the generalised programmes which their high-political leaderships are obliged to invent for them.

Colin Murray's chapter describes the single most appalling contemporary experience for the majority of South Africa's peoples. The forced removal of millions of 'surplus people' from their places of livelihood in recent years is a sharp reminder that while modern capitalism may need better skilled workers it can also make do with fewer of them, especially in times of recession. And South Africa's huge underclass, as it has now become, has no votes with which to influence the government and therefore no redistributional welfare payments to relieve its poverty. Murray also reminds us how carefully we must question both official statements and our own preconceptions. The repeal of the pass laws does most emphatically not mean freedom of movement for black workers; and Bantustans are rural slums, not peasant arcadias. But his account raises more difficult questions still, the fuller exploration of which is one of the many dimensions of the crisis which is absent from this collection.

With the Bantustans we enter a looking-glass world where nothing is quite what it seems and reality is difficult to identify. On the one hand they appear to be the pawns of a cynical regime. Bits of them are chopped up and allocated to a neighbour, their inhabitants are given invented identities, leaderships are conjured up from nowhere and fattened up with licences, loans and subsidies. But beneath the farce lies tragedy. For invented identities can come to embody real conflicts, especially when the resources at issue are so meagre. Africans really are divided by local competitions, it is not all done by mirrors. Local businessmen who hope to enjoy a protected market under the flag of Bantustan 'independence' can be violently opposed by working families who need free access to the white cities and whose cause is, improbably, championed by their local royal family. Bantustan nationalism can result in brutal chauvinism against residents of the wrong 'tribe'. All nationalisms are political inventions, not just in

Africa. Afrikaners are an invented people, an imagined community,[2] but no more so than the Ndebele, Tswana, Xhosa or Zulu. How far has the 'South African nation' in fact been invented by the economic integration in which, in their different ways, both white liberal and Marxist historians have trusted, or by the persuasive passion of the ANC and the UDF? How many nations are there now in South Africa and how many could there be? A nationality can be fused by revolution; it may also be torn apart. This is a question to which we will have to return.

William Beinart's contribution gives some indication of just how difficult a question this may be. For while we may imagine that South Africa's industrialisation – so much more complete than anywhere else in Africa – has uprooted the majority of Africans from the land, he shows that their experience has in fact been predominantly rural, even if much of the 'countryside' is now a commuters' slum. Blacks have indeed been largely separated from the possibility of their own production on their own property, but not entirely. They retain the potential of attachment to a local identity which confers rights to specific, historically hallowed, resources. Local nationalisms could well form around the effective presence of agrarian constituencies which would have to be consulted if any new South Africa (and the experience of other revolutionary states elsewhere in the modern world is not altogether auspicious) were not to suffer crippling food shortages. These local constituencies might have already been strengthened in any deepening of the revolutionary crisis, as peasants reoccupied white farmland and staked their claims to communal control. Beinart raises this possibility even now, in the context of the independent but contributory crisis of drought and recession, which perhaps affects marginal white farmers (through strains on their credit) more than blacks. Murray has similarly observed that some white farmers are quite prepared to liquidate their debts by a state-funded allocation of their land to expanded Bantustans. The greater visibility of conflict in the townships should not blind us to this continuing struggle on the land. It is not inconceivable that the present regime might try to mitigate agrarian conflict by coopting black capitalists into commercial farming, in parallel with its present strategy in the towns. This would

---

[2]   All students of nationalism ought to read Benedict Anderson, *Imagined Communities: Reflections on the Origin and Spread of Nationalism* (Verso: London, 1983).

be politically immensely difficult, but such reform would create still greater obstacles to revolution. Between rural capitalism (perhaps in the shape of state farms) and aroused peasant smallholders any new regime would have to steer a tortuous course.

Elaine Unterhalter confirms the foreboding of South Africa's generals, that unmediated counter-revolutionary violence will merely radicalise the opposition. Nor is that popular resistance confined to blacks alone. Some white mothers are appalled by what their conscript sons are being ordered to do in the streets of black townships, if not quite so appalled as black mothers who are on the receiving end. But women's political activism is more deeply rooted than in resistance to the present overt brutality. There is a much longer history of apartheid's silent violence – as our next chapter explains in the field of disease. Through the pass laws and their separation of families, apartheid has borne most heavily on black women; even African 'customary' law has been hardened against them. In other revolutionary situations, too, women have come to the fore, if only because the very survival of their households, in the midst of a social dislocation which puts the responsibility more squarely upon them, demands more defensive courage. Women's actions have obliged the ANC to consider more directly their claims to be the mothers of the future; they have inevitably put women's emancipation on to the agenda of liberation. But how far the restructuring of gender relations will not only forward the revolution but also survive its coming must remain for the time being an unanswerable question; the experience of other revolutions is not always happy.

There can be no clearer revelation of the power relations of apartheid than in the history of disease and medicine offered by **Shula Marks** and **Neil Andersson**. Disease has a social and political history as much as an epidemiological one. Its social history in South Africa presents a devastating indictment of the racially unequal distribution of public resources, especially in the current era of forced removals, the substitution of labour by capital, drought and recession. Africans' already meagre entitlement to public goods has been reduced still further in the rural areas, if the monstrously high levels of infant mortality are (and they are) a reliable guide. As in the field of possible future agrarian change so here, too, the remedies seem to point in opposite social directions. On the one hand, officially sanctioned reform appears to encourage the privatisation of health care for the minority among blacks, the regularly employed. On the other, a few brave doctors – backed up by some of the women's organisations mentioned in the previous chapter – are running clandestine surgeries for the victims of police action. In thus keeping activists out of the security dragnet, professional medicine is serving the people and their future rather than the present structure of power.

The complexities of keeping life going while at the same time challenging public institutions are also illustrated by the contemporary struggle for popular education. **Harold Wolpe**'s chapter provides further material germane to the themes of the unintended outcomes of reform and the uncertain questions of revolution which appear and reappear throughout the book. The apartheid programme of Bantu Education, designed to keep the Natives in their Proper Place, can have few equals in the diverting history of rulers tripping up on their own defences. Africans rebelled against their narrow educational bounds with the defiance of Black Consciousness; the schools expansion which provided industry with more semi-skilled workers furnished, as well, the educated youth who could help to coordinate resistance. But how resistance can be translated into progress is a ticklish question. The school boycott campaign of the later 1970s and early '80s, 'after Soweto', dramatised the illegitimacy of the existing regime but did nothing to enlarge popular opportunity and accountability in education. But the alternative strategy which is now being tried raises as many questions as it answers. In the present, how far is it possible to use the state school system, even for radically new approaches to learning, and even subject to the proviso that the army and police be withdrawn, without conceding the state's ultimate right of control? And, in the unpredictable future, how long will what one might call these educational soviets – just as one might talk of women's, peasant or township soviets – survive the imposition of a new state authority with a revolutionary legitimacy? Revolutions have a habit of consuming their children.

All states, all nations, are theatres, stages for cultural drama. An oppressive state is known by its closure of the stage to all but the leading actors, its obediently drilled choruses and index of banned books. A nation needs a plurality of voices, mutually intelligible but not for ever repeating the same tunes. **Elizabeth Gunner** ends our enquiry by asking whether South Africa's poets, songwriters and novelists are even now crowding on to the same stage and forging, by free experimentation, a mutually illuminating language from out of apartheid's polyglot discord of tongues. They have, as she shows us, a marvellously rich past to draw on, in which artists with a humane vision have been able to break down the internal containing walls of the system. All who were at her lecture were thrilled by her recording of the massed singing of the simple Anglo-Zulu refrain, 'Hlanganani: Come Together People of Africa'. It is a great loss that we cannot reproduce its cadences within the covers of a book.

There is one other feature of the lectures which cannot be reproduced here: the vigorous, impassioned but mutually respectful debate, rich with readily seized local allusion, metaphor and wit, which took place in the lecture hall and, afterwards, in the bar, between black and white South Africans, students and lecturers – and to which the English who were present could contribute only as hesitant outsiders. We were witnessing an emphatically **national**, patriotic, discourse which made humane nonsense of apartheid.

This example of instructive dialogue in an intellectually free environment raises a final question, particularly insistent for an academic readership: ought one's concern for the future of South Africa, and for its present agony, to be expressed in an intellectual boycott? One of our contributors, Adam Kuper, answered the question one way; Frene Ginwala argued, but not dogmatically, the claims of the other. At the moment, the ANC is inclined to distinguish between intellectuals who are in some costly way committed to liberation and those who are politically silent on their fence. It is a difficult question. If academics take our profession seriously, if we believe that truth has not only the power to set people free but can itself only be sought in freedom, then we must reject self-censorship and, by extension, the censorship of others. If we believe, as we must, in the power of free ideas to discredit unjust power; if we also accept the historical responsibility of the west, of Great Britain especially, in helping to create South Africa's white supremacy; if we admit that our own societies are tainted by racial injustice, then we cannot say that South Africa's problems are not also ours in a very intimate way, not just at the arm's length of international relations. Our own students give us a generous example of sanctions-busting by voluntarily funding black South African students' education in the west, believing, and not arrogantly, that each can learn from the other.

These reflections seem to make an incontrovertible case for distinguishing between an illegitimate regime with which one can have no dealing, and the individual patriots of what must some day be a free nation, with whom all intellectually and ideologically liberating contacts should be encouraged. It is, alas, not as simple as that. For all modern states strengthen their authority by interventions in civil society, by means of institutional privileges and public subsidy. One cannot therefore escape the issue of responsible authority – or authority which claims to be responsible for whatever apparently private transactions occur within, and between, civil societies. It is the essence of a revolutionary situation that authority is contested; it is not testable by constitutionally democratic means, the only known way of arriving at some poor approximation to political accountability to human needs. It is clear that intellectual truth must be guarded by all means against cooptation by a South African regime which is anxious to seize on any evidence which suggests acceptance of its legitimate authority: that is the problem which faces the current black strategy of 'people's education for people's power' within the state school system, as opposed to the previous schools boycott.

But does that mean that all academic interchange with South Africa must then seek the approval of another, revolutionary, authority which is also, for the moment, untestable by open constitutional means? The most, surely, that independent scholars can agree is that the ANC and other opponents of apartheid have earned, by costly sacrifice, the right to have their views taken seriously into account in any decision that we ourselves may take. To concede more than this, to grant unquestioned authority to a political body, is to allow it a right of unaccountable power which the ANC itself vigorously disclaims and which would, if granted, imply a wretched outlook for an ANC-ruled South Africa. The ANC has no wish to make our decisions for us. There is no escape therefore, in this as in other matters, from personal responsibility. The answer to this final question must, then, be given by our personal judgment which, crucially, one must be prepared publicly to justify in open discussion with those whose more costly efforts to bring justice to South Africa may be affected by our actions. In so fundamentally contested a situation there can be no middle ground. But in the end the decision has to be ours, each one of us.

1. Historians & Apartheid

CHRISTOPHER SAUNDERS

It is now ten years since Harrison Wright published his survey of controversies then current in South African historical writing. In *The Burden of the Present* he argued that historians of South Africa had allowed themselves to be so influenced by present concerns that they had over-simplified and so distorted the past. They should instead deliberately distance themselves from the present and, as far as possible, study the past on its own terms. Many historians of South Africa have indeed distanced themselves from the present and written detailed studies of little more than antiquarian interest. But those historians who have produced the more important work have not followed Wright's advice. Instead, they have in effect agreed with Edward Carr, who, in a lecture delivered at Cambridge a quarter of a century ago, said that 'history consists', and Carr implied that history, properly conceived, *should* so consist, 'essentially in seeing the past through the eyes of the present, in the light of its problems'. The more important historians of South Africa have seen the recovery of a past relevant to the present as a challenge rather than a burden. That South African historians of the past decade and more have been responsible for some of the liveliest and most exciting work done anywhere is in considerable part due, surely, to the very fact that they have been so profoundly influenced by the changing present. How indeed could it be otherwise, when the moral and political issues are so clear-cut, and the meaning of the past is so contested in the present?

The relationship between historians of South Africa and their presents will, I hope, emerge as a sub-theme of this chapter, for I intend to approach the debate about the relationship between white supremacy and economic growth historiographically. Though historians only became aware of such a debate in 1970, it is necessary, in order to place that debate in context, first to consider some aspects of historical writing in the century or so preceding 1970. Thereafter I shall

---

All the authors mentioned in the text will be found in the list of 'Further Reading' at the end of the chapter.

have to consider not only historians, but also what a number of semi-historians and non-historians wrote about the past - and about the present and the future, for the debate was by no means confined either to historians or to the past.

At least until the 1920s, and in a sense far beyond that, South African historical writing was dominated by the giant figure of the amateur historian George McCall Theal, who wrote most of his *History of South Africa* in the last three decades of the nineteenth century. That *History* was essentially the story of the triumph of white settlement in southern Africa, which Theal hoped would be capped by the reconciliation of English-speakers and Afrikaners. He was an historian of colonial nationalism, his nation - an adopted one, for he was Canadian by birth and upbringing - being that of white South Africa. That is not to say he ignored blacks - he gave them more attention than most later writers in the settler tradition he founded - but they were, in his eyes, barbarous, they had achieved nothing of significance and were almost always the cause of trouble. To help justify and legitimate white rule in South Africa, Theal propagated various myths that were to enjoy a long life, most notably that there had been an almost simultaneous arrival in the country of whites from the south and Africans from the north, or that when whites had entered the interior in the 1830s, it had been empty. For this late Victorian the establishment of white supremacy was essentially part of what he called 'the law of progress'; it did not require further explanation, and his *History* was largely descriptive, concerned merely to record those events - mainly political ones - which he thought significant.

Liberal historians

The new school of history-writing which emerged in the 1920s under the leadership of William Miller Macmillan developed in large part in reaction against Theal's brand of history. The historians of the new school were professionals, - Macmillan himself, trained at Oxford and in Germany, was Professor of History at the University of the Witwatersrand from 1917 to 1932. They sought to be more analytical than Theal, and to ask why South African history had taken the course it had. Macmillan rejected Theal's pro-colonist standpoint, his easy assumption that the establishment of white supremacy was right and proper, and many of his myths. Whereas Theal had accepted the racial order established in South Africa in his lifetime, Macmillan was critical of it. He not only searched the past for an explanation of South Africa's present ills, but also used his historical work to fight political battles in the present. His historical work of the 1920s was designed to challenge the segregationist policies of General Hertzog, Prime Minister from 1924. It told of how in the early nineteenth century Cape those called Coloureds had begun to be incorporated into Cape society, and Macmillan drew the lesson that in the twentieth century Africans could be incorporated progressively in a similar way as equal citizens in the Union of South Africa.

Macmillan was the first to assert the importance of economics in the country's history. One of his main arguments for the incorporation of Africans into a common political system was that the main theme in the country's history of the past century or more had been the growth of a single economy. The segregationist measures Hertzog proposed could not possibly be just - as some who called themselves liberals suggested in the mid-1920s - for economic growth had promoted, and continued to promote, integration. Segregation must inevitably, then, be a cloak masking repression. Territorial segregation might have been possible a century earlier, Macmillan allowed, but economic integration had now gone so far that what Hertzog proposed must mean *baasskap*, crude white domination. Macmillan was, then, the first to point to an apparent contradiction between the integration being promoted by the development of one economy, and the segregationist measures of the government; economic integration, he argued, was incompatible with policies designed to keep people apart.

Yet the theme of economic integration was not one which Macmillan investigated in any depth, nor did he explain how there had been increasing economic integration, on the one hand, yet on the other the development of racist policies which aimed to prevent such integration. And though he began to seek the roots of South African racism, he did so only in passing: only a few paragraphs in his *Agrarian Problem* lectures of 1919, and then in *The Cape Colour Question* and *Complex South Africa* began to argue that in the tradition, culture and character of the trekboer, the semi-nomadic frontiersman of the eighteenth century, was to be found the essential explanation for the racist policies being implemented in his own day, which he found so abhorrent. Eric Walker, who held the history chair at Cape Town in the 1920s and early 1930s, took up Macmillan's points and elaborated the theme which remained, until the 1970s, central to the liberal view of the way South Africa had developed.

Walker knew how Frederick Jackson Turner had in his famous lecture explained the course of American development in terms of the influence of the American frontier. In a lecture he delivered at Oxford in 1930, Walker made a central theme of Macmillan's idea that the origins of twentieth century racism, which he assumed explained the segregationist policies then being implemented, were to be found in the character of the early Afrikaner on the eighteenth century Cape frontier. By Walker's account, it was on the frontier that the trekboers had come to identify themselves as whites, superior to a black enemy, and the strong racial identity and prejudice then forged had been carried into the interior by the Voortrekkers in the 1830s and then been enshrined in the constitutions of the Orange Free State and the South African Republic, which proclaimed no equality in church or state between white and black. That the British in Natal were as racist as the trekkers was something most English-speaking liberals tended to ignore; there was an anti-Afrikaner element to their explanation of why things had gone wrong. By the twentieth century, by Walker's account, these same ideas and prejudices, forged in the eighteenth century, had come to dominate the Union founded in 1910, and they were, as he wrote in 1930, successfully challenging the Cape's non-racial tradition. Walker and his fellow liberals believed that the frontier ideas that lay behind the segregationist policies buttressing white supremacy were out of place in the modern world. There was, they implied, a contradiction between the old racism and the new forces of change, including the new economic growth. Segregationist policies, designed to preserve white supremacy in all fields of life, were hangovers from a past age, and were explained at the level of ideas, as the product of irrational white fears originating on a distant frontier, though now reproduced in the towns, to which the new trekkers - the poor Afrikaners - had moved in recent decades. But it was essentially the old fears, in Walker's view, that were leading the new trekkers to erect boundaries against black advancement.

The idea of a contradiction between an old racism and new forces of change was taken over and carried further by C.W. de Kiewiet, Macmillan's most brilliant student, in his masterly *History of South Africa: Social and Economic* (1941). Segregation, wrote de Kiewiet, had been tried since the days of van Riebeeck, founder of white settlement in the 1650s, and had never worked, for the forces bringing people together had always been stronger than the attempts to keep them apart. De Kiewiet followed Macmillan in believing that the history of South Africa had been one of growing interaction between people, and incorporation into one economic system. De Kiewiet may, too, have been influenced by the economic argument advanced by Herbert Frankel, a friend of his, in the *South African Journal of Economics* in 1927, an argument much used by those who challenged slavery in the early nineteenth century, that cheap labour was inefficient labour; therefore the segregationist devices to keep African labour cheap did not in fact promote economic growth.[1] But by the time he wrote his *History* there was another reason why de Kiewiet assumed that segregation could not work: the growth of secondary industry.

Before the 1930s, the economy was almost entirely based on agriculture and, from the late nineteenth century, mining - there was no more than a minute manufacturing sector. But after 1933, having left the gold standard and, in effect, devalued its currency, South Africa quickly pulled itself out of depression, and manufacturing industry for the first time began to grow rapidly. Liberals took heart from this: politically there seemed, after the implementation of Hertzog's segregationist measures in 1936, little hope of their achieving their goals, but it now seemed the economy could gradually achieve those goals for them. The growth of manufacturing industry would require more and more skilled labour. Given the small size of the white community, more and more blacks would have to be trained for such jobs. Migrancy would not be possible if skills had to be learned, and so blacks would have to be allowed to settle in the towns. So industrialisation and permanent African urbanisation seemed to go together, and permanent urban residents would, it was assumed, have to be given educational opportunities and welfare benefits, possibly even political rights. Colour bars, customary and statutory, would necessarily disappear, higher wages would have to be paid, and not only to those blacks who got skilled jobs, for the new manufacturing would need an ever-expanding domestic market, and, to make it possible for the mass of blacks to consume as well as be producers, they would have to be paid a decent wage. So it seemed that racial discrimination affecting jobs, education and access to the cities would go, and that South Africa would eventually, as a result of the operation of economic forces, be freed from racism.

This was far from being - as some later critics were to imply - a major argument in de Kiewiet's *History*, and it was essentially an *a*

---

[1]   I thank Saul Dubow for this point.

priori one, for secondary industry was new, and the evidence was not yet available on what the relationship between it and the state's racial policies would be. When de Kiewiet suggested the two were in conflict, he was not making an historical point relating to what had happened in the past, but a political one, against the segregationism then being introduced. Because of his opposition to segregation, he did not stress that in the early decades of the century the implementation of segregationist measures had in fact accompanied early industrial growth, though evidence on that was to be found in his *History*. Such evidence was also to be found in Frankel's book on capital investment in Africa, published in 1938, and in a book published soon after de Kiewiet's *History* by another economist, Sheila van der Horst. Both Frankel and van der Horst assumed, along with other liberals, that in the future there would be a growing incompatibility between industrial growth and the racial policies that underpinned white supremacy - but they did not fail to see that in the past such policies - and in particular those that provided and controlled a regimented labour-force - had been at the centre of the development of the mines and the commercialisation of agriculture.

In the early 1940s - in the interests of economic growth during a time of war - various aspects of segregation were relaxed, the job colour bar, the pass laws, restrictions on industrial action by Africans, and liberals could hope that their predictions were beginning to come true. But by the end of the war the old measures had been re-imposed, along with new ones, and then in the decades after the election of the National Party government in 1948 apartheid unfolded, extending racial discrimination into almost every area of life. Apartheid was in part a response to the increased black urbanisation during the war, a device to to control the effects of industrialisation and to prevent the breaking down of racial barriers. But the economic growth did not decline: there was a major crisis of confidence following the Sharpeville massacre in 1960, but then South Africa entered a new period of boom in the middle and late 1960s, when the growth rate was said to be second only to that of Japan, and manufacturing grew apace.

Yet liberals did not change their view that in the long run economic growth would destroy apartheid. As it became clear in the 1950s that there was no hope of removing the Nationalists at the polls, that view became, if anything, stronger. The very boom of the 1960s encouraged some liberals to elaborate the old argument about the incompatibility of economic growth and segregation/apartheid, and to predict far-reaching changes as a result of the development of the economy. In 1964 Michael O'Dowd of the Anglo-American Corporation advanced what some dubbed the Oppenheimer thesis: that the new economic growth would lead by the 1980s to the full dismantling of apartheid, which would usher in an era of mass consumption and a democratic welfare state on the British model. What had happened in England in the nineteenth century - the gradual extension of the franchise following industrialisation - would occur in South Africa. Liberal economists mostly accepted that the colour-blind market place would undermine apartheid. Ralph Horwitz, for example, predicted that conflict would grow between the polity - the state and its racial policies - and the economy, leading eventually to an explosion.

Liberal historians of the 1940s, 1950s and early 1960s wrote almost exclusively on political-constitutional matters, and gave no attention to the historical relationship between economic growth and the development of the racial order. They left any consideration of economics and economic history to those economists who taught those subjects at the South African universities, many of whom had little or no historical training. Macmillan, who might have tackled economic history, had left the country for good in 1932 and he wrote nothing original about its history thereafter. De Kiewiet was by 1932 settled in Iowa, and wrote his *History* there. When liberal history revived, after a long decline, in the 1960s, it was a revival that had as its central concern the recovery of the history of African societies, along the lines of what was being done in tropical Africa. Most of those who contributed to *The Oxford History of South Africa*, written in the mid to late 1960s, still assumed that apartheid was an ideology at war with economics, and was chiefly the product of irrational, archaic ideological and political factors - race prejudice, Calvinism, Afrikaner nationalism were all part of the explanation - not economic interests.

The hints of another kind of explanation to be found in Frankel and van der Horst were ignored, as was the argument of the sociologist Blumer in the mid 1960s that industrialisation - and the argument was not made specifically for South Africa - accommodated itself to the racial system it found. Economic development, in Blumer's view, was neutral, neither undermining nor shoring up any particular racial system. This argument suggested that any diminution of white control in South Africa was likely to come about for non-economic reasons, and also that capitalists, who had found themselves operating in a racial order, and had adapted to it, would happily work within some other system; their main concern was stability. But historians of the 1960s did not begin to ask whether Blumer's argument was correct historically in the South African case.

The revisionists

In the late 1960s, not only did South Africa enjoy massive economic growth, but segregationist policies were implemented more rigidly and thoroughly than ever in every aspect, from petty apartheid through to the grand apartheid of the Bantustans and the mass forced removals. In their classic of radical scholarship, *Class and Colour in South Africa* (1969), Jack and Ray Simons suggested a connection between the new economic growth and the intensification of apartheid, but they did not develop the point. That was left to a new generation of scholars, mostly young emigrés from South Africa, exposed to new ideas in Europe and America, including a revived Marxism. In the 1960s, posts opened up for historians of South Africa in other countries and the new work was in part a product of the new internationalisation of South African history; the main forum at which it was discussed was the University of London.

It was a Canadian, Frederick Johnstone - who had been led to do post-graduate work on South Africa by the emigré liberal historian Arthur Keppel-Jones - who, on his return to Britain from a research visit to South Africa in 1969, first elaborated an explanation for the compatibility of white supremacy and economic growth. He spoke of 'the relations between capitalist development, apartheid policies and the core structures of white supremacy' as being 'essentially collaborative' and of white supremacy 'continually being reinforced by economic development'. For him apartheid was a set of policies rationally conceived to restrict black advancement, by preventing blacks from acquiring education, accumulating capital or using their industrial bargaining power. Its purpose was to provide employers with the cheapest possible labour, and to arrange the reproduction and regulation of that labour. South Africa's industrial prosperity of the 1960s was, then, the result of ultra-cheap, ultra-exploited labour. Not only was there no antagonism between the system of racial domination and economic growth; on the contrary, the exact opposite was true; they were functional to, they benefited from each other. They were not only inseparable, they were mutually reinforcing. The more prosperity the whites enjoyed, the more secure was white supremacy. Racial oppression helped economic growth, and economic growth boosted white supremacy. What Johnstone called 'the conventional wisdom' - which was in fact a certain liberal position - was turned on its head.

This revisionist argument was developed by other scholars, and various implications for the present were drawn from it. If indeed segregation and economic growth were incompatible, then foreign investment, stimulating the latter, might be thought likely to heighten the contradictions and promote the demise of the capitalist system itself. But the argument advanced by Legassick, Innes and other revisionists in the 1970s was that foreign investment would, in furthering economic growth, bolster white supremacy. Therefore, because white supremacy was morally objectionable, foreign investment in South Africa should cease. As capitalism was firmly tied to apartheid, it was also argued, then both would and should be overturned together - one would not survive without the other. The liberal view of conflict between segregation and economic growth suggested that in the interests of the latter there might be a gradual, evolutionary dismantling of apartheid, and the possibility that capitalism might better function in a non-racial South Africa. The revisionist argument implied, on the other hand, that apartheid would have to be got rid of by revolutionary action, which the revisionists hoped would overturn apartheid and capitalism together.

Johnstone's argument in his 1970 paper almost entirely concerned white supremacy and economic growth in contemporary South Africa, but he and other social scientists - like Martin Legassick the other key figure in developing the revisionist critique, he was trained as an historian but became a lecturer in sociology - were quick to apply it to the past. In doing so they focused especially on the gold-mining industry, which for Johnstone was 'the play within the play', the key which explained everything else. The revisionists tended to attack an over-simple, stereotypical liberal view of that relationship, and it is easy to fall into the same trap when discussing them. In confining myself to the initial form in which their views were presented, I hope not to fall too far.

Segregation, the revisionists claimed, had always functioned for, had always benefited industrial growth. Industrial growth had not occurred despite white racism, but instead capital had used the state and racial policies and practices for its own ends. Though Legassick admitted that the roots of racism lay in pre-industrial South Africa - though in the slavery of the western Cape rather than on the outlying frontier - he argued in other papers that the racist policies that began to emerge at Kimberley and on the Rand in the latter part of the nineteenth century were quite different in scale and purpose to what had gone before. They were designed to obtain and control a black labour force and to keep it distinct from the relatively small, privileged white working class. Segregation - the name given to the new set of policies - had not always existed, but was deliberately created, mainly in the first decade of this century, to secure cheap labour for the mines and the farms. Industrial capital had not merely adjusted to an already existing racial order - as Blumer had suggested - but had shaped the new racial order of segregation. Stanley Trapido pointed out in 1971 that South Africa had not industrialised as Britain had; rather, like other *late* industrialising countries, it had used massive state intervention and coercion. Industrial development had taken a special form in South Africa because it was based so crucially on deep-level gold-mining, which needed vast amounts of labour. As the grade of ore was low, and the price of the metal fixed, labour costs were critical, and a massive ultra-cheap labour force essential. Explaining how this had been obtained, Harold Wolpe, a radical lawyer turned sociologist, suggested that the migrant labour system, created in capitalist interests, had allowed the mines and, later, secondary industry, to assume that the workers had homes and rural bases in the reserves; therefore they did not have to provide housing for the families of migrants, or welfare benefits. In this way the mineowners and other capitalists had derived profits from exploiting the pre-capitalist economies of the periphery, the reserves. Post-1948 apartheid was specifically a response to the disintegration of the reserve economies, and a way of propping them up to provide migrant labour for secondary industry.

This crude summary of the initial ideas of the revisionists, ideas which soon became nuanced, varied and complex, shows that their position on the relationship between white supremacy and economic growth was totally opposed to that which had suggested that economic growth was, and always had been, in conflict with the country's racial policies, and would ultimately undermine them. In the early 1970s, some assumed there could be no meeting ground between such starkly opposed positions, and spoke of two quite different, irreconcilable paradigms. But at the beginning of the 1970s very little historical research had been done on the relationship between white supremacy and economic growth. Liberal historians had, as already noted, tended to ignore the detailed study of anything related to the economy, while many of the new school, who were the first to consider the relationship in detail, were sociologists, economists or other social scientists who tended to argue from theory, or from scraps of historical evidence, and did no original historical research. When such research was done, it concerned aspects of the conundrum: the history of the reserves, of migrant labour, of relations between the state and the gold-mining industry, or, say, the reasons for the passage of particular segregationist laws; it was not focused centrally on the debate itself. Merle Lipton's *Capitalism and Apartheid* (1985) comes closest to the debate, and ranges over a wider field than her title might suggest, for her use of the term 'apartheid' embraces segregationist policies from the early twentieth century. She has many important points to make about the relationship between particular capitalist interests and particular apartheid policies, but she too is reluctant to address the broad relationship between white supremacy and economic growth, and for good reason, for that relationship is extremely difficult to pin down. Growth obviously occurred for many different reasons, some of them those which explained growth elsewhere in the world. But South Africa's growth was also the product of a peculiar set of circumstances, the main one being its immense mineral resources. Whether there might have been more or less growth had the country been governed differently was impossible to say; the world of counterfactuals makes ordinary historians uncomfortable. It was very hard indeed to imagine South Africa industrialising without white supremacy. For more than half a century the system of white supremacy, imposed on conquered people, helped produce a measure of stability, with state coercion and divide and rule policies combining with psychological dependence to prevent any major challenge to the system. Such 'stability' was conducive to economic growth, but beyond that the question seemed to boil down to the relationship between economic growth and South Africa's peculiar racial policies, which still left a lot of imponderables. And the problem was confounded by the large gaps in our knowledge of much of the economic history of the country.

Contemporary reflections on complexity

That said, let me now from the vantage point of 1987 attempt to offer some general reflections on what the work of the past decade and more has revealed about the historical relationship between white supremacy and economic growth. The single most important lesson to be learned from that work is an obvious one: that the relationship between white supremacy and economic growth was never as simple and straightforward as either of the views of 1970 suggested. And if the relationship was not simple, neither was it static - it changed over time. The view, then, that economic growth was *always* hampered by segregationist policies has long been discarded. Both mineowners and commercial farmers benefited from a racial system which helped provide them with the large, unskilled and docile labour force they wanted, and in limiting the mobility of workers helped to keep down wages or other rewards for service. It is now generally accepted that in the early phases of industrialisation, when a coerced labour force was extensively used, segregationist policies aided economic growth.

But the racial system both imposed costs and provided benefits, and different sectors of the economy benefited differentially. In *Working for Boroko* (1981), Marion Lacey stressed how commercial agriculture and mining capital, competing for labour in the decades after Union, differed in their attitudes to the reserves - mining capital wanted them maintained, to supply migrants: agricultural capital preferred them broken up, to provide labour that would live and work on the farms. Mining capital won much of that battle but, conversely, the racial system imposed costs of a different kind on the mineowners in the form of the job colour bar. In his major monograph, *Class, Race and Gold* (1976), Johnstone tried to downplay the importance of the job colour bar: for him it was marginal compared to the provision of a large, cheap, controlled labour force. Mining capitalists had, after all, opposed the job colour bar, and he wished to argue that the racial system had been devised in capitalist interests. But if the job colour bar was so relatively unimportant, how then could it have lain, as it did, at the centre of the white workers' Rand Revolt of 1922? Despite what he said, the evidence in fact seems clear that the mineowners did not merely want to adjust the job colour bar, as he suggested, but to get rid of it altogether, though after it was enshrined in legislation in 1926 they accepted that they could not do so. The early revisionists were wrong to suggest that capital had created the racial system which it desired. That system had in fact evolved for complex reasons, having in part, but only in part, to do with considerations of economic growth - which revisionists assumed to be the same as the interests of capital.

That capitalists did not invent the racial system in their own interests may also be illustrated with reference to the migrant labour system. For Lacey, 'segregation was not only compatible with economic growth but was designed as a coercive labour system geared to ensure capitalist production' (*Working for Boroko*, p.xi), and Wolpe, concerned to stress how the reserves functioned in capitalist interests, suggested that the capitalists created them, and began the migrant-labour system. In fact, later work showed that migrancy started well before the opening up of the Kimberley diamond mines, let alone the Witwatersrand gold fields. It was, to some extent, a deliberate form of African resistance to full proletarianisation. Conquest helped to shape the territories which were left as reserves, and forced men out to work, though why they went out as migrants from particular societies and not from others had much to do with local conditions and their social relations. Moreover, some mineowners were from the beginning opposed to migrancy, preferring a settled (stabilised) labour force, which would be more reliable than a migrant one, which needed constant training, and was thought potentially more likely to desert.

One of the unresolved questions raised by the debate about the relationship of white supremacy and economic growth is that of the importance of the mineral revolutions. Did the industrial system adapt to existing patterns, or should one follow the revisionists and stress discontinuity? In a book published in 1982 John Cell accepted Legassick's view that segregation was something quite new in the early twentieth century, but more recent work has, I think, tended to confirm the arguments of George Fredrickson and others, who have rather stressed continuities between segregation and earlier forms of domination such as the slave and indentured labour systems of the old Cape, and also continuity at the level of racial ideas and attitudes. Work on the countryside and on the 'dorps', by Jeffrey Butler and others, has suggested that in the twentieth century the Witwatersrand was not as all-important as Johnstone suggested.

The relative weakness of mining capital is confirmed by Alan Jeeves in his recent book on *Migrant Labour in South Africa's Gold Mining Economy*, which tells of how it took almost thirty years for the mineowners to create a recruiting monopsony. In characterising the relationship that came to exist between mining capital and the state as symbiotic, almost a marriage of equal partners, Jeeves' colleague David Yudelman probably exaggerates the extent to which the mineowners were in fact able to get their way. It was clearly in the interests of the mineowners to employ blacks in skilled jobs rather than whites at higher rates of pay. But the mineowners were not able to do this because of the resistance of the white workers who, after their Rand

Revolt was crushed, helped to elect a new government which re-established the colour bar, in a stronger form than before. If mining capital was not as powerful and influential as early revisionist writing suggested, neither was agricultural capital, as the recent work of Tim Keegan has shown. No sector, in fact, could dictate to the state.

If the reasons why particular racial policies were adopted be considered, it is clear that the economic interests of white workers who were concerned with job security, rather than those of capitalists, lay behind the job colour bar. Liberals had exaggerated the importance of racial prejudice and racial fear but that prejudice and fear could not be dismissed altogether, as revisionists tended to do. Segregation and apartheid were not adopted exclusively for political and ideological reasons; but the early revisionists had been wrong to exclude such reasons, or to regard them as insignificant. Recent work, such as Saul Dubow's on the making of racial segregationist policies in the 1920s, has again stressed the importance of political-ideological considerations, in particular the white fear that increased black urbanisation would create a dangerous proletariat in the cities, which would pose a threat to white security. Segregationist policies, which from 1948 went under the name apartheid, were in part devices to prevent that threat materialising, even at the cost of some economic growth. Hence the refusal to allow a stabilised labour force in the towns, which manufacturing industry wanted; hence the insistence on migrancy, and the measures to make life for those blacks who did live in the cities as difficult and insecure as possible; hence the increasingly rigid influx controls and, from 1970, the legislation which progressively stripped Africans of their South African citizenship and made them citizens of one or other Bantustan.

Segregationist policies might be economically functional where the labour force was unskilled and wages low, but the liberal argument was that it was manufacturing industry, in particular, with its concern for skilled labour and a domestic market, that would force changes in segregation policies. Certainly manufacturing and commerce were more vocal critics of such aspects of racial policy as the job colour bar and migrant labour than mining or farming before the 1970s, but, as the revisionists did not fail to notice, manufacturing did extremely well in the 1960s, despite having to rely upon migrant labour or having to use higher-priced white or Coloured labour. To what extent such extra costs were offset by the benefit of cheap, controlled labour remains unclear: we still lack anything like an adequate history of manufacturing industry. But let me notice here the recent restatement of the liberal argument by Merle Lipton. Segregation and apartheid, she has suggested, were incompatible with advanced capitalism, with economic growth dependent on advanced technology. Before the 1970s, the argument runs, only manufacturing was hampered by skill shortages, but from the early 1970s mining and commercial farming increasingly needed skilled labour, and so were led to criticise apartheid labour policies which prevented the stabilisation of labour. With increased mechanisation, farmers wanted more settled labour; with a rise in the gold price in 1970 the mineowners could begin to move away from a cheap labour policy - seen to be inefficient - and to think of finally buying off white labour, and eliminating the job colour bar. This at a time when there was an increasing concentration of capital in conglomerates which linked the various sectors of the economy, and in which Afrikaner businessmen played increasingly important roles. Afrikaner businessmen came to share the view of their English-speaking counterparts that certain key apartheid policies in the social and economic fields should disappear. This line of argument accepts that big business was not only worried by the direct costs of apartheid, but also by other costs, such as the huge, bloated bureaucracy spawned by the racial system, and perhaps too by the intangible costs of the long denial of rights and the refusal to respect the dignity of those constituting the bulk of the labour force, as well as by growing internal instability, increasing international hostility to the apartheid regime, the threat of sanctions, and the withdrawal of foreign investment. Essentially, however, the argument is that it was changes in the economy, and pressure from economic interests, that led the state to move away from rigid, all-embracing apartheid. It repealed some apartheid laws, accorded formal recognition to African trades unions in 1979, accepted the permanence of Africans resident in towns, removed the pass laws for those not living in the 'independent' Bantustans in 1986 and restored to some Africans the South African citizenship earlier taken away from them. Has, then, the liberal argument begun to come true? Has economic growth finally begun to dismantle white supremacy?

Let me conclude with two comments on the recent changes. (At the beginning of 1987 these seem to have come to a halt, as has - and the two are surely linked, economic growth.) We cannot know precisely why the government decided upon them - the records of cabinet and state security council meetings are not available. There is no doubt that pressure from big business, via, e.g. the Urban Foundation, did play an important role in the changes affecting the status of urban Africans. But quite clearly too there were other important reasons for the changes in policy: internal black resistance principally; changes in the regional balance of power, and especially the coming to power of black governments in the neighbouring states; growing international pressure, and a new concern by the government for international legitimation after the failure of the Bantustans to win any support abroad. All these have to be weighed and it is certainly not possible categorically to say that economic pressures were more important than other considerations in the making of 'reform'. If the changes were indeed enacted primarily for non-economic reasons, Blumer would then be vindicated.

Secondly, there is another reason why it is ludicrous to say - as the South African journalist Fleur de Villiers has recently - that 'capitalism has killed apartheid'. The reason is, of course, that apartheid is far from dead. Though the changes made in recent years constitute a move away from some of the more extreme varieties of apartheid, there is no evidence that the changes were designed to undermine, or to begin to undermine, white supremacy. On the contrary, it would seem that what has occurred has been a restructuring designed to get rid of certain aspects of apartheid not essential to the maintenance of white supremacy, in the hope that jettisoning them would save, or strengthen, the rest of the system. The changes reflected the victory of those (verligtes) prepared to compromise on less important apartheid legislation in the interests of preserving the core. They triumphed over those (verkramptes) who were more dogmatic, who feared that any diminution in apartheid would open the floodgates and permit the sweeping away of the whole system and a transfer of power. But the verkramptes were wrong: the pass laws, job reservation and denial of trade union rights were forms of domination that were not essential to the maintenance of white supremacy. Nor was that supremacy in any way threatened by bringing some Coloureds and Indians into central government on an ethnic basis as junior partners of the whites in a tricameral system. Nor would the co-option of some Africans threaten it - in the unlikely event that this could be achieved. Apartheid remains very much alive, and there is no evidence that economic change will lead to significant political change. Such changes as have occurred have been autocratically imposed and have been accompanied by massive repression. On present evidence, O'Dowd was certainly wrong that economic growth would lead to political liberalisation.

Mention of the present situation leads me to one final point. Obviously historians remain interested in the relationship between the state and its racial policies on the one hand and the development of the economy on the other. How closely capitalism was associated with apartheid in the past has obvious relevance for the debate about the nature of a post-apartheid economy. But in recent years work on aspects of the relationship between white supremacy and economic growth has diminished. (Though recently published, Lipton's book is the product of work mainly done in the 1970s). This shift of interests in part reflects the very difficulties of the topic, and changing historical fashion. But in part at least it also reflects changes in the present. In the early 1980s the state appeared all-powerful and what it did all-important. The nature of the state and its relations with capital seemed the central issue. But since the Soweto uprising of 1976 and more especially since the current wave of popular resistance which began in late 1984, the rising tide of black militancy, and the massive attempt to repress it, have moved to centre-stage. This has led historians to turn away from the state and its relationship with the economy, and from the role of white workers, and to look instead at the impact of industrialisation on those caught up in that process, at the making of the working classes, at their culture, their consciousness and local struggles - at many different forms of black resistance in the past. Segregationism is now seen not simply as something imposed from above, the product of what white capital, white labour or a white government wanted, but as shaped significantly by what happened on the ground, in Zululand or elsewhere. That the strengths and limitations of popular movements - and the recovery of previously 'hidden' struggles - have in recent years become a major area of historical enquiry is a reflection of current developments. Mass resistance will probably be the critical factor in the eventual dismantling of the apartheid regime. How black South Africans make the country's future will surely determine how historians come to question its past.

Further Reading

Blumer, H.,   'Industrialisation and Race Relations', Chapter 10 in Hunter, G., (ed.) *Industrialisation and Race Relations* (Oxford University Press: London, 1967).

Carr, E.H.,   *What is History?* (Penguin: Harmondsworth, 1961).

Cell, J.W.,   *The Highest Stage of White Supremacy* (Cambridge University Press: London and New York, 1982).

De Kiewiet, C.W.,   *A History of South Africa: Social and Economic* (Oxford University Press: London, 1941).

De Villiers, F.,   'Hutt revisited: capitalism and apartheid, 1986' in Lewis, R. *et al.*, *Apartheid – Capitalism or Socialism?* (Institute of Economic Affairs: London, 1986) pp. 21-34.

Dubow, S.,   'Segregation and "Native Administration" in South Africa, 1920 to 1936' (Oxford University D. Phil. thesis, 1986).

Frankel, S.H.,   *Capital Investment in Africa* (Oxford University Press: London, 1938).

Fredrickson, G.,   *White Supremacy* (Oxford University Press: New York, 1981).

Greenberg, S.   *Race and State in Capitalist Development* (Yale University Press: New Haven and London, 1980).

Horwitz, R.,   *The Political Economy of South Africa* (Weidenfeld and Nicolson: London, 1967).

Jeeves, A.,   *Migrant Labour in South Africa's Gold-Mining Economy* (McGill-Queen's University Press: Montreal, 1985).

Johnstone, F.R.,   'White Supremacy and White Prosperity in South Africa Today' *African Affairs* 69,

275 (1970), pp. 124-40.

—
Class, Race and Gold (Routledge and Kegan Paul: London, 1976).

—
'Most Painful to Our Hearts', *Canadian Journal of African Studies* 16, (1982), pp. 5-26.

Lacey, M.,
Working for Boroko (Ravan: Johannesburg, 1981).

Legassick, M.,
'Forced Labor and Racial Differentiation in South Africa' in Harris, R., ed., *The Political Economy of Africa* (Harvard University Press: Cambridge, Mass., 1975).

—
'The Frontier Tradition in South African Historiography' in Marks, S. and Atmore, A. eds., *Economy and Society in Pre-Industrial South Africa* (Longman: London, 1980).

Lipton, M.,
Capitalism and Apartheid: South Africa, 1910-84 (Gower: Aldershot, 1985).

Macmillan, W.M.,
The Agrarian Problem and Its Historical Development in South Africa (Central News Agency: Johannesburg, 1919).

—
The Cape Colour Question (Faber and Gwyer: London, 1927).

—
Complex South Africa (Faber and Faber: London, 1930).

O'Dowd, M.,
'South Africa in the Light of the Stages of Economic Growth' in Leftwich, A., ed., *South Africa: Economic Growth and Political Change* (Allison and Busby:

London, 1974), pp. 29-43. [O'Dowd's paper remained unpublished for ten years].

Simons, H.J.
& Simons, R.E.,
Class and Colour in South Africa (Penguin: Harmondsworth, 1969).

Theal, G.M.,
History of South Africa 11 volumes (Sonnenschein: London, 1887-1919).

Trapido, S.,
'South Africa in the Comparative Study of Industrialisation' *Journal of Development Studies* 7, 3 (1971), pp. 309-20.

Van der Horst, S.,
Native Labour in South Africa (Oxford University Press: Cape Town, 1941).

Walker, E.,
The Frontier Tradition in South Africa (Oxford University Press: London, 1930).

Wilson, M., &
Thompson, L. eds.,
The Oxford History of South Africa, 2 volumes (Clarendon Press: Oxford, 1969, 1971).

Wolpe, H.,
'Capitalism and Cheap Labour Power in South Africa' *Economy and Society* 1, 4 (1972), pp. 425-56.

Wright, H.,
The Burden of the Present (David Philip: Cape Town, 1977).

Yudelman, D.,
The Emergence of Modern South Africa (Greenwood: London, 1983).

2. Anthropology & Apartheid

ADAM KUPER

The South African debate

A few years ago a debate began on the special features of Afrikaner anthropology in South Africa. It was initiated by Martin West, in his inaugural lecture as professor of social anthropology at the University of Cape Town. His thesis was quite simple. There were in South Africa two traditions of anthropology. One, established at the English-speaking Universities, drew on British social anthropology and was concerned with the living realities of South African life. Its practitioners were liberals, and their work undermined the ideological bases of *apartheid*. The other, established at the Afrikaans Universities, purveyed a pre-war German romantic idea of race-bound cultures, destined ideally to develop in their own fashion, though threatened by contacts with others. Culture was the main determinant of behaviour.[1] This has come to be known as the *ethnos* theory. Later contributors to the discussion criticised the rather simple oppositions which West constructed, and with reason.[2] The *ethnos* theory is a recent development in Afrikaner anthropology. It was not the theory of such leading Afrikaner anthropologists as Van Warmelo and Eiselen, who were in fact educated in Germany. Moreover, if some Afrikaans anthropologists did indeed propagate a form of cultural determinism, they might justifiably

---

I am grateful to Saul Dubow, Robert Gordon, John Sharp and Peter Skalnik for their helpful comments on a draft of this paper.

1   M.E. West, *Social anthropology in a divided society.* (Cape Town: University of Cape Town, Inaugural Lecture, 1979).

2   See, e.g., J.H. Booyens and N.S. Jansen van Rensburg, 'Reply from Potchefstroom: anthropology in South Africa', *Royal Anthropological Institute News* 37 (1980) pp. 3-4; B.A. Pauw, 'Recent South African anthropology' *Annual Review of Anthropology* 9 (1980) pp. 315-38; J. Sharp, 'Two separate developments: anthropology in South Africa' *Royal Anthropological Institute News* 36 (1980) pp. 4-5; John Sharp, 'The roots and development of *volkekunde* in South Africa, *Journal of Southern African Studies* 8 (1981) pp. 16-36; and N.S. Jansen van Rensburg, 'Die verklaringswaarde van etniese grense - 'n verkenning' *Etnologie* 4 (1981) pp. 25-31.

argue that this placed them in a perfectly legitimate anthropological tradition; one, moreover, which is more fashionable today than the traditional structural-functional anthropology which West championed. Finally it could be said - and was said, more or less politely - that English South African anthropologists should not be too ready to cast the first stone. There have also been many illiberal English-speaking anthropologists, and more who have pretended to be quite apolitical, a difficult trick to bring off in South Africa.

Read from the Afrikaner camp, West's critique was apparently regarded as a continuation of the Boer War by other means. It may seem very odd to outsiders, but the English-Afrikaans opposition remains a genuine source of academic polarisation. I was invited to the meeting of the Association of South African Anthropologists in 1985, and was astonished to find that virtually all the participants were from the English-speaking and non-white universities. The association had been established as a country-wide structure a decade earlier, but the leading Afrikaans professors had broken away in 1977 because they found the proceedings too liberal for their taste. They had established their own, Afrikaans-medium association, and the government had provided funds for a journal, *Etnologie*. Their lecturers attended the conferences of the English-medium association thereafter at their peril.[3]

Some of the leading Afrikaans anthropologists still quite happily propagate traditionally hostile anti-'English' attitudes. For example, R.D. Coertze, Professor of Volkekunde at Pretoria University, writing in the official organ of the Afrikaans anthropological community in 1985, commented:

> There is a striking tendency among anthropologists in the English-speaking universities in South Africa to publish their research findings mainly abroad. This observation may be connected with the fact that a full 30% of the faculty of such anthropology departments are foreigners (*lands-vreemdes*) and that international recognition in disciplinary circles is important [for them]. If one takes the point of view that the results of anthropological research in South Africa are in the first instance for local judgment and application, then it is reasonable to expect that such research which is paid for by South African sources should be published within South Africa.[4]

---

[3]   See J.S. Sharp and J.C. Kotze, 'The conference of South African anthropologists: another failure of the liberal ideal?' *Anthropology Today* 1, 3 pp. 2-4.

[4]   R.D. Coertze, 'Prioriteitsterreine vir volkekundige navorsing' *Etnologie* 8 (1985) p. 71.

The implicit threat is quite clear, as is the recoil from the international community.

It is not for an outsider, however, to mount belated engagements in the Anglo-Boer war, and in any case the internal quarrels of English and Afrikaans speaking white academics are not the most interesting feature of South African anthropology. Yet it is important to stress that Afrikaans anthropology is less oriented to international academic developments than to the internal demands of Afrikaans culture. Its practitioners take their Afrikaner identity seriously, and so must we if we are to understand their work. Afrikaans anthropologists are by and large committed to the Afrikaner nationalist movement, in which the universities, like the churches, have traditionally been regarded as leading actors. The departments of *volkekunde* in the Afrikaans speaking universities were expected to contribute to the theory and practice of *apartheid*. They have generally done more or less what was expected of them.

I shall discuss the contribution of ethnologists to apartheid theory rather than practice, though they certainly did play an active part, particularly in the Ethnological Section of the Ministry of Native Affairs and its successors. Little has been written about these activities, but it is my impression that the ethnologists were initially occupied mainly with survey work (Van Warmelo's many publications bearing witness to this), but that later they were drawn into advising on the administration of the Bantustans. It has been reported that there is now an ethnological unit in the Defence Force. *Volkekunde* departments in the Afrikaans Universities have helped to train the bureaucrats in the ministries which deal with the Black, Indian and Coloured populations. What the practical impact of all this activity has been I cannot say. My theme here, however, is the contribution of anthropological ideas to the idea of apartheid.

I must begin by defining what I mean by *apartheid*, since it has come to mean so many different things. Like the radical changes of many revolutionary governments, *apartheid* exhibits, in retrospect, great continuities with previous policies, with established modes of 'native administration', and indeed with British colonial policies in Southern Africa. Nevertheless, I think it wrong to play down the distinctiveness of the policies introduced by Verwoerd as Minister for Native Affairs. Certainly from the point of view of the Afrikaner Nationalist movement, *apartheid* had radically novel features. Officially adopted in the early nineteen-fifties, *apartheid* was government policy until the late seventies, when (under the leadership of Vorster and, more especially, P.W. Botha) it was at least tentatively repudiated. Ministers now announce regularly that *apartheid* is dead, and perhaps in their sense it is (though, as the newspaper editor Percy Qobosa remarked, the body is still around and it is making a terrible stink).

Apartheid was an attempt to introduce radical changes in the position of the black population of South Africa by the imposition of new political structures. The plan was to restrict black South Africans to separate territories within the Republic, while the main areas of South Africa would be unequivocally white man's country. This disposition, Ministers explained, was in the deepest interests of all concerned. Administratively the critical new feature in *apartheid* policy was the notion that the reserves could be developed as viable political and economic entities, and that, at the same time, the white areas could be made independent of black migrant labour (a fantasy which has only recently been officially abandoned).

Apartheid was not just an intensification of traditional segregationist policies, although Verwoerd often preferred to present *apartheid* in a conservative idiom, as the continuation of historic practices. The idea that the destinies of White and Black in South Africa, interwoven for centuries, could somehow be disentangled was not a new one, of course, but it had not been a serious goal of policy for generations. And at the level of pure ideology, there was an even more radical departure from tradition. For centuries white South Africans - Afrikaner and English - had been accustomed to justify their political and economic domination by an appeal to white racial superiority. With the formulation of *apartheid* theory, racist language was avoided, racist arguments played down. For the first time, a new rationale was sought for segregation.

The official blueprint of *apartheid* was the 1954 report of the Tomlinson Commission - to give it its full title, the *Commission for the Socio-Economic Development of the Bantu Areas within the Union of South Africa*. It is a strange document, not least because it attempts to give *apartheid* a scientific gloss, justifying the separation of races on the basis of apocalyptic world history and home-made sociology. However earnest, the appeal to social science was not very professionally managed. To take one small but telling example, the first two maps in the appendix - illustrating respectively 'Racial Groups in Africa' and 'Indigenous Racial Groups of South Africa' - are taken (as the text acknowledges) from volume three of the Afrikaans *Childrens'*

Encyclopaedia. A less naive editor might have concealed the source. In the text itself, the sociology is presented in lumbering, child-like models: two triangles coyly overlapping illustrate the beginnings of assimilation, and so on.

Despite or perhaps because of this rather forced appeal to science, the logic of the report is elusive: or rather, the connecting thread is implicit, and some of the critical arguments are simply assumed. Consider this summary of the preliminary thesis - bear with me if it is rather long, but it makes up in authenticity for what it costs by way of tedium.

(i) The white colonist and settler came from the West European cultural *milieu* to South Africa, and established himself in a new home, where he entered into contact with unchristianised people who, in the course of years and in the same field of life, became an appendage to the European, with the latter as dynamic centre.

(ii) At an early date, the European, so far removed from his maternal culture, constructed a defensive wall around his intimate life, and from that time to this he has tried to ensure his own survival in these alien and unknown surroundings.

The European drew Africans into his service, and 'gave old clothes to his unclad Bantu employee, while the Bantu slowly assumed a new pattern of living, and now this tendency was continued in a more intimate connection...'

The consequences of this philanthropic attitude have been drastic:

a gradual process of overlapping has, however, taken place, for whereas at one time only a few Bantu were found on the roads with old motor cars, there are now many in possession of such vehicles and even some who drive the latest models.

(vii) Where at first, the European only knew the Bantu as labourers and tenants on the farm, as unskilled workers in the mining industry and as messengers and domestic servants, he now beholds the Bantu mason wielding his trowel, the Bantu teacher in front of his class, the Bantu doctor visiting his patients and the Bantu newspaper editor sitting at his desk.

The white South African did not behold these portents unmoved. But what was to be done?

The European is confronted with an inescapable choice. A large number of Europeans are seeking for safety in a *via media* which will not lead to a parting of the ways, at least in their own lifetime. But the leading groups at the head of the two formative poles now termed 'apartheid' on the one hand, and 'liberalism' on the other, are witnesses to the fact that in their minds the time has already arrived for choosing between the maintenance of separate identities and the process of coalescence, between the traditional South African and the Neo-Western way of life.

The balance of the report is concerned with the implementation of segregation: the consolidation and development of the 'Bantu Areas'. Significantly, its proposals for the development of these areas were judged to be far too extravagant by the Government, who were not prepared to spend the necessary funds for the development of black areas. Later an appropriately segregationalist rationale was developed: each population group should be taxed separately to finance its own development.

There is something very odd indeed about the argument of the Tomlinson Report. Here is one of the key official documents which launched *apartheid*, and yet it does not offer any real justification of *apartheid* at all. There seems to be no theory behind it.

In fact, of course, there was a theory - theories rather, if anything a surfeit of legitimising ideas. The problem, I believe, is that the theories made sense only within Afrikaner discourse. The most radical message of the Report is contained in the absence of some expected arguments. Above all, there is no suggestion that race is a crucial factor in policy. Indeed, in the chapter on race relations, the report explains the traditional segregation of South Africa's peoples in terms of differences of religion, in civilisation, in economic and social status, in the fact that they had fought each other, and in the demographic imbalance between them. The only reference to race is the brief comment that 'The physical differences and dissimilarities especially between European and Bantu, led to a feeling of aloofness and physical aversion'. Notice that this does not imply a real difference, but rather a felt difference. It is difficult to exaggerate the importance of this rhetorical shift, for it marked the first serious attempt to found a policy of discrimination on a basis other than simple racialism.

But what was to take the place of traditional racialist argument? The Tomlinson Report was an attempt to convey the same old message in a neutral - social science - language. It is a fumbling, lame attempt, but that is the aim. And this is where anthropology came in: both in the rejection of the old racist model, and in the construction of an alternative. Of course, this task was by no means left to the Afrikaner anthropologists alone, but they played a part. Nor can their contribution be understood solely or even mainly in terms of international anthropological debate. To understand the ideas which underlay *apartheid*, and the role of anthropology in its construction, it is necessary to penetrate the culture of Afrikanerdom.

I shall begin with the case of W.W.M. Eiselen, who signed the Tomlinson Report as Secretary for Native Affairs. He was one of the two leading Afrikaner anthropologists of his generation, and probably of the century.

The changing theories of apartheid

Eiselen was the son of a German missionary in Sekhukhuneland. He studied under Meinhoff at the Hamburg Colonial Institute, and became the first professor of ethnology at an Afrikaans-medium university, at Stellenbosch, in 1932. The following year, Verwoerd was appointed Professor of Sociology at the same University. In his department, Eiselen insisted on a balanced diet of British functionalist theory and German culture area and diffusionist ideas.[5] His fundamental political inspiration, however, owed little to either school. It is quite clearly set out in a lecture which he gave to the Filosofiese Vereniging at the university in 1929, later published under the title of 'Die naturelle-vraagstuk', 'The Native Question'.[6]

Eiselen began by remarking that white South Africans were inclined to identify themselves with all South Africa. 'Difficulties which arise because white and black must live side by side in this country, we call the native question. Seen objectively, the term "the white question" would have been as accurate, since it is an open question who is responsible for our race problems - the Bantu or the European'.

He then enquires whether there is any scientific basis for claims of racial superiority. The Greeks despised the Romans as barbarians, the Romans in turn despised the Germans. By analogy, 'no person knows what heights of culture the Bantu might reach in the future, because, as history shows, the past of a race does not count at all against it.' Intelligence tests apparently found differences in ability between racial groups in America, but these results were not reliable. Blacks did badly on them in America, but then so did Eastern and Southern European immigrants. There were evidently spiritual differences which paralleled racial differences, 'but nobody can decide today whether these are

---

[5] J.F. Eloff, 'Die Mens en die vakman' in J.F. Eloff and R.D. Coertze, (eds.) *Etnografiese studies in Suidelike Afrika* (Pretoria: Van Schaik, 1972) p. 9.

[6] W. Eiselen, *Die naturelle-vraagstuk* (Nasionale Pers: Cape Town, 1929).

differences of degree or differences of kind'.

These provocatively liberal observations were followed by a criticism of the reservation policy of the government. The reserves could not maintain the black population. Moreover, the administrative policies were muddled. The British favoured indirect rule, the French direct: South Africa was applying a confused mixture of the two forms of administration, but in practice their policy furthered assimilation and the devaluation of traditional culture.

The solution to this unacceptable state of affairs was separate development for the black population. There must be larger and better reserves, in which the rural black population could maintain itself properly; black workers in the cities must be properly paid; and there must be more white immigration, so that the industrial economy would be less dependent on black migrant labour.

The continuity of Eiselen's ideas is evident when one compares this early manifesto with his major policy document, the Eiselen Report on Bantu Education, produced for the Nationalist government which had just come to power, in 1948. Far more than the Tomlinson Report, this document illustrates the way in which Eiselen's ideas fed into the new *apartheid* policy. And it made explicit at least one of the theoretical links which the Tomlinson Report left out.

The main thrust of the report was that educational policy should begin by recognising and building upon cultural differences. Read as anthropology, its starting-point was diffusionist theory.

> After the earlier period of pacification of the Bantu there followed a period when both Europeans and Bantu favoured the adjustment of Bantu culture to European economic and political ideals. Bantu ideas of dress, morality, religion, economics, etc., were set aside in favour of European ideas and practices, and it seemed an accepted goal that Bantu culture should be done away with. This was conceived in terms of the individualism of the nineteenth century, which felt that it was feasible to lift an individual from one society and plant him in another, and that this process should be carried out on a large scale with nothing but happy results for all concerned. Bantu music and a few crafts were all that this school of thought conceived as having lasting cultural value.

Labour migration and urbanisation had further undermined the traditional way of life.

> These phenomena have given rise to two schools of thought: firstly, those who believe that Bantu culture is inferior and must gradually disappear; and, secondly, those who believe that while the old

traditional Bantu cultures cannot cope with modern conditions, nevertheless they contain in themselves the seeds from which can develop a modern Bantu culture fully able to satisfy the aspirations of the Bantu and to deal with the conditions of the modern world. (...it should be borne in mind that the term 'culture' is here used to embrace all aspects of the life of Bantu society.)

At this point the diffusionist account was buttressed by a distinctly functionalist argument. The 'relatively simple social organization of the South African Bantu has, in a limited space of time, undergone two major changes.' Subordination to the Europeans had undermined his social institutions, and the educational system to which he had been exposed reinforced 'the transmission of ideas, values, attitudes and skills which have not been developed in Bantu society and are often not in harmony with its institutions.' The organisational and ideological coherence of the Bantu system had been breached.

The solution was first of all to develop the reserves: 'if the Reserves can be developed economically and culturally those who come to labour centres will have a background sufficiently rich and respected to prevent their demoralisation'. Secondly, an appropriate form of education must be developed which did not alienate a child from his own culture.

It is worth emphasising once again that the Report emphasised culture here, and specifically rejected a simple racist argument:

The Bantu child comes to school with a basic physical and psychological endowment which differs, so far as your Commissioners have been able to determine from the evidence set before them, so slightly, if at all, from that of the European child that no special provision has to be made in educational theory or basic aims...But educational practice must recognise that it has to deal with a Bantu child, i.e. a child trained and conditioned in Bantu culture, endowed with a knowledge of a Bantu language and imbued with values, interests and behaviour patterns learned at the knee of a Bantu mother. These facts must dictate to a very large extent the content and methods of his early education.

The fantasy is that a special form of education might be devised to suit black South Africans to life in economically viable and politically free homelands - which, however, did not exist. It was education for life in a never-never land. The demand of black South Africans (as the Commissioners admitted) was for an education adapted to life in industrial cities.

Obviously the educational theory would only begin to make sense if something drastic was done about conditions in the reserves themselves.

Eiselen was certainly under no illusions about conditions there. The reserves, he told an audience in London in 1950,[7] were the lands left to the African tribes after the ravages of the wars of the nineteenth century. They were completely inadequate to sustain the population. However, there was no point simply adding to the area of land in the reserves if they continued to be farmed in an inefficient manner while the men went off as migrant labourers 'which contributes further to the retrogression of their agriculture'. Migrant labour 'brings temporary relief only in times of emergency, but in no wise touches the root causes of the chronic decline'. The solution was the development of agricultural education, especially for the traditional aristocracy, and the development of townships in the reserves with their own industry.

Eiselen was the intellectual force behind one particular official vision of *apartheid*, but in the early stages. In its early stages *apartheid* had something of the cargo cult about it, but a cargo cult in which the rights of others had to be sacrificed in order to prepare the way for a new dispensation. This millenarian attempt to revive an imagined past in which black and white societies had existed side by side became in practice a bureaucratic dictatorship which caused a generation of new suffering in the name of social engineering.

But the goals of classical *apartheid* were not attainable, at whatever human cost. Neither politically nor economically - nor, indeed, culturally or socially - could the complex institutions of South Africa be returned to some imagined initial state of nature, in which White and Black had each their separate destiny. Within a quarter of a century the policy was in ruins. Soon there were no believers left among the intellectuals. Already in the fifties and increasingly in the sixties, attitudes within Afrikanerdom began to diverge. This divergence can be traced on a small scale if one considers the careers of two of the next generation of Afrikaner anthropologists, Pieter Coertze and Pieter Koornhof.

Koornhof was born in the Transvaal in 1925, the son of a dominee. He won a Rhodes Scholarship and went from Stellenbosch to Oxford. Here he worked under the supervision of Meyer Fortes, and wrote a thesis on Zulu migrant workers entitled 'The Drift from the Reserves among the South African Bantu'. Meyer Fortes once told me that Koornhof's conclusions were so left-wing that he was astonished to

---

7   W. Eiselen, 'The development of South Africa's native reserves' (London: Information Office, South Africa House, 1950).

discover that he was determined to return to South Africa, and indeed to enter government service. He became a research officer in the Department of Bantu Administration, where Eiselen ruled, but soon became active in politics. In 1962 he became Secretary of the Broederbond, and in 1964 entered parliament. Between 1978 and 1984 he was Minister of Eiselen's - and Verwoerd's - old Ministry of Native Affairs, which had been rebaptised the Ministry of Bantu Affairs, and now, as *apartheid* went through its final convulsions, was rebaptised in sociologese as the Ministry of Plural Relations and Development. Once a member, it is said, of the Communist Party, Koornhof was a *verligte* Nationalist, and has apparently now paid the price: in the present convulsions he has been packed off to be Ambassador to Washington. He represents one clear development of the Eiselen tradition, for Eiselen remains something of a guru to the *verligte* nationalists.

Eiselen and Koornhof were (relatively speaking) pragmatic men, whose original starting point was the failure of what went under the name of Native Policy. A generation later, Koornhof was among the first of the leading Nationalists to declare *apartheid* a failure, but apparently Eiselen had himself harboured reservations from the start, never believing in total segregation. After the Soweto riots the *verligte* head of the Broederbond, Professor Viljoen, asked the elect in a secret meeting: 'Must we not think again in our inner circle about Dr Eiselen's idea of a neutral or grey area with political power shared by white and non-white, alongside a smaller, exclusive white state?'.[8] Mr Botha has been talking about grey areas in the past year, and there can be little doubt but that the *verligte* tradition, in which Eiselen and Koornhof must be placed, remains influential.

Another, very different student of Eiselen was P.J. Coertze. Born in 1907, Coertze studied at Stellenbosch between 1926 and 1928 and stayed on as a teacher until 1946. Then, when Eiselen and later Koornhof entered the government, he went on to the University of Pretoria as Professor of Ethnology. From this eminence he ruled Afrikaans academic anthropology for more than twenty years, establishing a tightly-disciplined cadre of ethnologists at several universities. The theory they propagated was the *ethnos* theory, which has been discussed so much recently.

---

[8] Ivor Wilkins and Hans Strydom, *The Super-Afrikaners: Inside the Afrikaner Broederbond* (Johannesburg: Jonathan Ball, 1979) p. 206.

Coertze himself summed up the ethnos theory in these terms:

By nature man is also a social being and cannot survive by living alone. As ants and bees, for example, have their existence in natural, organic, social entities, nests and hives respectively, so has man his existence in culturally determined, organic social entities, i.e. ethnies (sing. ethnos), whose structures and existential activities are culturally determined. Such units cannot be organised but originate organically as the outcome of the combined actions of the forces controlling and determining human existence.

Ontologically speaking, human existence is an existence within the framework of varying ethnical units, each having a separate corporal existence. This is man's normal existence, he cannot survive and lead a happy life in any other way.[9]

What is the relationship between an ethnos and a racial group? Is the ethnos just a posh way of talking about race? Coertze argues in fact that the ethnos comes first; if there is racial differentiation, it is a consequence of ethnos organization.

Even the process of differentiation into biological types was a consequence of ethnical differentiation. Biological differentiation can only take place when distinct groups of people have been isolated in separate regions for long periods, and then as a consequence of passive and active adaptation they become different biologically as well as culturally.

Even ethnos theory, then, is a form of cultural determinism rather than racial determinism. Yet while it can be placed in the Eiselen tradition, the theory is different in its emphasis and its presentation. One very distinctive feature is the direct appeal which Coertze makes to religious authority. Indeed, much of Coertze's rather small corpus of published work appeared in theological journals, and he worked closely with the Nederduitse Gereformeerde Kerk's policy-making bodies.

In the hands of Professor Coertze ethnos theory became an orthodoxy within most Afrikaans universities.[10] However, it must be said that his own academic contribution has not been impressive. He has published little and in contrast to most of his contemporaries he wrote no ethnographies. What he has published has been almost entirely in Afrikaans and non-academic. For their part, his students have on the whole preferred to contribute ethnographic descriptions rather than theoretical analysis. None of the dozen chapters in his

---

9   P.J. Coertze, 'Volkekunde' *Etnologie* 1, 1 (leading article).

10   See John Sharp, 'The roots and development of *volkekunde* in South Africa' *Journal of Southern African Studies* 8 (1981).

festschrift discuss the ethnos theory.

The Coertze line is now losing its authority. When the great split in Afrikanerdom occurred at the end of the seventies, Coertze and his son, his right-hand man, left the Nationalist Party to join the Conservative Party. His son, an equally *verkrampte* figure, succeeded to his chair in Pretoria, but their empire is crumbling. Kotze, a former student who became Professor of Ethnology at the *verligte* Rand Afrikaans University has broken publicly with the ethnos theory, and in Potchefstroom the new critical theology is feeding rejection of the classic *apartheid* ideas.[11]

What is the significance of these three careers for our story? First of all, it seems evident that both Eiselen and Koornhof started with a spirited rejection of traditional South African 'native policy'. The system of reserves and migrant labour was unacceptable: it impoverished the African people. Secondly, the educational system fed a rejection of traditional culture. In Eiselen's analysis there were two solutions: assimilation of the black group by the white; and *apartheid*, which was taken to mean the fostering of black culture in more viable reserves, and the improvement of the conditions of black labour outside these. Koornhof's policies reflected similar priorities, together with a commitment to more white immigration. Coertze, in contrast, showed no interest in the dry economic conditions of the reserves but took his stand on a much more abstract principle: the *ethnos* must persist.

In the long run, as has become evident, these different tendencies were seen to be antithetical. The division within the ranks of the Afrikaner anthropologists - of Coertze the younger and Kotze - mirrors the greater split within Afrikanerdom, and can be read back into the divergences between Koornhof and the older Coertze. Nevertheless, it is also clear that Eiselen and his students - and their students - were in search of a functional alternative to race in the ideological edifice of South African 'native policy'. With different emphases, and in different ways, they chose to identify 'Culture' as the alternative basis. For Coertze, the links between race and culture were clear enough, though biological differences were given no independent explanatory power in his theory. In Eiselen's case racial factors were completely discounted. They all clearly shared the view, derived from anthropological theory, that racial differences alone could not justify segregation and

---

[11] See J.S. Sharp and J.C. Kotze, 'The conference of South African anthropologists: another failure of the liberal ideal?' *Anthropology Today* 1, 3 pp. 2-4.

discrimination. That did not lead them to reject segregation, but rather impelled them to find an alternative justification for it.

Anthropology and Afrikaner nationalism

But why did they all assume that segregation was the answer? Why did the Tomlinson Report pose the alternatives - assimilation and segregation - and without any argument assume that segregation was the preferred solution? Ideologically the basic impulse comes from within the Afrikaner nationalist movement. This impulse was stronger for some than for others. A powerful statement comes, predictably, from Pieter Coertze:

> I am the heir and bearer of Afrikaner traditions for which heavy sacrifices have been made. I am pledged to my ancestors and to the future Great Afrikaner People that I must never be false in my friendship or to the Christian principles and national ideals which form the foundations of the Afrikanervolk.[12]

The basic commitment is to the integrity of Afrikanerdom: at its most idealistic, *apartheid* was a projection of the aims of Afrikanerdom onto others. All must wish to survive as distinct ethnic units, with their own language, religion and traditions.

But why should the Afrikaners wish to survive? I am not concerned here with the obvious economic and political advantages of white supremacy, since they do not explain the continued hostility of Afrikaners to English, and the emphasis on Afrikaner and not simply white political supremacy. This ethnic particularism has many sources, but one of the most important is religious. It is crucial that the Afrikaners believed that they were a people chosen by God to fulfil a special destiny in Africa. This is a Calvinist view of the world, in which one is chosen and cannot freely choose. Moreover, God has chosen others and given them their specific destinies too: and it is not up to mere men to muck about with the dispositions of the Lord.

I believe that the essential impulse of Afrikaner nationalism is to be found here, and that *apartheid* was only one possible expression of this ideology. It was, as it were, a social science version, to which anthropology and sociology contributed. (Verwoerd, it will be remembered, was Professor of Sociology at Stellenbosch when Eiselen was Professor of Ethnology.) The versions now in gestation will use different idioms - there is much play at present with the language of

---

[12] Cited in Eloff, *op. cit.* pp. 2-3.

political science. But the core will surely remain: the aim of *verligte* and *verkrampte* alike is to secure the future of the Afrikaner *volk*.

English-speaking anthropology

I want now briefly to turn to the anthropology of the English-speaking universities. As John Sharp has indicated,[13] it is too easy for the English-speaking anthropologists in South Africa simply to condemn their Afrikaans colleagues. The classic attitudes of white English South African academics towards the Afrikaner are self-congratulatory, indeed smug, laying claim to an international legitimacy as against the merely local, politically guaranteed respectability of the Afrikaans theorist. Yet the English-speaking anthropologists cannot claim always to have opposed the government in a principled, let alone effective, manner. There were certainly a few outstanding exceptions, but in general the English-speaking anthropologists in the South African universities have kept their heads down. One reason is that many of the more radical amongst them emigrated. Others left academic life for more committed work, most notably perhaps Agnes Winifred Hoernle and Ellen Hellmann.

I hasten to say that this comment is not intended as a condemnation. The problems which face teachers in the English-language South African universities are extremely complex, and while I personally chose to emigrate I never believed that this choice was more moral, politically more justifiable, than the decision of some of my contemporaries to stay. Nor is it reasonable to expect even committed opponents of the regime to fight every step of the way: indeed, some believe that it would be counter-productive to do so.

In case there are some who think that the dilemmas are quite straightforward, I should like briefly to recall the story of Volume 2 of the *Oxford History of South Africa*.[14]

The second volume of the Oxford history dealt with the modern period, and a central chapter was naturally devoted to the African nationalist movement. Leo Kuper wrote this chapter, and not surprisingly it failed to comply with the South African censorship laws,

---

13   In his article in the *Journal of Southern African Studies* (1981).

14   The story is told by Leo Kuper in his *Race, Class and Power* (London: Duckworth, 1974) pp. 289-314.

notably by citing speeches and writings of so-called 'banned' individuals. The Delegates of the Oxford University Press decided to censor the book on their own accord, and to publish a sanitised version in South Africa, which would meet the approval of the South African censorship authorities. It was enough to expunge Leo Kuper's chapter, since other contributors had complied with the regulations and refrained from citing 'banned' sources. The South African editor was Monica Wilson, and she argued that it was better to publish a reliable history, even if it was incomplete, than lose the opportunity to publish a broadly liberal history of South Africa in the country itself. In the event the Press published a censored version of Volume 2 for the South African market, but later, under pressure, submitted the international edition to the censors, who passed it. My own sympathies here are strongly against any form of self-censorship. Yet Monica Wilson's arguments are not devoid of all substance.

English South African anthropologists of the younger generation are more radical than many of their seniors. A number have become involved in local political action or in development work, and in general this has been at the expense of a more traditional interest and commitment to academic anthropology. They may be placed in the tradition of Agnes Winifred Hoernle and Ellen Hellmann, both outstanding academic anthropologists who left the university to work in the Institute of Race Relations. Unlike these predecessors however, to the extent that they share a theory, it tends to be a version of neo-Marxism.

Their political commitments affect their anthropological discourse in a negative way as well: they eschew all talk of culture. In part this taboo derives from the reluctance of the Radcliffe-Brown school to allow an independent explanatory role to cultural factors, but in part it must be ascribed to political motives. Yet it is clearly a very deleterious form of self-denial. Archie Mafeje has criticised this blindness to cultural factors, but he has treated it as though it were simply a flaw in their version of Marxism,[15] while in fact this evasiveness about cultural factors has deep roots in South African oppositional anthropology. Max Gluckman, writing on 'Anthropology and Apartheid' in Schapera's *festschrift*, which was published in 1975, was quite explicit about this. He attacked Leach for stressing cultural

---

[15] Archie Mafeje, 'On the articulation of modes of production' *Journal of Southern African Studies* 8 (1981) pp. 123-38.

difference, not because this was theoretically mistaken, but because of the political implications of this emphasis, in the South African context. He commented 'It is possible in the cloistered seclusion of King's College, Cambridge [...] to put the main emphasis on the obstinate differences: it was not possible for "liberal" South Africans confronted with the policy of segregation within a nation into which "the others" had been brought, and treated as different - and inferior.'[16]

South Africa's black anthropologists belong on the whole to the community of the English-speaking universities. The first generation - Soga and Molema and Plaatje and Z.K. Matthews, a student of Malinowski - were among the anthropological pioneers in South Africa, along with Bryant, Junod and Stayt. The next generation sought careers in Universities, and found them only abroad, becoming emigrés alongside some white colleagues. A similar fate awaited the leading black anthropologists of my own generation, Archie Mafeje and Harriet (Sibisi) Ngubane. Mafeje was in fact appointed to a lectureship in the University of Cape Town in 1970 by Monica Wilson, but the government refused to allow him to take up his appointment. Recently, however, Harriet Ngubane has been appointed to a chair in social anthropology at the very same University of Cape Town. There are also black anthropologists at some of the so-called tribal universities, although the chairs are usually held by Afrikaners. The anthropologist and musicologist Victor Raloshai has a leading position in the new Venda university.

Conclusion

My brief description of the anthropological profession in South Africa and its role in the development of *apartheid* raises questions of general interest which I should like to touch upon in conclusion. First of all, there is the relationship between a national intellectual culture and an international social science discipline. I am often struck by the divergent developments of anthropology in different countries. Teaching in Leiden, I was acutely aware of the differences between the traditions of anthropology even on the two sides of the North Sea. A cynical interpretation of this sort of differentiation would be that no academic discipline adds more than a new idiom to ideological perspectives

---

[16] Max Gluckman, 'Anthropology and Apartheid: The Work of South African anthropologists' in Meyer Fortes and Sheila Patterson, (eds.) *Studies in African Social Anthropology* (London: Academic Press, 1975).

which are entrenched in particular cultures. But I am convinced that international academic disciplines have their own power. They propagate ideas which can enter into and shift local intellectual discourse. R.D. Coertze may complain sourly about the tendency of his English-speaking colleagues to publish abroad, but the truth is that his own journal, *Etnologie*, cites international anthropological authorities and tries to come to terms with them, and is affected by them. And ideas do penetrate the laager. The replacement of 'race' by 'culture' in the high theory of *apartheid* was itself a consequence of the penetration of a local intellectual culture by international scientific ideas.

Moreover, within every anthropological tradition there is a stress on empirical work, and although empirical work is always blinkered and may be blinded by theoretical assumptions, there is always a possibility - occasionally realised - that ethnographic findings may break through the defences of any theory. I have met several Afrikaner anthropologists who have changed their views on anthropology and on politics because in their own fieldwork they had been forced to recognise the injustice which *apartheid* had caused in practice to the communities which they studied.

An important conclusion follows from these observations. If anthropological ideas do penetrate the laager, then scientific contacts should be fostered in every possible way. Therefore, and following from these observations, I would not support a boycott of South African anthropologists.

Further Reading

Booyen, J.H., &
Jansen van Rensberg, N.S.,   'Reply from Potchefstroom: anthropology in South Africa', *Royal Anthropological Institute News* 37 (1980) pp. 3-4.

Eiselen, W.,   *Die naturelle-vraagstuk* (Nasionale Pers: Cape Town, 1929).

Eloff, J.E.,
& Coertze, R.D. (eds.)   *Etnografiese studies in Suidelike Afrika* (Van Schaik: Pretoria, 1972).

Gluckman, Max,   'Anthropology and Apartheid', in Fortes, M. & Patterson, S. (eds.) *Studies in African Social Anthropology* (Academic Press: London, 1975).

Kuper, A.,   *South Africa and the Anthropologist* (Routledge, Kegan Paul: London, 1987), esp. Introduction.

Kuper, L.,   *Race, Class and Power* (Duckworth: London, 1974).

Mafeje, A.,   'On the articulation of modes of production' *Journal of Southern African Studies* 8 (1981) pp. 123-38.

Pauw, B.A.,   'Recent South African anthropology' *Annual Review of Anthropology* 9 (1980), pp. 315-38.

Sharp, John,   'Two separate developments: anthropology in South Africa' *Royal Anthropological Institute News* 36 (1980) pp. 4-5.

——   'The roots and development of *volkekunde* in South Africa' *Journal of Southern African Studies* 8 (1981) pp. 16-36.

West, M.E.,   *Social Anthropology in a Divided Society* (University of Cape Town, 1979).

3. Capitalism & Apartheid

MERLE LIPTON

Introduction

There are two sharply divergent views of the relationship between capitalism and apartheid, each of which disparages the other as the 'conventional view'. The first is that apartheid was created by, and serves the interests of, capitalists, who benefit from the plentiful supply of cheap, coerced labour - and that this is proved by the success and rapid growth of the South African economy. The opposing view is that apartheid is the outcome of racist feelings, particularly among the Afrikaner Nationalists who have been politically dominant for most of the period since the Union of South Africa was formed in 1910. Apartheid policies were often opposed by many capitalists on the grounds that their costs and inconveniences conflicted with the requirements of running their enterprises.

The relationship between capitalism and apartheid raises large questions about the relative importance of class and racial factors in accounting for South African development; and also questions about the nature of capitalism and its relationship to the state - whether it is Marx's 'committee of the bourgeoisie', or whether the state has autonomy, and often acts in its own interests, or in the interests of other more amorphous groups such as voters, among whom capitalist interests might not predominate. These questions are not just of theoretical interest; they have implications for political strategy. If significant sections of capital are opposed to apartheid, then they are potential allies in the fight against it. But if apartheid nurtures capitalism - indeed is the raison d'etre for it - then obviously the destruction of the one must involve the destruction of the other.

Before exploring this argument it is first necessary to define briefly the terms used. By apartheid is meant the system of legalised, institutionalised race discrimination and segregation that had its origins in the policies and measures of the four colonies - two of them former republics - that formed the Union of South Africa and were extended and systematically tightened by the National Party (NP), which was elected to power in 1948. There are other important dimensions to the South African problem, such as class inequality and authoritarianism. But while these interact closely with apartheid, they are conceptually distinct from it and are not unique to South Africa. By capitalism is meant a social system in which there is a substantial degree of private, as distinct from state or communal, ownership of the means of production, and in which owners hire workers for a wage, or rent their property, for private profit.

The argument of this chapter is that the relationship between capitalism and apartheid has been complex and changing, and cannot be encompassed by either of the two partial explanations given above, although each contains some elements of truth. It will be suggested instead, that capitalists could co-exist with, and gain from, apartheid in cases where their businesses were dependent upon large supplies of cheap, unskilled labour, particularly if they were also export-oriented, and did not require a domestic market. This was the case in most mining, and in white agriculture up to the 1960s. But apartheid was not required by, and was often costly for, employers who needed more skilled labour, and/or a larger domestic market. This has long been the case in manufacturing and commerce. Over time, as these sectors have become more capital-intensive and mechanised, their need for skilled labour and for longer production runs has increased, and this has raised the costs to them of apartheid, which keeps skilled labour scarce and expensive, and limits the domestic market because of low black wages.

The question whether capitalists support or oppose apartheid, and whether economic growth strengthens or erodes apartheid, is therefore too crude and needs reformulation. The point is - what kind of economic growth? If it is growth that is dependent upon large supplies of cheap, coerced workers, then it can co-exist with apartheid. But if it is growth that requires more skilled labour and a larger market, then it is likely to lead to pressures to erode apartheid policies. Moreover, the fast growth of the South African economy cannot simply be attributed to apartheid. There is a whole range of other factors which has contributed to this: mineral endowments, the availability of capital, entrepreneurship and skills; and effective economic policies such as protection. In some sectors, and at some times, apartheid has contributed to economic growth; but in other sectors and at other times (including the present) apartheid has constrained it.

This broad thesis will be illustrated by an examination of the changing policies and pressures of employers. It is only possible to do this briefly here, but the detailed arguments and evidence on which this argument is based are set out in my recent book, *Capitalism and Apartheid: South Africa 1910-86*, which covers the evolution of the interests, attitudes and pressures of employers from Union until the present.

White farmers

The primary sectors, agriculture and mining, dominated the South African economy until about the 1960s, and their needs were crucial in shaping the institutional and political structure of South Africa.

White farmers were among the leading advocates of apartheid policies such as the 1913 Land Act, which reserved 86% of the land for whites and the pass laws, which controlled the movements of Africans and was aimed at keeping down their numbers, and restricting their permanence, in the towns. These measures obviously enlarged the supply and reduced the cost of African labour, which they tied down on the farms. They also reduced competition from black farmers. White farmers also supported a wide range of other apartheid policies which segregated blacks socially and excluded them from political rights.

However, there was an important exception to the implementation of apartheid in agriculture. Farmers evaded the imposition of the job colour bar, which gave preferential employment to white workers and excluded Africans, and often Coloureds and Indians, from the more skilled, and even from some of the semi-skilled jobs. By excluding the majority of the population from competing for skilled jobs, the 'job bar' restricted competition and greatly raised the cost of skilled labour. But farmers managed to evade this major cost of apartheid labour policies. On the farms, skilled and managerial jobs were increasingly done by Africans and Coloureds, despite very high white unemployment in the period before the Second World War. The result was that the poorer rural whites were driven into the towns to look for work. Ironically, white farmers then supported their former dependents in their struggle to impose the job bar on the mining and industrial sectors, where white workers were provided with protection from what they regarded as 'unfair competition' and undercutting by black labour.

It is significant that white farmers, regarded as pillars of support for apartheid, escaped this major cost inflicted on other capitalists. It is also an indication of their political power. Another sign of this power was their success in securing preferential access to unskilled black labour, of which there was a scarcity throughout southern Africa until the 1960s. Pass laws were implemented in a way that tied Africans down on the farms, and kept their wages very low, by reducing the competition from the mines and towns where wages were higher.

From about the 1960s, major technological changes made farming more capital intensive, mechanised and larger-scale; this led to important changes in labour policy. First, it reduced the need for such large numbers of unskilled workers. Second, it led to an increasing need for a more skilled workforce to operate the tractors and other machines and to cope with more scientific, highly-organised farming methods. It meant that workers could not just be taught on the job, but required education and training - with all that this implied for the somewhat feudal master-servant relationship. Third, greater capital-intensity meant that wages became a smaller proportion of total costs, so that farmers became less concerned to keep down the wage bill. Finally, farmers became increasingly interested in the domestic market and therefore developed an interest in raising the general wage level, as employers in manufacturing and commerce had long wanted to do.

These effects led to a gradual shift in the policy of the South African Agricultural Union (SAAU). Since the 1970s, SAAU has been pressing for higher wages, improved working conditions, better access to training and education for farm workers, and also for increased mobility. In its recommendations to the 1979 Riekert Commission, SAAU recommended the scrapping of influx controls, of which it was once a major advocate.

However, there are differences over these issues among farmers. The less efficient, marginal farmers, especially in the Transvaal, do not support these more progressive policies. Instead, they remain an important source of support for right wing parties such as the Conservative Party and the Herstigte Nasionale Party (HNP). But the trend among leading farmers is towards less racist policies; this now extends to the question of political rights, as was shown in their support for the Lombard-Buthelezi Commissions, which recommended an experiment in multi-racial 'power-sharing' in Natal. Those familiar with the record of white agriculture will recognise that, whatever the inadequacies of such programmes, they signify that there has been since the 1970s (and not just recently) an enormous shift from the policies which white farmers have advocated since Union.

Mine owners

Mine owners, like farmers, supported the Land Act and pass laws that made black labour plentiful, cheap and rightless. They also forced their workers to live in the notorious migrant labour compounds and ruthlessly suppressed the trade unions that periodically emerged. However, unlike farmers, mine owners were unable to escape the job colour bar which the white unions succeeded in imposing on the mines. Recurrent attempts to erode the job bar led to violent conflicts with white labour, culminating in the 1922 Rand rebellion, which shook the newly established South African state to its foundations. The fact that mine owners went to such lengths to challenge the job bar is an indication of its high costs to them. After 1924, however, they were forced to acquiesce in the job bar because of the superior political power of white labour.

This had important consequences for a whole range of labour policies, because the whole system hung together. The fact that the mines could not use blacks in skilled jobs contributed towards the perpetuation of the migrant labour system, because employers only develop an interest in stabilising their workers at the work-place with their families, when these workers become more skilled. Employers then want to retain them so as to avoid the costs of high labour turnover. Other factors which contributed towards the perpetuation on the mines of the exceptionally repressive and highly institutionalised form of apartheid were: first, the fixed price of gold, which did not rise from 1934 until 1970. This made it difficult to pass on costs, as employers could in other sectors. Second, the fact that technology on the gold mines changed more slowly; it remained very labour intensive, dependent on large numbers of unskilled workers. Third, farmers had preferential access to black labour and this meant that mine owners became increasingly dependent for African labour on foreign sources, particularly from Mozambique, which they were less likely to be able to stabilise. Fourth, the cost constraints on the mines - initially largely foreign-owned - were increased by the fact that they were subject to higher taxes and other charges such as freight rates than were other sectors, particularly agriculture. These contrasts with the successes of white workers in securing the job bar, and of white farmers in securing preferential access to black labour, show that mine owners had less political power than might be expected from their predominant economic position, measured in terms of their contribution to GDP, government revenue and foreign exchange. The argument is not that mine owners were powerless, but that in matters in which they were in conflict with local white farmers and white workers, it was generally these 'national' interests that prevailed.

During the 1970s, the labour policies of the Chamber of Mines began to shift. Mine owners renewed their pressures against the job bar, as there was by now an acute shortage of skilled labour. They also began to press for the right to stabilise some black workers; and they supported the demands of secondary industry for socio-economic reforms, including mobility of labour, higher wage levels, trade union rights and, more recently, even political rights.

Among the reasons for this long overdue shift were: first, the rise in the gold price since 1970, which meant that they were better able to pay higher wages, stabilise labour and institute other industrial reforms. Second, the widespread unrest amongst the black labour force since 1973 intensified the need for such reform. Third, there was mounting overseas criticism, to which the huge multi-national mining companies, all of which had investments abroad, were very sensitive. Fourth, mine owners faced pressure from within the white oligarchy, particularly from the manufacturing and commercial sectors, which were playing an increasingly important role in the economy and wanted reform.

However, policies and attitudes are changing more slowly on the mines than in secondary industry. In particular the migrant labour system has remained intact. Moreover, there are differences within the Chamber of Mines between the progressives, who are beginning to align their policies with manufacturing and commerce, and employers such as the Afrikaans firm, Gencor, and the British-based Goldfields, which have dragged their heels over wages and have been hostile towards black unions. Nevertheless, despite significant differences among employers, by the mid-1980s the trend was clearly towards the scrapping of apartheid policies.

Manufacturing and commerce

The secondary and tertiary sectors (manufacturing and commerce) have long been a source of pressure for less racist policies. These pressures were evident from the 1920s, soon after the establishment of employers' organisations like the Federated Chambers of Industry (FCI) and the Associated Chambers of Commerce (ASSOCOM). Their pressures focused on some specific aspects of apartheid.

The first among them was the job colour bar and the related question of black access to training and education. There has long been a struggle over the job bar in these sectors between employers and the white unions, the latter supported by the Afrikaner Nationalists and the English Labour Party. (It should be noted that support for apartheid has not come exclusively from Afrikaners.) Urban employers were not as successful as white farmers in evading the bar, but it was more difficult to enforce on them than on the mines, partly because of the numerous small firms in these sectors; partly because there was less effective unionisation amongst white workers, by contrast to the mines, where a few giant mining companies could be more easily policed by strong unions backed by government inspectors. Another factor contributing towards the erosion of the bar in these sectors was more rapidly changing technology. Mechanisation led to the emergence of a grey area of semi-skilled jobs for machine operatives. Jobs were also frequently fragmented and reclassified. There was not, therefore, a simple skilled/unskilled division and this made the job bar more difficult to enforce.

The resultant higher skill levels among black workers had important implications for a further range of apartheid policies. For instance employers developed an interest in stabilising their black workers so as to reduce turnover. This conflicted with the major aim of government policy, viz, to prevent Africans from settling permanently in the towns with their families. The government argued (correctly) that urbanisation and the breaking of Africans' ties with their 'homelands' would eventually lead to their incorporation into a common society and inevitably, therefore, to the demand for political rights.

There were conflicts also over labour mobility. Urban employers did not need to coerce blacks to work for them. On the contrary, it was the aim of the pass laws to prevent blacks from flocking into the towns where wages (while low) were higher than on the mines and farms, and life was somewhat freer, with more educational and cultural opportunities. Any labour shortage in the towns was caused by the pass laws, which also led to harassment and bureaucratic rigmarole for employers and workers, and to a constant stream of criticism from employers of these laws and of the laws restricting stabilisation.

Urban employers also pressed for a generally higher wage level on the grounds that this would improve productivity and broaden the domestic market on which they were dependent. Finally, some employers supported the recognition of black trades unions. Amongst the reasons for doing so were that this would provide them with allies in their fight against the job bar and would lead to an improvement in communications with the workforce. From as early as the 1930s some employers had already recognised black unions, especially in the garment industry.

However, as one would expect, there were variations among employers, according to such factors as their size, capital-intensity, product and profitability, ethnic affiliation and political attitudes. More progressive policies were advocated by the FCI and ASSOCOM, representing the majority of employers. But they were not supported by some of the more marginal, less efficient employers, particularly those represented by the Afrikaanse Handelsinstituut (AHI). In 1960, it still accounted for under ten per cent of urban employers, but it was politically influential because of its close connection with the National Party.

Furthermore, while progressive employers advocated reform both of labour relations and in some socio-economic spheres, there were other aspects of apartheid which they did not challenge. They did not question residential and educational segregation and the exclusion of blacks from political rights - even though they did not usually support the Nationalists when they took away these rights, for example, from the Africans and coloureds in the Cape - preferring to keep the door open to the gradual extension of rights. Their attitudes were thus contradictory and ambivalent, most clearly illustrated by the case of influx control. Many employers shared the fear of urban whites of being 'swamped' by Africans streaming into the towns and feared that greater numbers would somehow threaten white security and lead to disorder, crime and even revolution. They did not therefore generally propose the complete scrapping of influx control. But, *qua* capitalists they wanted a larger labour pool, and the right to settle their workers in town; they pressed consistently for the easing of restrictions. Theirs was a cautious, somewhat paternalist policy that would lead both to more material benefits for the workforce and to the gradual incorporation of blacks into a common society. This would open up various possibilities, including the increasing black bargaining power which would arise out of better education and wages, and secure urban tenure. All this pointed in the opposite direction from the strengthening and tightening of segregation and discrimination that had been enforced by most South African governments since Union.

The exception to this general trend was the United Party government during the Second World War, which was more responsive to the pressures of commerce and manufacturing, partly because of the growth and importance of these sectors during this period. This government eroded some segregationist policies by accepting, for example, the principles of black stabilisation and the legality of black trades unions. But their limited and cautious reforms were reversed by the Afrikaner National Party government elected in 1948, and representing a white agricultural and worker base. It set out to shore up the crumbling structures of segregation under the new ideology of apartheid, and to extend them more systematically to the secondary and tertiary sectors.

This attempt coincided with the expansion and modernisation of secondary industry during the post-war period and with a fundamental change in the labour supply situation. The pool of unemployed white workers had dried up as a result of economic growth; there was indeed an increasing shortage of skilled labour. Conversely, the former shortage of cheap, unskilled labour in the primary sectors was gradually transformed into a surplus, as a result of rapid black population growth and the mechanisation of production.

Industrialists and other critics warned that a skewed pattern of economic development was emerging, which would lead to an artificial shortage and therefore high cost of skilled labour (becoming increasingly important with mechanisation in all sectors), at the same time as there was growing unemployment among blacks, who were excluded from filling the skilled jobs. There were continued conflicts between industry and government over labour, and related socio-economic policies, from the time of the election of the NP. The fact that the government persevered with its policies up to the 1970s is yet another indication that political power was not a simple correlate of economic power in South Africa.

After the 1960 Sharpeville crisis, which led to a flight of foreign capital from South Africa and the most intense business criticism yet, the Prime Minister, Verwoerd, began to take these complaints more seriously. He formulated his 'separate development' policy which he claimed would make it possible to reconcile economic growth in secondary industry with apartheid. First, labour-intensive industries should be decentralised to the Bantustans or their borders. Here there would be freer employment policies: capital would be subject to fewer constraints on the number and skill levels of black workers. This was tolerable because black advances in these areas would increase neither black numbers nor their right to permanent settlement in the 'white' areas that it was the major object of government policy to prevent. Nor would black industrial advance on the borders disturb the hierarchical race structure as a whole.

Secondly, in return for some industries decentralising to the Bantustans, the government would permit somewhat more flexible labour policies in the 'white areas' for those industries which could not decentralise. In particular, more job fragmentation would be permitted, with the less skilled part of the job going to blacks. This 'floating job bar' would make room for some black advance, but blacks would move up the ladder under whites, so that the hierarchical race structure would remain intact.

The government made great efforts to enforce this elaborate experiment in social engineering on industry. If it had worked, it would have constituted the modernisation of apartheid, not its erosion, because it would have left the apartheid structures intact. But, for a variety of reasons, it did not work. One of the reasons was that it was opposed by capitalists, who mostly resisted the attempts to force them to decentralise under the terms of the 1967 Physcial Planning Act. Employers also insisted that the floating job bar was inadequate. They wanted the bar scrapped and a competitive, mobile market in skilled labour established.

There was an intense struggle over these issues from the mid-1960s, led by the FCI and ASSOCOM. From 1970 they were also joined by more conservative employers like those in the AHI which, while it had initially agreed with the aim of the separate development policy, in practice found it too costly and unworkable. This growing group of urban capitalists in the NP was an important factor in shifting government policy.

The 1970 election, in which Verwoerd's successor, Vorster, defeated the HNP, paved the way to the first government concessions to business pressures. Changes in the job bar were followed by concessions in the related area of access to education and training and later by the gradual concession of permanent urban rights, more mobility, property rights etc. These developments contributed to the increasing political debate, black political activity and trade union pressure which came to a head in the 1973 Durban strikes. Their actions, which received increasing international support, especially after the 1976 Soweto riots, jolted and pushed capitalists towards a still wider reform programme. Employers now extended their objectives to cover the complete scrapping of measures such as pass laws, and to extend to all blacks (including those in the Bantustans) citizenship and political rights which would be negotiated with black leaders, including those in the ANC. This programme was set out in a series of policy documents, such as the 1985 Business Charter, signed by practically all business organisations. The fact that this programme was now supported by conservatives in the AHI and the Chamber of Mines was among the reasons why business pressures became more effective. The previously separate interests of capital were now converging. But the inadequacies and limitations of the reforms, and the difficulties in implementing them, indicated the continuing limits on capitalists' power. Ranged against it were white labour, now largely transformed into a bureaucracy in the state sector, and the NP political establishment, which wanted to retain its grip on power and which feared the consequences of losing control, both for their economic interests, and also for security reasons.

Conclusion

Against this view of the progressive role played by at least some sections of capital in the erosion of apartheid it is sometimes argued that, while capitalists have on occasion pressed for some reforms, these have been very limited and have merely led to marginal adjustments in apartheid. Moreover, they did so only when they were under pressure and to suit their own interests. But, as this account shows, there has been a long history of opposition by important sections of capital to some major apartheid policies from which three conclusions may be drawn.

First, while their pressures were often indeed limited, the overall thrust was towards less racist policies and the erosion of apartheid. They pointed in the opposite direction from racist and segregationist policies.

Second, capitalists' policies had dynamic consequences: for example, the erosion of the job colour bar led to changes in a number of other policies - education and training, wages, the stabilisation of labour and urban rights, job mobility and, eventually, trade union rights. These changes, in turn, strengthened black bargaining power both as consumers and producers, which raised a whole further series of pressures and changes. The whole system hung together and, when some of its pillars were eroded, this set in train a process which undermined the whole structure. Moreover, reform elsewhere in the world surely often happens in this seemingly ad hoc, piecemeal and incremental fashion.

Third, people's intentions are often difficult to gauge, they invariably include a large element of self interest. In this respect South African capitalists were hardly unique. Whatever their intentions, it is the consequences of their actions which are most important.

However, the argument here is not that South African capitalists were liberals - though some of them were and more of them have become so. The argument is rather that, whether they were liberals or not, their interests led them into conflict with some apartheid policies. This conflict in turn had far-reaching consequences whether or not this was intended. The end result was that pressure from capital contributed to the erosion of major aspects of apartheid, and to the increase of black bargaining power, in a situation that otherwise looked very immobile. Wittingly or not, capitalists thus helped to create political possibilities.

All this has implications for strategy: it suggests that capitalists should not all be lumped together as supporters of apartheid and the government. Instead, distinctions can be made between those who are progressive and those who are not, and pressures applied to push the latter towards less racist policies. Progressive capitalists are potential allies in the struggle that still lies ahead to destroy apartheid.

Further Reading

Consult the list under Ch. 1 by Christopher Saunders.

4. South Africa at War

GAVIN CAWTHRA

To understand the current crisis in Southern Africa, one has first to grasp its military dimension. For the foreseeable future this will be at least as important as the economic, political and social factors. Similar processes of militarisation (if not on the same scale as will emerge in South Africa) have occurred in other countries in the region - Zimbabwe, Mozambique and Angola, where the military side of the struggle for freedom was of vital importance.

The process of militarisation

During the 1960s it was fashionable to describe South Africa as a police state. Today it ought to be called a military state. Under the leadership of P.W. Botha, first as Defence Minister and for the last eight years as Prime Minister and President, the South African state has been transformed and is now armed to the teeth. Three aspects of this militarisation process can be identified.

First, it is clear that the military now plays a decisive role in the state's decision-making. A silent military coup has taken place; the security establishment headed by Botha himself and General Malan, the Minister of Defence, has replaced Parliament and the Cabinet as the country's legislature and executive. We can trace this process back to the 1950s and still more to the 1960s when the South African Defence Force (SADF) developed a national security doctrine. This stressed that war was won not by military means alone but by psychological, social and economic struggle as well. In modern times no war is a one-dimensional armed conflict; it entails all aspects of social life. This doctrine was gradually codified by South Africa's generals and became known as the 'Total Strategy'.

This chapter summarises many of the main points in the author's book: Brutal Force: The Apartheid War Machine, *(International Defence and Aid Fund: London, 1986).*

SADF publications in the late 1960s and 1970s constantly referred to the necessity of this total strategy, to counter what was seen as an equally total onslaught against the South African state. The forces of world communism, the normal term applied by the South African regime to any of its opponents, were said to be seeking to overthrow the state. These forces were undermining morale by psychological leverage over the population, and threatening the country's economic infrastructure with international sanctions campaigns in western countries. South African military commanders saw these various forces as co-ordinated elements of a total onslaught, which demanded their own total counter-strategy. The implication was that the military itself must become involved in all these different fields. All sectors of public life would have to be brought under the control of the government and then centralised through the military. The activity of each sector would be directed to one overall aim, the survival of the South African state. Botha himself was the principal mover of this strategy; when he became Prime Minister, he could implement it.

One of Botha's most important steps was to establish a new framework for making and implementing policy decisions which completely cut across, and indeed replaced many of the existing constitutional structures. This framework has become known as the National Security Management System. At its apex is the State Security Council (SSC) of which Botha is President. The SSC is technically a Cabinet Committee but in effect it has replaced the Cabinet as the chief decision-making body. It meets before the Cabinet, and more regularly; it meets in secret; its non-Ministerial members are more important than Ministers, the chief of the SADF for example. Underneath the SSC is a Work Committee which does the routine work of the Council. There is also a large Secretariat composed of permanent SSC employees. They are recruited from the National Intelligence Service, Military Intelligence or the regular SADF. They are dominated by security personnel. The Secretariat is divided into three branches: Communications, Strategy and National Intelligence Interpretation. It also has an administrative component. Information is fed to the SSC, via its Secretariat, by the three intelligence agencies of the state: the National Intelligence Service, the Security Police who do the groundwork by interrogating people, and the Department of Military Intelligence which is probably the most important of the three agencies today.

All the major decisions taken by the South African state are made in secret by the SSC. It decides what to do next in Namibia and whether to attack the Front-line States or to declare a State of Emergency. In May 1986 it was the SSC not the Cabinet which decided to sabotage the Commonwealth Eminent Persons Group's negotiating initiative, to attack the capitals of Zimbabwe, Botswana and Zambia and to declare a State of Emergency. Parliament knew nothing of these decisions until after the event. Beneath the SSC are fifteen Inter-departmental Committees on which sit representatives of various government departments. On each committee there is always a representative of the Police or the Defence Force. The object of these committees is to co-ordinate government strategy in various areas: social action, psychological action, telecommunications, and so on. These fifteen committees cover the whole spectrum of South African society.

The most important components of the National Security Management System are the Joint Management Centres (JMCs) beneath which are Mini-Joint Management Centres and Sub-Joint Management Centres. The eleven JMCs are organised around the territorial command structures of the SADF, thus demonstrating their military application. They are the local organs of the State Security Council. Members of the provincial administration, local government departments, administration boards and of course the Police and the Army sit on these bodies. Their object is to co-ordinate state strategy in each region. Towns, villages and certain sensitive districts have Mini- or Sub-JMCs. These centres are intended to monitor all developments in their area, to know who is heading what organisations, what their grievances are, and what types of demonstration are likely to occur in which streets. The centres are responsible for day-to-day intelligence, which is fed upwards through the system in order that the appropriate repressive steps may be taken.

The whole country is covered by this secret, military-dominated system. This has made democracy, even for whites, a charade, since decision-making on all vital issues is rooted in the National Security Management System, not in the ruling party or Parliament.

Having taken state power, the military establishment has, secondly, mobilised the white population for a protracted war against the black population of South Africa and its neighbours. This process has a number of aspects. It starts with ideological and psychological preparation. Radio and T.V. propaganda, with its constant use of militaristic images, harps on about the total onslaught against South

Africa through educational institutions, particularly schools. The regime has also tried to indoctrinate people with a militaristic attitude. Approximately 200,000 white schoolboys are now mobilised into Cadets; these are directly controlled by the Army, which uses them to instil military values in the young.

Civil Defence is also used to mobilise the white population. This voluntary system has a hierarchical organisation which reaches down to street level. It involves white civilians in support of the security forces and emergency services.

Conscription has been responsible for the greatest level of involvement by whites in the military process. White males were first conscripted in 1967. Ever since, there has been a steady increase in both the number of people eligible for conscription and in the length of time they have to serve. Some years ago military service was nine months, then it went up to a year, then to two years. Now it is two years initially followed by 'camps', which are periods of operational duty of up to three months annually for twelve years. This means that white males are constantly in and out of the army for fourteen years of their lives.

Conscription of older white men began in 1982 with the institution of the Area Defence System. Individual magisterial districts are proclaimed and all locally resident white men between the ages of 18 and 55 are required to register for military service within them. This process is being extended to cover the whole of South Africa. It started in the border areas of the Northern Transvaal and is now being extended southwards to include some urban areas of the Eastern Cape. Men who register are not necessarily called up, but the army has their details and can mobilise them at need. It usually calls them up for short periods, say twelve days a year in the local Commando - white South Africa's militia. In this way virtually every white male between the ages of 18 and 55 has been forced to play his part in defending apartheid. The SADF has also campaigned to recruit volunteer women soldiers. There has been some talk of female conscription but this is unlikely, given the male chauvinism of white South Africa.

There has also been talk of conscripting blacks into the army. It was one of the reasons for the new parliamentary system, which in 1984 granted limited rights of representation to people classified as 'Coloured' and 'Indian'. Government representatives argued that 'you can't ask a man to fight unless he can vote'. The franchise extended to the 'Coloureds' and 'Indians' was meaningless, because it was always overridden by an inbuilt white majority in parliament. Government nonetheless believed that it provided the moral basis for conscription. In the event the regime has never gone ahead with black conscription, because of the very strong resistance to it in these communities.

The third aspect of South Africa's militarisation is seen in the attempt to secure strategic industries and to build up a military/industrial complex to provide the regime with its own domestic arms industry. Steps have been taken to secure oil supplies and to establish iron and steel plants. ARMSCOR, the state's Armaments Production and Development Corporation, is today one of the largest industries in South Africa. It employs 30,000 people directly and claims that through subsidiary corporations and contracts with local suppliers, it involves 100,000 people in arms production.

Despite its tremendous investment in this field, it is clear that the South African regime is not self-sufficient in armaments. It can equip the army with rifles and other small arms and it has certain capabilities in the missile field. It can manufacture armoured cars and other basic vehicles. But more sophisticated items like military jet aircraft or highly complex electronic communications are beyond its capacity. This is not surprising; even developed countries such as Britain find it difficult to make modern military aircraft without help from the United States or other European countries. South Africa can never be self-sufficient in arms. It will always need to import key components, if only because it would be far too expensive to establish its own domestic production lines.

Pretoria had always relied on the West for its military capacity. That is why the mandatory arms embargo, imposed on South Africa in 1977, was so vital. South Africa has already started to lose the air superiority on which it relied to carry out large-scale attacks against neighbouring countries. The arms embargo is steadily eroding South Africa's capacity to wage war in the region.

Forces at the disposal of the South African Government

It is impossible to put exact figures on the number of men in the SADF because it does not publish them. My estimate of the Defence Force's total strength is in excess 600,000 personnel. Many of these are 'Reserves', people who have undergone their full-time military training and are now going through their period of liability to annual call-up, first for up to three months in the SADF and then in the local

Commandos. A full-scale mobilisation of these men even for brief periods would have a crippling effect on South Africa's economy as they were pulled out of key posts. The day-to-day strength of the regular and full-time conscript SADF is somewhere in the region of about 200,000. This is still a considerable force. It is much stronger than any of the neighbouring countries' armies. Indeed, it is stronger than all of them combined.

In addition to the SADF itself, which consists of the army, air force and navy, the South African regime can call on a number of other forces. Each of the so-called 'independent' Bantustans has its own 'army'. These are very small and their discipline is questionable. But the SADF is training them; within the Bantustans there is very close liaison between the various forces; effectively they are under the SADF's command. In Namibia the SADF has set up a nominally separate structure called the South West Africa Territory Force, recruited mainly from Namibians, in some areas by conscription. This force is about 20,000 strong.

The South Africa Police is also a para-military force. Its current strength is about 56,000 but this will almost double over the next few years. All policemen are armed and have been given military training in counter-insurgency warfare. They travel in armoured vehicles and carry automatic weapons. They are not so much a police force, more an auxiliary army. In addition to the South Africa Police, the regime has established a range of other police forces. The town councils or equivalent black local authorities through which the South African government rules the townships and which have been attacked consistently over the last two or three years by popular movements, now have their own police.

About 6,000 town council police have now been trained; a further 10,000 are to be recruited. They are given fairly rudimentary instruction for about three months. Over the past couple of years the regime has set up yet another force, currently about 1,000 strong and soon to reach 6,000, which people call 'kitskonstables' (instant police). These are 'trained' in three weeks. Many of them are recruited from the vigilante groups which have been operating against the 'comrades' in various townships, in collusion with the South Africa Police. It is clear that the regime is greatly increasing the number of police that it can throw into the townships as the first line of defence.

SADF strategy

The SADF's national security doctrine stresses that war must be fought on all levels and that these must be co-ordinated under centralised control. South African commanders draw much of this strategy from the French theorist Beaufre.[1] He specialised in what he calls the 'indirect mode of warfare', that is, the non-military aspects. They have also studied counter-insurgency warfare in numerous situations: Algeria, Vietnam, Malaya, Greece, and so on. General Malan got experience on the spot with the French in Algeria; he was also at the U.S. Staff College during the period of America's war in Vietnam.

South African commanders have learned from these other wars and adopted their own counter-insurgency strategy. They argue that guerrilla war can be divided into four stages. The first is the organisational stage where political movements organise among the people and adopt their grievances. The second is termed the 'terrorism' stage, when limited guerrilla warfare is directed against specific targets. The third stage, 'guerrilla warfare', describes the situation in which large numbers of guerrillas - thirty, forty, a few hundred - can move more freely and attack targets more widely. The final stage is that of mobile, semi-conventional warfare. The guerrilla force has by now transformed itself into something like a conventional army, equipped with heavy weapons to attack cities and major military targets.

This is a very mechanical approach which looks rather inappropriate to the South African situation. Nevertheless, South African strategists accept it as a model and argue that their objective must always be to turn the guerrilla army back to the previous stage. In addition, they stress the need to use the guerrillas' own tactics. The SADF must be prepared to consolidate and defend its own territory before counter-attacking in order to wipe out the enemy. The regime must also win the hearts and minds of the people, by psychological and social warfare. Conversely, white strategists also advocate the immediate use of maximum force to maintain the initiative against any guerrilla enemy.

The war in Namibia

Much of Namibia is desert or semi-desert. At least half the population live in the northernmost area called Ovamboland, which is where the war is mainly being fought. SWAPO has considerable political support.

---

[1]   André Beaufre, *An Introduction to Strategy*, (Faber and Faber: London, 1963).

Even the South African army has admitted that over the whole of Namibia (even outside Ovamboland) some eighty per cent of the people support SWAPO. The origin of the conflict lies in South Africa's occupation of Namibia during the First World War, when it was a German colony. Under a League of Nations Mandate, but contrary to its terms, South Africa set about turning Namibia into a fifth province of South Africa and then imposed its apartheid policies.

For the past twenty years and more the world community has been calling on South Africa to withdraw, as it has no legal standing in a country which is nominally under the Trusteeship of the United Nations. In addition to waging a diplomatic struggle the liberation movement has, since 1966, taken up arms. For several years most of the fighting was in the Caprivi Strip, in the far north-east. It was then a 'low-intensity' war, fought by the South Africa Police, with the army only in a supporting role. Since the independence of Angola in 1975, under the MPLA government, there has been a tremendous increase in Namibia's armed struggle. Many thousands of South African troops have been moved into the territory. Estimates put the total number of troops, including the Territory Force and the militarised police, at 100,000. As the population numbers only about one and a half million, there is one soldier or armed policeman to every fifteen civilians. Namibia today must be one of the most militarised countries in the world.

Most of the fighting is in the north where the majority of the people live, where SWAPO support is strongest and where most guerrilla activities are focused. Guerrillas carry out frequent strikes on army bases, convoys and various strategic and economic targets. Huge numbers of troops scour the bush searching for guerrillas but seldom make contact. Frustrated by their inability to pin SWAPO down, the police and troops have become increasingly brutal in their methods. There have been mass round-ups, torture, indiscriminate killing and rape. Most of the northern areas are under martial law, which prevents media access. Troops are ordered to shoot on sight after the curfew.

The population in Namibia is clearly subject to official terrorisation. The South African regime nevertheless clings to the ideology that it is winning hearts and minds and that the SADF is waging war in its psychological and social dimensions. The SADF itself repeatedly claims to have won the war; in fact they are no nearer to ending it than they were twenty years ago. They continually maintain that they are buying time for a political solution, but they are further away from a solution than they have ever been. They keep on trying to install puppet governments in the capital, Windhoek, which collapse after a couple of years. The South Africans know that they would lose any internationally supervised election. They know they do not have the people's support.

Attacks on neighbouring states

The Namibian war has spilled over into southern Angola. South African troops constantly cross into Angola from their Namibian bases. The reason they give for these operations is to attack SWAPO, which the SADF states has bases in Angola. But South Africa's raids on Angola go far beyond attacks on SWAPO; they are aimed at bringing down, or at least seriously weakening the Angolan government.

The SADF's first intervention in Angola was in 1975 after the downfall of the Portuguese dictatorship. South Africa wanted to install a compliant regime in Angola, so it invaded the territory in support of the UNITA movement. South African armoured columns penetrated to the gates of the capital, Luanda, but were stopped and then retreated back into Namibia. They brought with them remnants of their UNITA allies. These forces were reconstituted, retrained, re-armed and then relaunched back into Angola. Southern and central Angola have since then been in a constant state of generalised warfare, partly through UNITA operations and partly through South African intervention. In 1981 South African troops launched a major invasion of southern Angola and occupied several hundred square kilometres of Cunene province. They remained there until 1984, when they made a partial withdrawal. The south and south-eastern areas of Angola have been devastated by South African and UNITA activity. Several hundred thousand people have been made homeless, the economy of the area and whole towns have been destroyed by bombing.

South Africa has also attacked Mozambique, making similar use of a 'surrogate' force. The Smith regime, in what was then Rhodesia, had recruited a small group called the Mozambique Resistance Movement and started deploying these people inside Mozambique to carry out acts of sabotage behind the Zimbabwean guerrilla lines. After Zimbabwe's independence the MNR (generally known now as RENAMO) were pulled back to South Africa and given an infusion of arms and money. The MNR began to infiltrate Mozambique, attacking outposts and villages. As a result large areas of Mozambique have suffered economic dislocation, which has caused starvation and political set-backs for the FRELIMO government.

Zambia has been attacked on a number of occasions by South Africa. Troops in the Caprivi strip have crossed into the south-western area of Zambia to carry out sabotage bombings. In Zimbabwe surrogate forces seem to have been used. In Swaziland, Lesotho and Botswana regular South African troops have repeatedly violated the borders.

The whole of southern Africa has been drawn into this conflagration. The object of the aggression is first, to prevent these countries supporting the liberation movements in South Africa and Namibia and, secondly, to reduce their independent status to that of vassals of Pretoria. Pretoria talks of a constellation of states, under South Africa's economic and political control. But even when South Africa manages to secure political leverage over these countries, it continues to attack them. It signed a so-called peace agreement with Mozambique, very humiliating for FRELIMO, yet Pretoria broke the agreement even as it signed it; it continued to deploy bandits in Mozambique. Swaziland signed a secret agreement with South Africa and yet South Africa continued cross-border attacks.

It is clear that the South African regime is not interested in negotiated peace or stable co-existence with its neighbours; it wants to reduce them to a level where they do not pose any threat, real or potential, to the regime.

The war in South Africa

It is convenient to divide the conflict in South Africa into rural and urban sectors, although there is considerable overlap between urban and rural areas, as in any country.

In rural areas the basic military unit is the Commando, a part-time force made up of local whites who are often farmers. They are supposed to know the local terrain. They carry out part-time military duties, mainly patrols, and have an intelligence function. As soon as they are aware of guerrilla activity or labour unrest, or any other disturbance, the local Commandos will feed their information through the National Security Management System. The Commandos act as a trip-wire; if they detect a group of guerrillas they will call up reinforcements from a nearby army base.

In the Bantustans, or 'homelands' as they are called by the regime, the Bantustan 'armies' carry out the same sort of function, and they can always call on the SADF for reinforcements. Some of the rural areas are now largely militarised, particularly in the northern Transvaal which borders Swaziland and Zimbabwe. The white farmers along the northern borders are responsible for keeping records of the black people on their farms, their workers and any strangers who come into their area. They have to erect security fencing, they patrol roads and so on. They get cash subsidies and other inducements from the government to stay on their land, and they are obliged to join the local Commando. These farmers act as South Africa's first line of defence; that is why the ANC has been attacking them.

The urban areas have been the site of the most intense conflict over the past couple of years. It is only recently that the army has been deployed in the urban areas in any number. During the 1976 uprisings in Soweto it was the police who were responsible for suppressing resistance; the army was mainly kept in reserve. It is only since P.W. Botha became Prime Minister that the army has been used to any appreciable extent in the townships. During the school boycotts and workers' strikes of 1980-81, mainly in the eastern and western Cape, there were reports of army units being involved in clashes with strikers or students. In 1981 a major military operation was launched in Westbury township in the Transvaal. The army surrounded the town, sealing it off completely. The police then moved in and searched from house to house, rounding up the leaders of a local schools boycott.

The army has been most visibly active since September 1984, when the current wave of resistance erupted. The first major operation was in October 1984 when some 7,000 troops were put into the townships of the Vaal triangle, where the resistance first started. They surrounded Sharpeville and Sebokeng, two of the major townships, and carried out a systematic house-to-house search with a considerable show of force. Troops handed out leaflets announcing 'We are your friends - we are here to help you' and stamped people's hands with stamps saying 'Friendly forces'. Given that they were waking people up at gunpoint at 4 a.m., this hardly had the desired effect of winning affection! The operation also failed in its other objective, which was to capture 'revolutionary elements'. Nevertheless, the operation set a precedent for massive army intervention in the townships. The Sharpeville/Sebokeng operation was deliberately carried out in the full glare of publicity. Since then things have changed: the SADF is now doing everything in its power to keep the media out.

For the past two years not a day has gone by without the army being involved in some capacity in South Africa's townships. Some townships have several garrisons either inside the townships or just outside. The SADF says these are temporary but in some cases they have been in place for two years. Virtually all South Africa's townships are being patrolled on a daily basis by armoured vehicles. Various tactics have been tried - troops have set up searchlights on nearby hills or built watch-towers around townships with searchlights mounted on them. They have surrounded townships in the eastern Cape with barbed wire, and closed off all but one or two entrances which have then been patrolled with armoured vehicles. They have attempted to stop school-students' resistance by occupying the schools, particularly in July 1986. Troops moved into the schools, positioned armoured vehicles in the playgrounds and tried to determine which students could enter school and to issue identity cards. There were even reports of troops in the classrooms, listening to what the teachers were saying.

The state of emergency has given extraordinarily wide powers to the SADF. Any soldier, whatever his rank, has the power to arrest anyone and to detain that person without trial for two weeks - a period which can then be extended indefinitely by the Minister of Law and Order; to interrogate anyone; to use such force as they deem necessary; to search anyone, any building, any vehicle; to seize and impound vehicles, objects, even aircraft, and to order anyone to leave an area in which they are not usually resident. They can enforce all the emergency regulations, including restricting people to their houses, preventing children from going to school and so on. One would think that some attempt would be made to check the behaviour of troops who wield such immense power. On the contrary, they have been given a blanket indemnity from civil or criminal prosecution for any act they choose to carry out. In the last resort, this is a licence to kill. Furthermore, nobody need know about it, because the media have been excluded from the townships. A blanket ban has been put on any report of any incident anywhere. The black areas of South Africa have now been invaded by young white troops who enjoy the most extraordinary martial law powers.

The irony is that the South African generals have fallen into precisely the trap which they warned against. General Malan himself has said that 'Bullets kill bodies, not beliefs' and, on another occasion, that 'in this type of battle you can never win on a military field, you can only win in the political field'.[2] Yet it is clear that the South African regime is politically bankrupt, totally incapable of satisfying the political aspirations of the majority of the people. It is trying to do what its generals have warned against - to win the war by brute force alone.

Further Reading

Cawthra, G.,	*Brutal Force: The Apartheid War Machine* (IDAF: London, 1986).
Committee on South African War Resistance,	*Resister*, bi-monthly journal of the COSAWR, B.M. Box 2190, London WC1N 3XX.
Frankel, P.H.,	*Pretoria's Praetorians: Civil-Military Relations in South Africa* (Cambridge University Press: Cambridge, 1984).
Grundy, K.W.,	*The Militarization of South African Politics* (Tauris and Co.: London, 1986).
Hanlon, J.,	*Beggar Your Neighbours: Apartheid Power in Southern Africa* (CIIR, James Currey: London, 1986).
Johnson, P. and Martin, D.,	*Destructive Engagement: Southern Africa at War* (Zimbabwe Publishing House: Harare, 1986).
Konig, B.,	*Namibia: The Ravages of War* (IDAF: London, 1983).

---

[2]   Cited in IDAF, 'The Apartheid War Machine', *Fact Paper* No. 8 (1980).

5. The Regional Crisis

ROGER RIDDELL

Introduction

In all situations of conflict, fact, myth and propaganda intertwine to enlighten, confuse and conceal, with different interest groups competing to have their own particular viewpoint heard and accepted as the conventional wisdom. The escalating conflict evolving in southern Africa is no exception. The present contribution broadens the main theme of this collection to consider the regional crisis in southern Africa which the political, military and economic defence of apartheid within the international borders of South Africa is causing to its neighbours outside.

South African dominance

There can be no doubt that in comparison with South Africa, its neighbours are economically weak. The eight independent states of southern Africa - Angola, Botswana, Lesotho, Malawi, Mozambique, Swaziland, Zambia and Zimbabwe - have a combined wealth that is only one fifth that of South Africa. In 1984, the joint gross domestic product (GDP) of these eight countries was valued at $18 billion compared with $73 billion for South Africa. One effect of this wide difference in economic power and, additionally, its relative concentration - for the land area of South Africa's neighbours is three times as great as that of South Africa and its total population one and a half times greater - is that South Africa's view about the region tends also to dominate and be heard - and therefore be absorbed and internalised - far more readily than those of its neighbours. In short South Africa's economic (as also its military) dominance is reflected in the influence that its own assembly of the facts, its own world-view and perhaps its own myths about the region have on the manner that the problems of southern Africa are perceived not only within South Africa but also internationally. One only has to look a little more critically into one recent event, the way in which the death of President Machel of Mozambique has been reported, to appreciate the relative powers of the different countries of the region to present events as they unfold. The President's plane crashed in a remote hilly area as it

77

approached Maputo airport where it was scheduled to land. The site of the crash was far closer to Maputo than to Pretoria and even closer to Mbabane, the capital of Swaziland. Yet the flight had also been monitored by the South Africans who arrived at the scene of the tragedy first, within hours of the crash, and who were able both to identify the President and break the news to the world press. Indeed for some 24 hours after the crash occurred the South African view of events was the only one available to the world's media and thus its particular interpretation was extremely influential in the attempt to explain the causes and circumstances of the crash. Far less credence was given subsequently to claims by Mozambique, Zambia and Zimbabwe that the crash was no accident and to the detailed comments of experienced local pilots that faulty instrument data in the aircraft or isolated human error could not have caused it.[1]

Fact and Fiction

This particular example leads to a more general question about the interpretation of events as they develop in southern Africa: in what way is the South African view of the crisis that is unfolding in southern Africa correct and in what manner does this view influence the common international perception of this crisis? The widespread publicity that the escalating violence within the borders of South Africa has had internationally has raised the question about the spreading of violence and chaos to the neighbouring states. And on the economic plane are growing fears that retaliatory action by South Africa on its neighbours to the threat and growing reality of sanctions imposed by western governments, international companies and banks will add to that chaos and even lead to total debility. On the one hand South Africa argues either that economic sanctions against it won't work or else that its economy will survive, with its own black majority suffering the most, and on the other hand it puts forward the view that sanctions it might impose against its neighbours will work and that the effects will be dramatic. A widely-held South African view about the regional effects of sanctions initiated by South Africa is highlighted in a recent paper by Dr Leistner, Director of the Pretoria-based Africa Institute of

---

[1]   See, for instance, 'Mozambique: Pandora's Boxes' *Africa Confidential* 27, 23 (12 November 1986) and B.P. Andrews, 'A Professional Look at some of the Technical Aspects of the T134-B Disaster' *The Financial Gazette* (Harare), 7 November 1986, p.4.

South Africa which begins as follows:[2]

> The advocates of economic sanctions against South Africa usually fail to consider how the damage they propose to inflict on South Africa may affect other countries in the region. The degree of suffering, naturally, would depend on the severity of the sanctions imposed against South Africa. In practice this could imply anything - from token, those designed only to serve as a warning, to measures intended to cause severe disruption, such as total embargoes on all trade with South Africa and the severing of air and telecommunication links.

These South African perceptions of the regional crisis are also shared by western leaders and form a dominant view in the international press and media. For instance as recently as October 1985 the Australian Foreign Minister explained his government's policy towards South Africa thus: 'we want to bring it (SA) to its senses and we want to so do before the violence in South Africa spreads beyond its borders'.[3] More recently, in August this year, the United States Administration put out a news release which contained the following statement:[4]

> Punitive boycotts of exports imposed by South Africa's major trading partners...would (also) have a direct negative impact on the economies of neighbouring black countries...An unintended impact of sanctions on South Africa is Pretoria's apparent intention to retaliate economically with counter sanctions against its black neighbours. The South African Government is even now instituting slowdowns at border posts, and with the actual advent of sanctions it could do much more. It could: - Expel tens of thousands of migrant workers; - Cause severe shortages of food, petroleum products, and energy; - Restrict South African investment, soft loans, and grants; - Constrain access to South African ports and rail facilities, causing decreases in export earnings from mineral and other products; and - Create shortages of imported industrial supplies and manufactured goods leading to sharp price hikes.

The statement ends with the illuminating comment:

> Historically, punitive economic sanctions seldom have been effective. Whatever the case may be with South Africa, one thing is clear: its

---

[2]   G.M. Leistner, 'Sanctions Against South Africa in Regional Perspective' (Africa Institute of South Africa: Pretoria, 1985) (mimeo).

[3]   Quoted in *The Observer* (London), 13 October 1985.

[4]   'Meaning of Sanctions and Counter Sanctions for South Africa's Neighbours' *GIST* (Bureau of Public Affairs, Department of State) August 1986.

black neighbours would suffer substantially.

The food shortage argument is one recently used by the British Prime Minister. In an interview in July 1985 she commented thus:[5]

> I sometimes get the map out and say look at it. Have you looked at how goods are going to get in and out of Zambia and Zimbabwe. Close Beit Bridge and how are you going to do it? That's the maize route. When there was drought, that's the route through which maize went to keep people alive. I ask them, have you looked at it? Have you looked at the poverty and hunger and starvation - just when we're after all trying to give things to Africa, to see she doesn't suffer in this way?

If these perspectives and evaluations of the nature of the regional crisis were correct and complete then the counter-comments and policy proposals of South Africa's neighbours appear odd, to say the least. Why, for example, should the majority of southern Africa's independent states be in favour of sanctions against South Africa and some who are members of the Commonwealth be among the most vociferous lobbyists for concerted international action against South Africa? Why, too, should the leading private sector business organisation in all the independent states - the Confederation of Zimbabwe industries - pass a resolution at its annual congress, in July 1986, supporting the stance the Zimbabwe government has been taking on the sanctions issue?

In the following section an attempt will be made not only to answer these questions but to explain why such a response can be seen as both rational and understandable. By implication it will be inferred that the South Africa-based perspective and its policy conclusions are either extremely partial and therefore misleading or else incorrect. We can start with Mrs Thatcher's comment about food. Although she is quite right about the strategic importance of Beit Bridge and the rail line linking South Africa and the north, she is wrong about the recent use of this particular transport route for food supplies. Even the cutting off of the Beit Bridge link will have little effect on the supply of food to the major food defecit countries of either Africa as a whole or of the independent states of southern Africa. It is not the Beit Bridge link which is used to provide food to the food deficit countries of Angola, Mozambique or even Botswana. But what is of more importance is that in 1986 it has been South Africa and not the main land-locked nations of the southern African interior that have been experiencing food deficits. In 1986 Zambia had a maize surplus and Zimbabwe had over

---

5   Interview with Mr H. Young, *The Guardian*, 9 July 1985, p.23.

one million tonnes of maize in excess of its domestic requirements. Early in 1986 the Beit Bridge rail link was used to transport 20,000 tonnes of maize from Zimbabwe to South Africa.[6] And it is not only maize which has been in short supply in South Africa: in September 1986 Canada delivered 55,000 tonnes of wheat to South Africa for domestic consumption.[7]

Regional destabilisation

Moving from this specific misconception to the more general theme, the major reason for the apparently self-destructive attitude to sanctions taken by the majority of the Front Line States (FLS) lies in appreciating the economic destruction that South African destabilisation has inflicted on the independent countries of the region and is continuing to inflict. Contrary to the view of the Australian Foreign Minister, cited above, the violence in southern Africa has for many years spread beyond the borders of South Africa and has led to substantial costs, direct and indirect, on the economies of the independent states.[8]

Hanlon records that since 1980, in the 8 majority-ruled states of the region, South Africa has: - invaded three capitals (Lesotho, Botswana, Mozambique) and four other countries (Angola, Swaziland, Zimbabwe and Zambia); - tried to assassinate two prime ministers (Lesotho and Zimbabwe); - backed dissident groups that have brought chaos to two countries (Angola and Mozambique) and less serious disorder in two others (Lesotho and Zimbabwe); - disrupted the oil supplies of six countries (Angola, Botswana, Lesotho, Malawi, Mozambique and Zimbabwe); and - attacked the railways providing the normal import and export routes of seven countries (Angola, Botswana, Malawi, Mozambique, Swaziland, Zambia, Zimbabwe).

The human costs have been considerable, though given little prominence in the international press and media compared with the, albeit belated, coverage given to the famine in Africa further north. As

---

6   *The Financial Gazette* (Harare), 21 February 1986.

7   *The Financial Gazette* (Harare), 12 September 1986.

8   For a detailed account of South African destabilisation on the region see J. Hanlon, *Beggar Your Neighbours* (CIIR, James Currey: London 1986) and P. Johnson and D. Martin, *Destructive Engagement: Southern Africa at War* (Zimbabwe Publishing House: Harare, 1986).

Professor Reg Green summarizes it in a recent paper:[9]

> Recent analysis (carried out for UNICEF) suggests 8,500,000 peasants dislocated and over 4,500,000 persons in danger of starvation as a result of South African and proxy force aggression. Deaths from starvation as a result of war dislocation and blocking of relief supplies over 1983-85 probably totalled over 200,000. On reasonable estimates of mortality without and with the war, infant and child war deaths, from war related food shortages, dislocation and disruption of health services, in Angola and Mozambique are of the order of 120,000 a year or one every four minutes.

But it is the economic costs of destabilisation that particularly need to be highlighted. The Southern African Development Coordination Conference (SADCC), consisting of the eight independent countries of Southern Africa, plus Tanzania, is a grouping of these nine countries established in 1980 among whose objectives are to increase mutual economic development and, *inter alia*, reduce current levels of economic dependence on South Africa. At the annual SADCC summit held in 1985 a paper was tabled itemising the estimated costs of South African destabilisation efforts. In the period 1980-84, the paper judges, on fairly conservative assumptions, that these amounted to some $10 billion, or $2 billion a year.[10] Extrapolating these figures forward to 1985 and 1986 would add an additional $9 billion, giving $19 billion in all or some $2.7 billion a year.[11] Using slightly different assumptions, figures of up to $30 billion or over $4 billion a year in this period have also been estimated.[12] Putting the lower estimates of destabilisation costs into some perspective, they are equivalent to approximately 10 per cent of gross domestic product lost, and some 30 per cent of SADCC's export earnings. For Angola and Mozambique, destabilisation costs have been even more significant, equivalent to perhaps some 30 per cent of GDP. In the years 1980-84, the SADCC countries, excluding Tanzania, received $8.6 billion in aid, suggesting that in that

---

[9] R.H. Green, 'From Economic Disaster Toward Recovery and Renewed Development: Toward African Action' (Institute of Development Studies, at the University of Sussex) October 1986, p.3 (mimeo).

[10] 'An Illustrative Assessment of the cost of Destabilisation on the Member States of Southern African Development Co-ordination Conference' reproduced in Hanlon (1986), pp. 265-270.

[11] Hanlon (1986), p. 270.

[12] R.H. Green, 'The SADCC Economies and Sanctions Against South Africa: Notes Toward Cost Containment and Benefit Attainment' (Institute of Development Studies, at the University of Sussex) 1986, p.4 (mimeo).

period, destabilisation costs exceeded all aid inflows from all sources, with the gap between aid received and destabilisation costs widening substantially over the most recent 1985-86 period.[13]

Table 1 provides a breakdown of these destabilisation costs by sub-category:

Table 1. *Estimated Accumulated Cost to SADCC States of South African Destabilisation (1980-84 $Million)*

Direct war damage	1610
Extra defence expenditure	3060
Higher transport and energy costs	970
Lost exports and tourism	230
Smuggling	190
Refugees	660
Reduced production	800
Lost economic growth	2000
Trading arrangements	300
Total	10120

Source: Hanlon (1986) p.265.

Direct War Damage Costs relate to costs of direct military activities in the neighbouring countries such as the attack on the Zimbabwe airforce, the oil refinery in Angola and the port and oil installations in the Mozambique port of Beira.

Extra Military Expenditure refers to the increased defence expenditure incurred arising from the direct and indirect measures taken

---

[13] For aid flows see OECD, *Geographical Distribution of Financial Flows to Developing Countries* (OECD: Paris, 1986) p. 28.

to counter South African aggression or to defend economic installation and supply routes. For instance, at the end of 1986, over one quarter of Zimbabwe's armed forces were stationed in neighbouring Mozambique to keep open the oil pipeline which supplies all the country's imported petrol and diesel oil and the crucial rail link to the port of Beira.

Higher Transport and Energy Costs. Perhaps the most visible sign of South African destabilisation has been its success in restricting access to the sea by the land-locked nations of the region and switching extra-regional trade through South Africa. The impact of these actions can be seen from the estimated traffic flows shown in Table 2.

Table 2. *Comparative Estimate of Use Made of SADCC and South African Transport for Extra-Regional Trade %*

	1982		1985	
	SADCC	SOUTH AFRICA	SADCC	SOUTH AFRICA
Botswana	5	95	5	95
Lesotho	-	100	-	100
Malawi	95	5	5	95
Swaziland	67	33	30	70
Zambia	64	36	40	60
Zimbabwe	33	67	10	90

Source: C.W. Davids, 'The Impact of Economic Sanctions against South Africa on the SADCC States', Ottawa, CIDA, 1986.

The potentially efficient and most economic rail route out of Zambia and Zimbabwe is the Southern Mozambique rail route through Chicualacuala in south-east Zimbabwe to the Mozambique port of Maputo.

Since mid-1983 this rail line has been unusable because of guerilla activity and the northern Beira route has been underutilized. As a result, over 90% of this extra-regional traffic has had to use the direct and indirect South Africa rail route. The economic costs of this diversion can be illustrated with reference to Zimbabwe's steel exports. In 1985, the rail freight costs of taking a tonne of steel from the factory in central Zimbabwe to Maputo would have been Z$30. The actual cost of taking it to the South African port of Durban was Z$88 a tonne.[14] Not only does this cost differential affect the competitiveness of Zimbabwean steel (the cost charged by the producer, the Zimbabwe Iron and Steel Corporation [ZISCO], has been lowered to well below cost to maintain exports), but it also affects the foreign exchange equation for freight charges. The switch to Durban entails larger train distance in South Africa which means for Zimbabwe higher payment of Rand vis-a-vis domestic currency for the steel to reach the coast, an absolute loss in foreign exchange to Mozambique and a more than proportional gain in foreign exchange for South Africa.[15]

Lost Exports and Tourism. Transport disruption has decreased reliability of transport routes which has reduced the ability of southern African countries to supply export markets leading to a loss of orders, while their tourism has also been seriously affected. The beach resorts around Maputo and Beira used to house a thriving hotel and tourist industry: today the hotels are used by squatters and the homeless.

Diamonds, ivory and game skin *smuggling* have all increased leading to substantial losses in foreign exchange. For instance, there is evidence of a growing illegal trade in Angola teak-wood. Trees are cut down by UNITA forces in south-east Angola, sometimes under the supervision of South African conscripts, floated down the river to South Africa military check-points in Namibia where they are sawn and shipped to a company in Johannesburg.[16]

Data related both to smuggling and to reduced production and lost economic growth are clearly difficult to determine accurately. However, there is little doubt that the effect of channelling scarce resources of foreign exchange for increased freight and insurance charges, the loss of production in agriculture and industry, falling levels of production

---

14 Figures calculated by the National Railways of Zimbabwe.

15 In 1980 revenue for port charges in Maputo amounted to $96 million but by 1985 this source of revenue had fallen to about $20 million.

16 'Namibia (2): The Caprivi Strip', *Africa Confidential* 27, 21 (15 October 1986).

investment and the delays experienced in a wide range of development projects have led to losses running into several hundreds of millions of dollars.

Boycotts and Embargoes of products have been a frequently-adopted tactic used by the South Africans to cause economic disruption within the region leading to higher costs, lost markets and the slower movement of goods. Two such measures carried out in September 1986 were the deliberate delaying of goods traffic at the Zimbabwe/South Africa border of Beit Bridge affecting Zimbabwean and Zambian goods, and the South African decision to institute customs deposits on transit traffic. A less recent but most dramatic event was the complete halting of road traffic to Lesotho and the slowing of rail traffic on 1st January 1986 which lasted until the coup in Lesotho in late January. Not without significance, South Africa's Customs Union treaty with the three former High Commission territories, Botswana, Lesotho and Swaziland, stipulates the free movement of goods, between the countries of the contracting parties.[17]

It is in this context of South African destabilisation, stretching over a considerable number of years, and the increased costs that this is causing the economies of the independent states of the region that the debate about sanctions needs to be placed. No one doubts, least of all the South Africans, that their country is the regional economic power and has the potential to disrupt the economies of the region, indeed as it is presently doing. The neighbouring countries are calling for sanctions not only because of their abhorrence of the apartheid system but because they believe that the extra costs that are likely to be incurred with increased sanctions need to be evaluated in relation to the past, present and increasing future costs of destabilisation, and the efforts of South Africa to increase their economic and transport dependence upon their southern neighbour.

Economic dependence: a two-way relationship

There is, however, another element in the sanctions debate that needs highlighting. It is too readily assumed in the discussion about sanctions in the wider southern Africa context that, because South Africa *is* the dominant and dominating economic power in the region, it *will* react to further international sanctions imposed against it by inflicting more

---

[17] Quoted from S.R. Lewis, *Some Economic Realities in Southern Africa* (Overseas Development Council: Washington D.C., September 1986) p. 17

widespread and damaging economic measures on its neighbours simply as a matter of course. Certainly there *is* evidence to support this simple relationship of cause and effect, for in September 1986 South Africa announced the prohibition of recruitment of Mozambican workers on the South African gold mines. In mid-1986 there were 50,000 Mozambican workers employed in the South African gold mines remitting some £70 million annually back to Mozambique in repatriated earnings, valued at about one third of its total annual foreign exchange earnings.

What is often not appreciated, however, is that, taken together, the SADCC countries are an important element in the continuing health and strength of the South African economy and that with increasing international restrictions on South Africa imposed from outside Africa this dependence of South Africa on her neighbours is set to increase. A few figures illustrate this particular aspect of the relationship.[18]

While the independent states of southern Africa are trade dependent upon South Africa, South Africa, too, is dependent upon the region. In 1984, South African exports to the SADCC countries were valued at $1.7 billion, accounting for 10 per cent of all South Africa's export earnings and nearly 20% of South Africa's non-gold exports. SADCC's exports to South Africa are far smaller, amounting in 1984 to $415 million. Thus South Africa runs a visible trade surplus of some $1.3 billion with SADCC countries, equal in 1984 to 44 per cent of its total trade surplus for the year. This figure of $1.3 billion is comparable to South Africa's total foreign earnings from the EEC, Japan and the U.S. received for all its food and agricultural exports and slightly more than its world-wide exports of coal. Economically speaking, therefore, to cut off trade with its regional neighbours or to cause such havoc as to reduce significantly their imports from South Africa is, in effect, to shoot itself in the foot and impose sanctions on itself.

The increasing dependence of South Africa's neighbours on the South African transport network leads additionally to large and rising invisible earnings to South Africa. Together with insurance costs, clearing and forwarding charges and port charges, South Africa earned some $300 million in invisibles in 1984, again a far from insubstantial amount. There are, too, other invisible earnings of note. Botswana, Lesotho, Swaziland and Mozambique all receive electrical energy supplies from South Africa - Lesotho 100% of its electrical energy

---

18   Much of the data in the following paragraphs are derived from Lewis (1986).

needs, Swaziland over 70%. Zimbabwe pays out over $50 million a year in pension remittances to former residents and citizens who now reside in South Africa. Together these foreign currency flows amount to at least another $80 million a year.

Another element in the South Africa-SADCC linkage is the considerable stake that South African companies have in a number of SADCC countries. For instance, South Africa's giant companies De Beers & Anglo-American have investments worth over $150 million in Botswana, while in Zimbabwe the South African stake is even greater, with South African interests controlling one quarter of all private capital stock, valued at over $1 billion. Not only do these amounts constitute 'captive' South African assets but the dividends and profits from South African capital, valued overall in excess of $80 million a year, add yet another sizeable inward revenue flow to the South African economy from the neighbouring states.

Of course, not all invisible payments accrue to South Africa. The largest invisible outflow of funds from South Africa relates to the remittances of foreign workers, largely mineworkers of whom those employed in the gold mines are the most important. Official South African figures suggest that there were in 1985 some 350,000 such foreign workers in South Africa of whom nearly 300,000 were employed in the mines. The net outflow of remittances of these workers to the SADCC countries in 1984 amounted to some $200 million.[19] Taking this outflow into consideration, the two-way flows discussed suggest that South Africa probably has net invisible earnings obtained from the neighbouring states of some $200 million overall.

---

[19] The recent decision against workers from Mozambique, taken in the context of rising black unemployment in South Africa itself, probably of the order of three million, might suggest that an escalating policy of repatriation would be a smooth and beneficial move for South Africa to embark upon. However, as Lewis remarks (1986) p. 12: 'It is important to remember that employment of SADCC nationals has economic benefits to South Africa, too. The Chamber of Mines, a private sector organisation heavily involved in the recruiting efforts, has made it quite clear in public statements that the threats of repatriation of SADCC citizens in the face of sanctions against South Africa would not be in the interest of South Africa. With around 300,000 of the total of just over 600,000 black mine workers in the South African mines, the replacement problems would be significant, even in the face of South Africa's unemployment situation. New recruiting was cut back substantially some years ago, so the people now employed in the mines are experienced workers, and the cost of replacing them is not something that could be done costlessly, either to the South African economy or to the mining companies.'

The final major financial linkage between South Africa and some countries in the region relates to the Customs Union existing between South Africa and Botswana, Lesotho and Swaziland. The revenue these countries receive from the Customs Union is considerable, amounting to an average of $300 million a year over the past few years. The importance of this revenue source can be appreciated when it is realised that Customs Union revenue constitutes some 25% of all government revenue for Lesotho and Swaziland. These figures would suggest that South Africa has a potentially enormous grip over the BLS countries and that the turning off of this particular tap could quickly produce havoc in their respective economies. Indeed this argument has recently been used by the South African authorities in their own contribution to the sanctions debate. For instance, last year South Africa's Department of Foreign Affairs put out a document stating that: 'if the South African economy were to be damaged by sanctions to the extent that the flow of imports into southern Africa were substantially diminished, this most important source of revenue to the BLS countries would be eroded, with serious consequences for the economies of these countries.'[20] What this document suggests is that South Africa has the power to manipulate the Customs Union revenue through its control of trade to the BLS countries going in and out of South Africa. However this statement is factually incorrect. The Customs Union agreement specifically states that the revenue obtained by member countries is calculated in reference to *all* imports from *all* sources. Hence if, for instance, the Botswana/South African trade routes are cut off or even if Botswana obtains relatively fewer of its imports through South Africa but is able to switch its source of supply through, for instance, Zimbabwe, then to the extent that its total imports are not reduced neither is its Customs Union revenue. In short, the room for manoeuvre is greater than a superficial view of South African action against its Customs Union neighbours would initially suggest.

In general, therefore, the simplistic view that South Africa has both the economic power and, most importantly, the economic will to strangle the economies of the states of southern Africa needs considerable qualification. There are strong forces at work suggesting that a massive increase in action by South Africa would not be in its

---

[20] South Africa, Department of Foreign Affairs, *South Africa: Mainstay of Southern Africa* (South Africa, Department of Foreign Affairs: Pretoria, 1985), quoted in Lewis (1986) p. 17.

interests, most particularly if sanctions against South Africa by the international community did effectively cut its own foreign exchange earning base and reduce domestic employment. The states of Southern Africa provide a significant source of foreign exchange earning and therefore also a significant source of employment within South Africa.

While these conclusions are clearly important for understanding the complex inter-relationship existing within southern Africa, it is also important not to go too far the other way and argue that the states of southern Africa have nothing to fear from South African action. In this context, three points need to be highlighted.

First, as the discussion on destabilisation costs revealed, South African action has already done considerable damage to the economies of the region which has had costs for South Africa. Overall economic decline, rising defence expenditure and economic disruption has reduced economic activity in the SADCC countries, leading to a loss of South African trade opportunities in the region and reducing South Africa's foreign exchange and employment opportunities, even though damage to the transport system will have provided direct economic and financial gains to South Africa.

Second, this itself indicates the potential and actual conflicts between different parts of South Africa's state system and a less than consistent overall strategy in the region. Clearly destabilisation action and strategy have a far broader purpose than covered by the realm of economics; while one part of this strategy has been to maintain and indeed increase the economic dependence of the region on South Africa, political and military issues have also played a dominant role, frequently resulting in economic harm to South Africa.

But, third, it also needs to be acknowledged that the most significant economic action taken by South Africa has been directed against its *weaker* economic neighbours. Mozambique has clearly been a prime target while Zimbabwe has not. But even in the case of Mozambique, South African policy has by no means been totally consistent. For instance, following the Nkomati Agreement in early 1984, South African businessmen flew into Maputo to attempt to intensify the South African economic presence in Mozambique and over $20 million worth of investment and contracts from South Africa flowed into the Mozambican economy while South African personnel still work at the port of Maputo - hardly a sign of a universally-agreed policy of destabilisation and destruction of the Mozambican economy.

An uncertain future

The final issue that needs to be considered is of course what will happen in the future. There are four sub-questions that need to be addressed. First, what effect will increased international sanctions on South Africa have on the region? Second, what regional action is South Africa itself likely to take? Third, what should the SADCC states do in response? And finally, what action should the international community take to cushion those adverse effects on the region which are likely to result? Clearly there is a whole array of different sanctions possibilities one could postulate in a crystal-ball gazing exercise. Some particular types of international sanctions against South Africa have had a more dramatic and rapid effect on its economy than others.[21] It seems unlikely that trade sanctions directed at South Africa will provide a quick and effective rupture to South Africa's economic survival, and comprehensive mandatory sanctions are not yet on a realistic international political agenda. However, financial sanctions, and particularly action by international creditor banks, have had significant effects. Most dramatic in relation to the effects on the economies of the region has been the fall in the value of the Rand. In relation to this effect, the SADCC states on balance have benefited. Undoubtedly, the falling Rand has had negative effects for the region. Most particularly, the resulting increase in inflation has spread to South Africa's neighbours, the lowering of South African export prices has reduced the competitiveness of goods produced in SADCC countries and exchange rate management has certainly become more difficult. However, the fall in the Rand has overwhelmingly led to increased quantities of South African exports going to the region and at lower foreign exchange values, providing overall a balance of payments gain in at least six of the SADCC countries. To the extent that increased international action against South Africa continues to erode the value of the Rand then this particular gain to most countries of the region needs to be kept firmly in view.

For the future, clearly transport links remain as crucial as they always have been. One of the first initiatives of the SADCC grouping in 1981 was to set up a Transport and Communications Commission whose task was to initiate projects expanding, upgrading and building new transport links to reduce dependence on the South African

---

21 For a more detailed discussion of these issues see 'Sanctions and the South African Economy' *ODI Briefing Paper* (December 1986).

transport system. In the recently-initiated Beira Corridor project, the extension of Zambia's oil-pipeline, the recent decision in Zimbabwe to rebuild its oil refinery and attempts to improve the rail links north through Zambia to Tanzania, crucial projects are under active consideration or under way to address this problem. Of all these, the Beira Project is of paramount importance. Consultants believe that by the end of 1986 up to 60% of the region's present traffic could pass along this route, a quite massive shift in traffic routing away from South Africa and, after three years, nearly complete independence from the South Africa transport system could be achieved for transit trade.[22] However, past experience suggests that these figures could be wildly optimistic, depending as they do not only on aid commitments being fleshed out into finished projects but also on action South Africa is quite capable of taking to disrupt this particular initiative. While uncertainties are present, what does seem evident is that one needs to be extremely wary of the 'catastrophe' scenario of South African action to cut off the rail links with the north causing complete economic havoc; a view which the pessimists have attempted to persuade an uncritical public will necessarily result.[23]

Finally, however, the preceding discussion has tended to treat the SADCC countries as a homogeneous grouping. This is certainly unhelpful when looking at the very different problems that particular countries have so far experienced and which they could face in the future.

Financial aid and material support is needed and will be needed in far greater quantities for some countries than for others. Today, the Mozambican economy is in a perilous position and aid is desperately needed. For the future, Lesotho and Swaziland will be particularly vulnerable to South African action and, in the event of this type of targetted action escalating, they will need widespread and sustained assistance. Botswana, Zimbabwe, Zambia and Tanzania remain far more able to resist an escalation of economic action by South Africa, if it were ever to arise, even though present economic plans and projections would be severely undermined and specific targetted assistance would be needed.

---

[22] See 'Shipping: Threat of Disruption stimulates Search for New Routes' *African Economic Digest*, 8 November 1986, p.13 and 'Freight and Materials Handling in Zimbabwe' *The Financial Gazette* (Harare), 28 November 1986, p. 17.

[23] See, for instance, 'Catastrophe Theory Based on a Fallacy', *The Financial Gazette* (Harare), 4 July 1986, p. 1.

Conclusion

Over the past few years southern Africa has gone through a period of exceptional turmoil and this is likely to increase in the years ahead.

In this context it remains more important than ever to analyse clearly the complete picture of what is happening in the southern African region both so as to target policy in directions that could help to resolve the escalating conflict and to take cognisance of the weapon of propaganda that is used to misinform and distort events as they unfold. South Africa is, without a doubt, the dominant power in the southern African region. It has used this power to inflict economic damage on its neighbours but its power is also in part determined by the economic gains it obtains from them. It is the ambiguities arising from these conflicting inter-linkages which provide the essential background for assessing southern Africa's uncertain future.

Further Reading

Hanlon, J., *Beggar Your Neighbours* (CIIR, James Currey: London, 1986).

Hayes, J.P., *Economic Effects of Sanctions on Southern Africa* (Trade Policy Research Centre: London, 1987).

Johnson, P. and Martin, D. *Destructive Engagement: Southern Africa at War* (Zimbabwe Publishing House: Harare, 1986).

Lewis, S.R., *Some Economic Realities in Southern Africa* (Overseas Development Council: Washington D.C., September 1986).

Overseas Development Institute, 'Sanctions and the South African Economy' *ODI Briefing Paper* (London: December 1986).

—— 'Sanctions and South Africa's Neighbours' *ODI Briefing Paper* (London: May 1987).

UNICEF, *Cutting Off the Flowers, The Macroeconomic and Human Cost of War to Southern African* (UNICEF: Nairobi, 1987).

6. The Case for Sanctions

FRENE GINWALA

Introduction: the analysis of the 1950s

The appeal from the oppressed majority in South Africa for the international community to impose sanctions against the apartheid regime was first made more than 25 years ago and was articulated by the then President-General of the African National Congress, Chief Albert Luthuli. The case for sanctions does not rest on its antiquity, but on its current relevance and any discussion on the merits of sanctions must be located within the political reality of South Africa in 1986. Yet the basis on which the initial call was made is as valid today as it was when first made. What has altered is that there are now *additional* reasons for imposing sanctions - on legal, political and humanitarian grounds, while the need for international action to avert a ghastly catastrophe has never been more urgent.

Let us look briefly at the South Africa of the 1950s, out of which came the call for sanctions. This was a decade in which popular mass struggles had reached a peak, and the regime responded by shutting down the few legal avenues open for opposing apartheid.

THE DEFIANCE CAMPAIGN, which took the form of non-violent resistance through organised and systematic defiance of apartheid laws, had to be brought to an end, because merely asking people to disobey a law, even sitting on a bench reserved for whites, became a criminal offence subject to severe penalties.

This was a period when on the one hand South Africa was being fashioned to the nationalist design of ethnic division, white supremacy and entrenched exploitation. On the other hand, the ANC, which had been formed in 1912 to unite the African peoples, was in the vanguard of forces seeking to unite all South Africans. The very attempts to entrench a white South Africa and delineate and exclude other so-called 'nations', led to a determination to assert one South African nationhood and a common South African society.

The alternative society was outlined by popular participation in a nationwide democratic process (little publicised or known about) designed to ascertain what kind of South Africa people wanted. Views collected were put together in the Freedom Charter which was adopted at a Congress of the People, attended by more than 3,000 delegates. This was the first occasion in the history of the country when people of all races had come together and collectively set out their perspective on the kind of society in which they wished to live. The declaration in the Freedom Charter, that South Africa belonged to all who live in it, black and white, was considered to be treason by the state - and 156 leaders were arrested and so charged.

Already, the ANC had begun to reassess the organisational forms in which the struggle was being conducted. A broad alliance had been formed with Congresses of the other racial groups: Coloured, Indian and White and with the trades unions. But leaders of all these organisations were being banned, restricted and house arrested. There was a growing awareness that though charges of treason might fail this time, the regime was determined to wipe out all opposition, and that sooner or later the organisation itself would be banned. It was at this stage, in the late 1950s, that plans were made and personnel designated to establish what was to become the external mission of the ANC, whose function would be to mobilise international support for our people's struggle.

In looking at South African society we were increasingly aware of the extent to which it was a product of foreign influence and the degree to which its political and economic character had been determined by outside interests. Looking first at the political dimension, it was a British Parliament which entrenched exclusive white power in the constitution. South Africa thereafter claimed to be part of a 'democratic free world', whose other members did not dispute that claim - they welcomed a racist, undemocratic regime and incorporated it in the defence of this 'democratic free world'. They aided and protected it internationally, and by this acceptance tried to give it a credibility and respectability; notwithstanding that those who took power in 1948 had been supporters of the Nazi regime that the same democratic free world had sacrificed so much to fight against. By continuing to relate only to the regime they also tried to give it a legitimacy, and by inference and action, set themselves up as opposed to our own struggle for freedom and democracy.

High Commissioners and later Ambassadors were accredited to a regime which, to this day, exclusively represents white interests. They discussed the politics of our country and exchanged strategic information with our oppressors. Similar discussion about the future of our country still goes on in our absence, while academic, cultural and sporting links with white South Africa have been maintained, building up the morale and confidence of those who support and impose apartheid.

When we looked at and analysed the internal dynamics of oppression in the country, we began to appreciate just how international connections were operating to give not only political but also economic and military strength to our oppressors. We did not need to seek external intervention anew. Foreign interests were already involved in the country. Over the years, British, U.S. and West European companies and finance houses had helped to build apartheid and were continuing to prop it up:

- flourishing trade and foreign investment permitted the apartheid economy to fund ever-increasing expenditure on the state's repressive machinery, and it still does;

- new technology flowed in to help refine that machinery and make it more efficient, that too continues;

- military collaboration brought it arms and built an armaments industry, and despite a mandatory arms embargo, collaboration goes on.

It was clear that these international connections were helping to sustain the very forces we were fighting. Hence, as the battle lines for the 1960s were being drawn, an appeal was made to the international community to stop this aid flowing to apartheid South Africa.

TO THE EXTENT THIS INTERNATIONAL SUPPORT COULD BE DECREASED, TO THAT EXTENT THE FORCES WE WERE FIGHTING WOULD BE LESS STRONG, AND OUR TASK WOULD IN THAT DEGREE BECOME LESS DIFFICULT.

Thus, sanctions were conceived as a **weapon** in our liberation struggle, and remain so today. They were a weapon that would complement our people's efforts, not be a **substitute** for them. And they remain so today.

The present situation

After the banning of the ANC in 1960, the severe repression and the effective illegalisation of all forms of peaceful struggle, the ANC decided that it could no longer exclude armed struggle from the means used to fight apartheid. Today, we remain convinced that the responsibility for destroying apartheid and liberating our country rests with the oppressed. We are engaged in the mobilisation of the entire population and its organisation into mass political action, which is being complemented and reinforced by armed struggle. Within this strategy we still see the need for international sanctions - even more urgently than before.

In the intervening years the reasons for imposing sanctions have increased and added strength to our original demand. But the basis on which the original call was made, and the purpose which sanctions were designed to serve remain unaltered. The original call for sanctions was simply a request to those who were strengthening the regime to desist from doing so - it was a **political** demand. So long as it remained merely a political demand, an appeal to governments to act, it was possible to equate the situation in South Africa with that in a number of other countries, and the argument 'why should we impose sanctions on South Africa and not on tyrannies in country X,Y or Z', according to one's political perceptions, had some validity.

However, in the years since, political developments in southern Africa and the development of international law have combined to distinguish the South African situation from all others where there is an absence of democracy and repression, and has placed a **legal obligation** on member states of the United Nations to impose sanctions. This is what makes the South African situation unique:

- Apartheid South Africa is not an ordinary law-abiding member of the international community, but a state that has violated almost every single norm of international behaviour and several specific provisions of international law.

- The apartheid regime stands in violation of more than 150 resolutions of the Security Council and General Assembly alone, as well as almost every single clause of the Universal Declaration on Human Rights.

- Under the International Convention for the Suppression and Punishment of the Crime of Apartheid, the policy itself and practices associated with it such as forced removals, or preventing any racial group from participation in the political and cultural life of the country are recognised as crimes violating the principles of international law.

- By continuing to maintain its illegal occupation of Namibia, the apartheid regime is in further violation of its international obligations.

- And last but not least, aggression against member states of the UN and economic sabotage and destabilisation, are amongst the most serious violations of the Charter possible. By its frequent acts of aggression, the Pretoria regime has repeatedly breached the peace of the region and stands as a threat to international peace and security.

These constitute additional reasons for imposing sanctions. One should take note that there is a **duty** on the international community and in particular upon the veto-holding members of the Security Council to bring this illegality to an end. By refusing to act, these powers are violating their own obligations under the UN Charter. The International Law Commission of the United Nations has declared that states have a duty to refrain from any co-operation with such gross illegality and further, that they are under the additional duty to assist in the removal of such illegal situations.

Far from acting to support international law, three members of the Security Council persistently abuse their power of veto, using it to protect this international criminal, and thereby reassure the regime that it is immune, at least relatively so, to the full action that could be taken by the international community. These obligations on members of the international community do not change the relationship of sanctions to our liberation struggle. That remains as already outlined. They merely add additional reasons why sanctions should be imposed.

The arguments put forward against applying sanctions totally ignore this international obligation, and apart from drawing attention to it, I do not wish to dwell on what would inevitably cause debate among lawyers.

Before looking at some of the arguments against the imposition of sanctions that are frequently put forward, I would like to set the present context in which questions of feasibility of sanctions, their effectiveness and consequences need to be considered.

As we have seen for over two years now, by banning, detaining, harassing and charging those engaged in peaceful political protest, such as activists of the United Democratic Front, the Pretoria regime has shown once more that it still does not tolerate opposition and remains determined to maintain white domination, whatever the cost in human suffering and lives. Despite the rigorous censorship there are reports of torture in prisons and brutality in the streets. Deaths mount up as troops and police fire on unarmed civilians including babies. In the current state of emergency, that is over the past five months, over 23,000 people have been detained, including trade unionists, and church leaders. Children as young as seven are not only detained but have been charged with public violence.

Notwithstanding, life continues under the state of emergency - with security perimeters and mounted searchlights around many black townships, road blocks outside and armed police and military vehicles patrolling the streets within. A new meaning has been given to the concept of compulsory education as street curfews are imposed during school hours, armed police and troops herd children into classes and mount guard to ensure they remain there.

The struggle also continues: the schools remain empty. People of all ages are daily demonstrating that however intense the repression, whatever the sacrifices demanded of them, they will not be cowed into submission, but will continue to fight for liberation until victory.

Since even Botha claims that he is opposed to apartheid, let me clarify what we understand by liberation. We do not consider as sufficient changes that simply reduce the brutalities of apartheid or ameliorate its effects, whilst the shackles that bind the oppressed are left intact. Liberation requires the destruction of the apartheid system in its entirety: its ideological roots, its institutional branches, its violent seeds and its bitter fruits of oppression, racism and exploitation.

Liberation must entail the transfer of power to the people of South Africa, so that they can collectively shape the society they desire, create the institutions and structures that are required and decide by whom and how they will be operated. Liberation must lead to the creation of a non-racial, democratic and united South Africa. In effect, it means a political system of one person one vote, one electoral roll. That I believe is what you understand by democracy in this country.

A great deal of money and public relations expertise has been put into promoting the notion that the regime is engaged in a process of reforming apartheid. In the face of resistance that will not be suppressed, the regime has been forced to conclude that South Africa can no longer be ruled in the old way. But without any strategy to regain control of the country or of political development, the regime has sought to pre-empt for itself the role of initiator and agent of change based on a professed opposition to apartheid, and a belated acknowledgement that it is an outdated concept.

By this stratagem, Botha has tried to retain control over the process of change, to slow its pace, and to steer its direction away from fulfilment of the people's aspirations. Most importantly, the regime desires acceptance of itself as the agent of change, and thereby, recognition of the right of the white minority to continue to decide the destiny of South Africa. Those who continue to insist that change can only come to South Africa through reform, are in effect accepting that apartheid must continue, and the white minority should retain the monopoly of decision-making.

In the attempt to bolster the image of the oppressor-turned-liberator, new and hitherto unfamiliar words have entered the regime's vocabulary, but their commonly accepted meaning has been distorted. Thus there is a 'common citizenship', which must be exercised in differentiated and discriminatory political institutions and which does not carry, or even imply, equal political rights. The words, 'a united South Africa' are uttered, but refer to the fragmentation of the Bantustans. 'Power sharing' is much favoured, but as used by Pretoria means that the oppressed will be allowed to share in the implementation of apartheid, while 'full political participation' will permit them to become actively involved in the various mechanisms of oppression.

The oppressor may be able to alter his language, but can no more change character than the leopard his spots. When we look at the reforms that have been implemented, promised or presaged, the new rhetoric cannot disguise the reality of Pretoria's objectives. None of the proposed reforms is a translation into policy of the wishes of the majority. Rather, they are an expression of the ideas of the ruling group acting in its own interest, not those of the oppressed.

The so-called reform programme, for which Mrs Thatcher wishes us to give credit to Pretoria, is a set of measures elaborated and implemented in the context of Pretoria's doctrine of national security.[1] They have the sole aim of trying to defuse the crisis in the country, with a view to ensuring the permanence and security of the apartheid system and of white minority domination. That is not to say that all the changes have been purely cosmetic, but rather that none springs from an intention to dismantle apartheid.

Since the reforms originate from those with a vested interest in maintaining apartheid, the outer limits of the programme are defined by the requirement that everything is subject to amendment, provided that such change will extend the life of the apartheid system in its most fundamental essentials. Apartheid will be reformed in order that it may survive. **That** is what Botha needs time for, to shore up and strengthen apartheid, to adapt it, so that it can better withstand pressure.

---

[1]   For which, see Chapter 4 by Gavin Cawthra, above.

In such circumstances to put forward the view that Botha needs to be encouraged and given time to implement reforms is a nonsense. The rejection of the reforms by the majority is not based on their measure, that they do not go far enough or fast enough, but rather, on the recognition that they are simply a refashioning of apartheid and merely combine its essential ingredients in a new way.

Replies to arguments against sanctions

1. **Sanctions won't work.** This argument is frequently thrown out, without any explanation or consistency about what is meant by the word 'work'.

a) It has been said, I believe by a British Minister, that sanctions will not bring down the apartheid regime as an historical trumpet once allegedly brought down the walls of Jericho. Sounds impressive. But who introduced such a notion? Not us - not those who called upon the international community to impose sanctions. No, it is the **opponents** of sanctions who put forward such a possibility, and set up the Aunt Sally so that they can knock it down.

Because they are opposed to the very notion of acting against the Pretoria regime, they do not bother to even examine the basis on which the call for sanctions was made i.e. that sanctions are a **complement** to our own struggle. With or without sanctions we will continue to fight, and with or without sanctions we will win. **But** sanctions will weaken the regime and forces against us and will thereby significantly affect the length of the struggle, the economic cost, the destruction of the infrastructure of the country, the agony of our people, the loss of life - all these can be minimised by sanctions.

Sanctions will work therefore in terms of what **we** have seen to be their purpose. The ANC has never seen sanctions as simply a punishment, nor as a means of exacting revenge on our oppressors. Sanctions are a viable and effective method of putting pressure on the regime, affecting its capacity to continue to pursue apartheid policies and maintain them by force and at the same time undermining support for apartheid among the white minority.

b) Another reference to sanctions not working is put in the form that sanctions, far from persuading white South Africans to move away from apartheid, would in fact push them into a laager and make them more intransigent. Taken to its logical conclusion such an argument would also suggest that the people of South Africa should not struggle too much or too forcefully as it would drive whites into laager and increase support for the right wing.

The underlying assumption of this argument is that apartheid will be destroyed by the miraculous conversion of its present supporters. How this event is to be realised is never explained. As already indicated this is not feasible - it is the struggle of the people of South Africa that will lead to the destruction of the system.

Not only is this argument based on a false assessment of the dynamics of change in South Africa, but also on a failure to take into account why so many whites support the system. Quite simply, it is profit, wealth, comfort, privilege, and a lifestyle that is based on incomes that are amongst the highest in the world.

Would whites who now support apartheid continue to do so if they had to live within the laager? - armed behind barriers, on guard and fearful of the people around them, hankering after a lost glittering lifestyle, isolated from international contact and having to risk death to defend a declining standard of living? The evidence says not. Already both individuals and companies are preparing their bolt-holes. In the past 12 months alone over 300 accountants have left the country, and the number of doctors and other professionals is many times more. Entire classes of professional graduates have left. Anglo-American is just one of the largest of the companies that have gone off-shore - the easier to engage in sanctions busting but, equally, a prudent each-way bet.

One must bear in mind that South Africa's society and economy are not standing still; they are in a state of great upheaval and growing instability under pressures of internal resistance. Far from uniting whites, these pressures have resulted in divisions among white South Africans such as have never been seen before. Growing numbers of them are exploring ways out of the morass into which Botha's policies have cast them. Within the last few months alone delegations from Cape Town university, NUSAS, the Catholic Bishops, the Dutch Reformed Church and a variety of other groups have begun to enter into dialogue with the ANC, and many more are calling for an end to the spiral of ever greater repression, seeking another way out.

While at the one extreme you have the overt facists jackbooting around behind a newly-designed swastika, you also have whites like Marion Sparg who only a week ago began serving a 25 year sentence, because she chose to become a soldier for freedom in our people's army Umkhonto we Sizwe. Marion was not the first white to do so, and many more will follow.

c) The third aspect of the sanctions won't work argument is that sanctions will be circumvented. Oddly enough this argument is put forward most vehemently by the very people and governments who have done their utmost to ensure that sanctions are not made mandatory, by persistently vetoing resolutions in the Security Council, and when public opinion forces them to take action they take great pains to ensure that any measures are riddled with loopholes. Did you know for instance, that when the EEC finally decided to impose some sanctions in September, they deliberately decided that Namibia should be excluded? So everything they prohibited is permissible if it is stamped 'made in Namibia', or the destination is declared to be Namibia. And who controls Namibia?

The problem is not that sanctions won't work, but that a number of governments, particularly Britain, America and West Germany are opposed to sanctions against the apartheid regime precisely because they believe they will work. We have seen that when it suits their political purpose all the objections to sanctions disappear: Zimbabwe, Iran, Nicaragua, Libya, Falklands and, most recently, Syria. I do not recall any speeches about how sanctions did not work when Pretoria blockaded Lesotho last year, or when it held up traffic to Zimbabwe and Zambia a few months ago.

The fact is that sanctions not only do work, but that already one can see the effects in South Africa of even the inadequate sanctions that have been applied. In addition to the oft-quoted sanctions by bankers, there is the effect of the oil embargo. For many years the major oil producers (except of course Britain and the USA) have imposed an embargo on the sale of their crude oil to Pretoria. Earlier this year, Botha confirmed the figures published by the ANC last year, that in order to circumvent the oil embargo the regime was wasting nearly $2 billion annually. In April, the Parliament was told that over the 11-year period between 1973-1984 R22 billion had been spent because of the oil embargo! Over this period the Rand and the US$ were approximately at par.

If sanctions did not work, the regime would have no cause to fear them. Yet we find that in the Proclamation declaring the state of emergency in June 1986, it was made an offence 'to encourage or promote disinvestment or the application of sanctions or foreign action against the Republic'. If sanctions are not effective, why bother with such a provision?

2. Nothing could better illustrate the political perspectives of those governments which oppose sanctions than their new-found concern with **the suffering of blacks in South Africa** which they use to justify continued support for Pretoria. This argument is hypocritical, presumptuous and racist. Are we supposed to believe that Mrs Thatcher, for one, is unaware that blacks have been suffering for decades because of apartheid and are suffering even now? From Pretoria, from anti-sanctions capitals, from city boardrooms and universities have come streams of figures and guesstimates trying to quantify future black suffering in terms of poverty, deprivation and unemployment, and prognostications on the future of a free South Africa as a consequence of the destruction of the economy that will follow sanctions. According to your politics and your audience you can take your pick.

What is definite however, and can be accurately quantified, is what is happening **at present** to the majority as a direct result of apartheid policies. South Africa boasts that it is among the top seven food-producing nations in the world. Every year, one billion dollars' worth of agricultural products are exported including grain, beef, vegetables and fruit, much of which finds its way into the supermarkets of Western Europe. But black South African children are denied this food and die of malnutrition - 136 children every day, nearly 1,000 each week, nearly 5,000 per month, almost 50,000 every year, year in and year out. These deaths are not a consequence of drought, flood or natural disaster, but a direct result of the policy of apartheid; their very regularity bears testimony to the deliberate intent of the authorities.

In pursuance of the objective of an ethnically divided South Africa, nearly four million people have been moved, never by choice, often by force - moved from their homes and communities of long standing. Two million more live under the threat of imminent removal. This is demographic engineering and population control on a scale unknown in peacetime. By way of comparison consider: An estimated 10-20 million people were forcibly transported from the African continent to the Americas in the course of the slave trade, but this was over a period of three centuries. Now, in one country, South Africa, in our lifetime, over a mere 20 years, 4 million people have been uprooted and dumped in the barren wastelands called Bantustans. Within one decade the population of the Qwaqwa Bantustan increased by more than 500%, that of another, KwaNdebele, by 414%. Is it any wonder that there is malnutrition and starvation? Can there be any doubt where the responsibility lies?

Botha does not need sanctions to destroy the South African economy and create black unemployment. Apartheid policies of successive national party governments have done so without any outside help. **Without sanctions** the numbers employed in agriculture, construction, trade and transport have fallen between 1980 and 1985. Between 1968 and 1981 permanent employment on white farms fell by 50% and seasonal employment by 70%. In one year alone, 1983, 250,000 African workers were laid off by farmers. Overall in 1985, unemployment was as high as 37% of the economically active population, and well over 50% among Africans.

The decline in the economy is not simply a reflection of world-wide recession. The racist regime boasts its superiority compared with what it describes as 'economic mismanagement' throughout Africa. But the facts show a different picture. In the decade 1973 to 1982, in real terms, the South African average annual growth in GNP per capita was 0.5%. Across the border, landlocked Lesotho had 4% annual per capita growth, Botswana 5%. The explanation of the contrast can only be apartheid.

The country's resources are being squandered in pursuit of an apartheid ideal, with its proliferation of parliaments, ministers, and separate departments, overlapping local government institutions, and so on *ad infinitum*. There are 18 or 19 ministers of education, 15 ministers of health, and on through the Ministries, with vast overlapping and segregated bureaucracies. Billions more are being spent on the repressive and coercive machinery of the state, on the purchase of arms and equipment, and on a military machine that is used to terrorise and intimidate African people in South Africa, Namibia and throughout the southern African region.

Therefore in this debate, the one thing that we can be absolutely sure about is that unless apartheid is brought to an end, there will be even further poverty, deprivation, unemployment and suffering for black South Africans. And this is even without the bloodshed and murder in our streets. Only a democratically elected government representative of the people and responsible to them, can bring an end to this waste and introduce sensible economic policies to develop our resources, distribute the wealth equitably and thus reduce the poverty of the majority.

Those who argue against sanctions by professing concern for black suffering would do well to examine their own actions and responsibility. They should pay heed to what the people of South Africa are saying and come to terms with the fact that the days when white Britons decided what was good for blacks, and told them so, have passed and will not return. Support for our liberation must begin by accepting our people's right to self-determination in the methods used to conduct our struggle, the help we seek and receive, and in the sacrifice we choose to make.

We are no less concerned about the potential for bloodshed and destruction in South Africa, and we have no desire to inherit a country reduced to a wasteland. That is precisely why we have called for international pressure through sanctions. Neither the oppressed people of South Africa nor those of Namibia will suffer anew as a consequence of sanctions. That it will add in some measure to their present suffering is acknowledged, but this is weighed against the cost to our people of letting apartheid last longer. The sacrifice now is worth making in the context of bringing a speedier end to apartheid and its continuing bloody toll. Surely, genuine concern on these counts is best expressed by providing assistance to minimise the consequences rather than by adding to the suffering through a failure to act.

3. It has also been argued that **economic growth will destroy apartheid,** and therefore, there is a need to maintain and even increase economic links. Associated with this is the proposition that greater foreign investment can promote peaceful changes in the system by improving the conditions of workers. Both are equally fallacious.

The aspirations of the majority of South Africans are not confined to better wages and working conditions. Of course workers want these, but they cannot be a substitute for liberation. Slavery was never and cannot in future, be made acceptable by providing good food and comfortable slave quarters. The role of foreign investors in creating and establishing apartheid institutions and practices within the economy has already been referred to. There is nothing in their record of action, as distinct from rhetoric, which supports the proposition that they are now about to make a 180 degree turn and begin to undo the racist and exploitative system they helped to establish. Nor indeed can they.

Foreign companies cannot democratise the political system. They cannot stop the harassment, torture and murder of our people. They cannot end residential segregation, Bantustans, Bantu Education or any other laws of apartheid. They cannot return to the African people the land that was alienated by whites.

What they can do, but do not do, is refuse to collaborate in our oppression. Employers, including British companies, use the repressive system in labour disputes, call in the police, and dismiss workers. So long as these companies remain in South Africa, they are drawn into participation in the repressive machinery of the state directly. They follow local commercial practice and make up the salary differentials of employees called up to do national service. British companies are thus actually paying wages to the men who are deployed in the townships and whom you have seen on your television screens, shooting and whipping unarmed youngsters.

British companies, including Shell and British Petroleum (BP) and most others, are required by law to organise their employees into militia, to finance and provide military training for them, to facilitate the storage of arms on their premises, and to integrate their installations including refineries, storage depots and factories into regional defence plans. The nature of the 'defence' they will be required to undertake is revealed in the fact that the SADF provides the training, of which an important component is counter-insurgency and riot control. These are just some of the ways in which collaboration with apartheid leads to participation in repression.

It should be noted that not a single British company has stood up and refused to be involved in these ways. That is a measure of their opposition to apartheid. It is only when companies refuse to collaborate with the regime that one can begin to take seriously their protestations of being opposed to apartheid. This is as true of multinationals as it is of South African business. Nothing could be more absurd than the suggestion that sanctions will only hurt the businessmen, and that they are against apartheid anyway.

If mere words were sufficient, the apartheid system would have drowned in the avalanche of statements claiming opposition to apartheid, including a deluge emanating from the Pretoria regime. It is by their actions that we know them. This is true of companies and of governments. Regrettably, on the basis of the record, Britain has chosen to add to the verbiage, but dilute any action. The action we seek is comprehensive mandatory sanctions.

Selective incremental measures give the regime time to adjust and ameliorate the effects. Sanctions conditional on lifting the state of emergency and the release of political prisoners are merely an attempt to dilute our objectives. It is comprehensive mandatory sanctions that are needed.

By their actions, the majority in South Africa have revealed their determination to continue the struggle. Our victory is certain. What remains to be decided is how long it will take, what will be the price in the agony of our people, and what role will the international community play? Both the time scale and the agony can be substantially diminished by international action *now*. ACTION IN THE FORM OF SANCTIONS. NOW.

Further Reading

Consult the list under Ch. 5 by Roger Riddell.

7. Displaced Urbanisation

COLIN MURRAY

Introduction

The pass laws were formally repealed in July 1986. They have been regarded for decades as a lynch-pin of the system of apartheid, since they comprised the discriminatory legislative framework, the cumbersome bureaucratic apparatus and the vicious daily harassment through which access for black South Africans to jobs and housing in the 'white' urban areas was rigidly circumscribed. Their abolition was accordingly welcomed in many quarters as a significant step along the road to reform. The pass laws were replaced, however, by a strategy of 'orderly urbanisation', elaborated in the President's Council report of September 1985 and a White Paper of April 1986. There is still much confusion about what this implies in practice, for a number of reasons. First, influx control now depends primarily on access to jobs and housing. It is administered in terms of legislation nominally passed for other purposes, such as the Slums Act and the Prevention of Illegal Squatting Act. It is to be regulated by the 'local state' and the 'market' rather than by the central state. One consequence is that influx control is differently administered in different regions of the country. Housing shortages are more or less acute. People experience variable combinations of direct and indirect pressures to live in designated residential zones at greater or lesser distances from the main urban centres. Second, what is meant by the 'local state' in this context remains obscure. The White Paper of April 1986 explicitly connected the management of 'orderly urbanisation' with a proposed third tier of government, that of the Regional Services Councils. But their political constitution and strategic responsibilities have never been clearly defined. Indeed, this whole reformist initiative has run into the ground,

I am grateful to William Cobbett for helpful comments on an earlier draft of this chapter. Various versions were presented at the ASAUK meeting in Canterbury in September 1986, at seminars in London and Oxford in October and November 1986, and in the public lecture in Cambridge for the present series in November 1986. This revised version was completed on 31 March 1987 and takes no account of events subsequent to that date. It is also published in African Affairs *86, 344 (July 1987).*

it appears, since the declaration of the present Emergency in June 1986. Third, while the freedom of movement of black South Africans is constrained in practice by their lack of access to employment and accommodation, people already identified as citizens of the four 'independent' Bantustans (Transkei, Bophuthatswana, Venda and Ciskei) remain aliens and are therefore formally precluded from a right of access to jobs and housing in 'white' South Africa. South African citizenship is to be restored only by a complex formula of administrative concession to TBVC citizens who were 'permanent residents' of 'white' South Africa in July 1986 - an estimated 1.75 million out of a total of approximately 9 million TBVC citizens. The political boundaries between these Bantustans and 'South Africa' (in the reduced sense used by Pretoria to exclude the TBVC states) are therefore extremely important formal barriers to the freedom of movement of many millions of people who consider themselves to be South African.[1]

This chapter suggests that the key to understanding the confusion lies in an analysis of the phenomenon of 'displaced urbanisation'. This term describes the concentration of black South Africans, over the last ten to fifteen years in particular, in huge rural slums which are politically in the Bantustans and economically on the peripheries of the established metropolitan labour markets. Two such cases are examined here. One is the huge slum of Onverwacht/Botshabelo in the heart of the eastern Orange Free State (see Map 3). The other is a string of slums comprising the newest Bantustan, KwaNdebele, in the central Transvaal to the north-east of Pretoria (see Map 4).

---

[1]   For valuable critical analysis of 'orderly urbanisation', see D. Hindson, 'Urbanisation and Influx Control' and 'Creating New Controls', *Work in Progress*, Nos. 40 (January 1986) & 41 (April 1986); and the Special Edition on Influx Control Policy, *South African Labour Bulletin* 11, 8 (September/October 1986), especially V. Watson, 'South African urbanisation policy: past and present', pp. 77-90; and W. Cobbett, ' "Orderly urbanisation": continuity and change in influx control', pp. 106-121. For a summary review of experience since July 1986, see *Weekly Mail*, 20 March 1987.

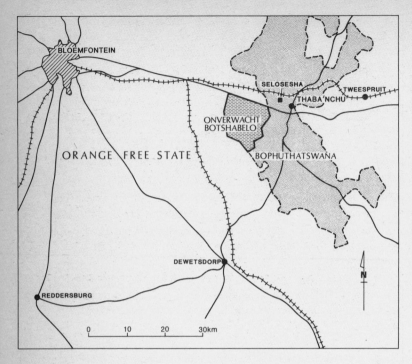

Map3 *Onverwacht-Botshabelo*

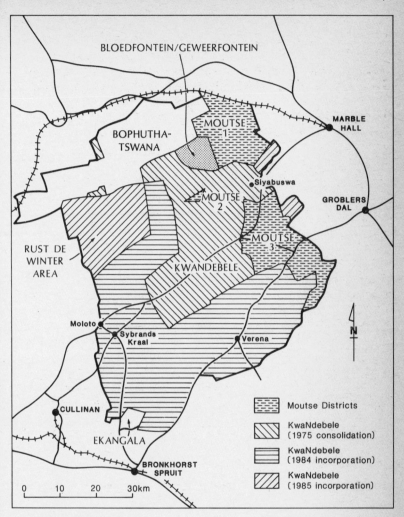

Map 4 *KwaNdebele*

Onverwacht/Botshabelo was bare veld in 1979.[2] Now it accommodates perhaps half a million people. It is the largest relocation slum in the country, or the second largest black township (after Soweto). Its population is predominantly Southern Sotho, since most people who have been moved there since 1979 have come from the northern, central and eastern districts of the Orange Free State. But Onverwacht/Botshabelo is physically adjacent to the Thaba 'Nchu district of Bophuthatswana, part of the 'independent' Tswana Bantustan; and it is a long way from Qwaqwa, the 'non-independent' Southern Sotho Bantustan on the boundary of Natal, the Orange Free State and Lesotho. The original establishment of Onverwacht as a site for Southern Sotho refugees from Thaba 'Nchu, within commuting range of Bloemfontein but at a great distance from Qwaqwa, the other pole of physical concentration of the Southern Sotho population, obviously contradicts the ethno-national/territorial logic of the Bantustan strategy. Such contradictions, reflecting some of the injustices, the failures and the absurdities of the original strategy, were acknowledged in President Botha's formulation of an alternative strategy of regional development in 1982.[3] Nine Development Regions have been identified. They are supposed to transcend the political and economic boundaries of grand apartheid under which South Africa was divided into ten Bantustans on the one hand and 'white' urban and rural areas on the other. Onverwacht/Botshabelo is the core of Development Region C which embraces both the provincial capital of Bloemfontein, with its own black townships in 'white' South Africa, and also the Thaba 'Nchu district of Bophuthatswana. The burgeoning slum was explicitly adopted as a prime site of experiment for the pragmatic modernisers within the

---

[2]   In 1979 and for some years afterwards it was known as Onverwacht to its inhabitants, after one of the farms in a block compulsorily purchased from white owners by the government. Its official name of Botshabelo is intended to reflect its initial function as a place of refuge (*botshabelo*) for 'illegal squatters' in the Thaba 'Nchu district of Bophuthatswana. The official name has only recently been generally adopted by the people who live there. Accordingly, I use both names in the text.

[3]   For a critique of regional development, see W. Cobbett, D. Glaser, D. Hindson & M. Swilling, 'South Africa's Regional Political Economy: a critical analysis of reform strategy in the 1980s', *South African Review III*, South African Research Service (Ravan Press: Johannesburg, 1986), pp. 137-168.

state, committed to technocratic reform of apartheid 'from above'.[4] Accordingly, one of the critics of 'regional development' has recently analyzed Onverwacht/Botshabelo as a test case for the strategy of 'orderly urbanisation'.[5]

By contrast with the relative political passivity of Botshabelo, KwaNdebele has been a seething cauldron of violent confrontation. There are two main reasons for looking at KwaNdebele in some detail. First, it represents an extreme case of displaced urbanisation. Second, it was a prime site of popular struggle throughout 1986 against the implementation of Bantustan 'independence'. It illustrates the complexity of factional conflicts which are transposed to the Bantustans from the sites of direct confrontation between the people and the state in the black townships of 'white' South Africa. Although they are politically transposed in this way, I would argue that the outcomes of such conflicts are of fundamental and by no means peripheral importance to the outcome of the larger struggle in the country as a whole.

Displaced urbanisation and regional development

There are three important elements of the phenomenon of displaced urbanisation. They are, first, the relative concentration of population in the Bantustans over the last three decades; second, the diversion of state expenditure on housing to the Bantustans, albeit on a grotesquely inadequate scale, with a corresponding deliberate freeze on black housing in the 'white' urban areas; and, third, the widespread commuterisation of the black labour force. The simplest evidence of the first trend is Charles Simkins' estimates of the distribution of the black population of South Africa at decennial intervals between 1960 and 1980. He calculated that, while 39.1 per cent (of a total black population of 11.5 million) were living in the black reserves or Bantustans in 1960, 52.7 per cent (of a total black population of 21 million) were in the Bantustans in 1980. While there was an absolute

---

4   See, particularly, a series of articles by P. van Zeyl, Manager, Research and Corporate Planning, South African Development Trust Corporation (STK): 'An Evolving Development Axis', *Growth* (Autumn 1985); 'IDPs on the Development Axis', *Growth* (Winter 1985); 'Botshabelo: increasing emphasis on regional co-operation set to bolster development impetus further', *Growth* (Summer 1986).

5   W. Cobbett, 'A Test Case for "Planned Urbanisation" ', *Work in Progress*, No. 42 (May 1986), pp. 25-30.

increase in the numbers of Africans living in both urban and rural areas of 'white' South Africa over the period, there was a slight *relative* decline in urban areas from 29.6 per cent in 1960 to 26.7 per cent in 1980, and a very substantial relative decline in rural areas from 31.3 per cent in 1960 to 20.6 per cent in 1980.[6] This redistribution of the black population reflects overwhelming state pressure against the tide of black urbanisation that would otherwise have occurred in 'white' South Africa, consistently with deepening poverty in the black rural areas, with rapidly rising black structural unemployment in white capitalist agriculture, and with rates of urbanisation prevalent elsewhere in the Third World.

What *has* happened, in summary, is massive 'urbanisation' in the Bantustans, in terms of the sheer density of population now concentrated there. One recent estimate is that 56 per cent of the population of the Bantustans are now 'urbanised'.[7] Several million people have been relocated from white farms, from 'black spots', from small town locations and from the metropolitan areas.[8] In addition, some densely populated zones have been formally incorporated into the Bantustans by the re-drawing of boundaries on the map. Some of the concentration has taken place in 'proclaimed' (officially planned) towns in the Bantustans, whose population was 33,500 in 1960, 595,000 in 1970 and 1.5 million by 1981.[9] But most of the concentration has taken place in huge rural slums which are 'urban' in respect of their population densities but 'rural' in respect of the absence of proper urban infrastructure or services.

Most housing in the rural slums is self-built. For many years central and local government authorities have used the acute shortage of black housing as an administrative device of influx control. The 'orderly urbanisation' strategy which has replaced the pass laws has merely made this more explicit. In many townships new building has been frozen as a deliberate tactic to enforce 'voluntary' removal to new

---

6   Figures adapted from C. Simkins, *Four Essays on the Past, Present and Possible Future of the Distribution of the Black Population of South Africa* (Southern Africa Labour and Development Research Unit: Cape Town, 1983), pp. 53-57.

7   J. Graaf, cited in Cobbett, ' "Orderly Urbanisation" ', p. 121.

8   For details and analysis, see L. Platzky and C. Walker for the Surplus People Project, *The Surplus People* (Ravan Press: Johannesburg, 1985).

9   F. de Clerq, 'Some Recent Trends in Bophuthatswana: commuters and restructuring in education', *South African Review II*, South African Research Service (Ravan Press: Johannesburg, 1984), p. 272.

towns or closer settlements in the Bantustans. Estimates and projections of housing shortage differ widely, of course, depending on premises and methods of calculation. One official source in 1984 estimated that the backlog of housing for Africans in 'white' areas was a staggering 420,000 units, contradicting the then Minister of Co-operation and Development's claim of less than half that number. Only 11,902 houses were built for Africans in 1984.[10] Irrespective of formal repeal of the pass laws, it is clear that, despite small increases in the rate of construction in recent years, the continuing acute shortage of housing affords an administrative barrier to black urbanisation in 'white' South Africa which state officials at various levels have repeatedly exploited.[11]

Associated with the trend of rapid 'urbanisation' in the Bantustans is an increase in the numbers of frontier commuters, defined as people who live in a Bantustan and commute daily or weekly to work in a 'white' area. Official figures record 615,000 in 1978 and 773,000 commuters in 1982; while the total number of migrants from the Bantustans officially recorded in 1982 was 1.395 million.[12] Thus there are still substantially more migrants than commuters but, taking into account unofficial estimates from different areas and booming bus transport in the early 1980s on certain key routes, it is evident that commuters represent an increasing proportion of the black labour force as a whole. A particularly stark indication of this development was recorded by Joe Lelyveld in his excellent book *Move Your Shadow*. The number of daily buses running between the desolate slums of KwaNdebele and the Pretoria region, operated by the major private bus company Putco but heavily subsidised by central government, was 2 in 1979, 66 in 1980, 105 in 1981, 148 in 1982, 220 in 1983 and 263 in 1984. Lelyveld commented: 'In a period in which South Africa is alleged to be changing and phasing out apartheid, the expansion of Putco into... the homeland provides as accurate a measure as can be

---

[10] *Survey of Race Relations in South Africa 1984* (South African Institute of Race Relations [SAIRR]: Johannesburg, 1985), p. 374; L. Platzky on behalf of the National Committee Against Removals, 'Reprieves and Repression: Relocation in South Africa', *South African Review III*, p. 396, fn. 5.

[11] For a review of state housing policy, see P. Hendler, A. Mabin and S. Parnell, 'Rethinking Housing Questions in South Africa', *South African Review III*, pp. 195-207.

[12] SAIRR, *Survey 1984* (1985), pp. 258, 259.

found of the real thrust of change'.[13]

The significance of this trend is that the black labour force is no longer simply divided (as in the Riekert philosophy of 1979) into relatively privileged urban 'insiders' with Section 10 (1)(a)(b)(c) rights to live and work in 'white' South Africa on the one hand, and disadvantaged 'outsiders' from the Bantustans and from foreign labour reserves who have no such rights and must seek work in the 'white' areas as temporary migrants on the other hand. Rather, frontier commuters from the slums of KwaNdebele, for example, or from those of the Moretele-Odi block of Bophuthatswana to the north-west of Pretoria, are effectively integrated into the metropolitan labour market, in terms of their access to and dependence on wage incomes in the industrial region of Pretoria-Rosslyn-Brits. But housing is not available for them in those industrial centres, and they and their families must find a place to live in the fragments of this or that Bantustan which are not wholly beyond the reach of the Putco buses.

Corresponding, then, to the state's refusal to accommodate blacks residentially within 'white' South Africa is a strategy of industrial decentralisation intended to disperse productive activities to the metropolitan fringes, away from the established industrial cores.[14] This strategy depends on generous wage and transport subsidies and tax incentives. Thus, in the eastern Free State, for example, Bloemfontein was identified in 1982 as an Industrial Development Point (IDP) along with Botshabelo outside Thaba 'Nchu and Selosesha inside Thaba 'Nchu. Now rising on the veld beside the Bloemfontein-Thaba 'Nchu main road, and one third of the way along it, is a site called Bloemdustria which is intended to develop in relative proximity both to Bloemfontein and to the vast pool of potential labour concentrated at Botshabelo. Writing recently of Botshabelo and Ekangala, another IDP in the central Transvaal which is supposed to be incorporated into KwaNdebele, William Cobbett has pointed out that they show 'how far labour provision has moved from the simple traditional division

---

13 Joseph Lelyveld, *Move Your Shadow: South Africa black and white* (Michael Joseph: London, 1986), p. 122. The desperate half-life of KwaNdebele's commuters on the Putco buses is movingly described by the journalist Joe Lelyveld, pp. 127-131 above, and by the photographer David Goldblatt in O. Badsha & F. Wilson (eds.), *South Africa: the cordoned heart* (Gallery Press: Cape Town, 1986).

14 For analysis of industrial decentralisation as one element of the strategy of regional development, see Cobbett and others, 'South Africa's Reform Strategy'.

between urban workers and long-distance migrants. Peripheral labour pools form part of extended urban labour markets, by complementing controlled residential exclusion with labour market inclusion'.[15] This is what 'orderly urbanisation' is all about: partial labour market inclusion and controlled residential exclusion. On the one hand, the rapidly 'urbanised' inhabitants of the rural slums have been integrated, to a degree, into metropolitan labour markets. On the other hand, they are kept at arm's length, as it were, from the major 'white' industrial and residential areas.

The constitutional corollary to these 'regional development' initiatives is that frameworks have to be devised to administer the distribution of local services. Accordingly, elaborate and ingenious proposals have been put forward for Regional Services Councils (RSCs), on which all communities will be represented in proportion to their consumption of services provided. Since white municipalities have a much greater capacity to consume services than black townships, it may be inferred that the RSCs are intended to manage the putative incorporation of the rural slums into a loosely federal political framework without making any concession to the demand of black South Africans for a unitary democratic state. This 'solution' is sponsored by reformists within the state who acknowledge, apparently, that the Bantustans will eventually be re-incorporated but who are anxious to retain the substance of white power. The implementation of RSCs has been substantially delayed, however, for the obvious reason that, in the wake of the demise of the black local authorities, they are fatally deficient in political credibility. They also conflict with, and are opposed by, the established administrative authorities of the Bantustans.

Thus·struggles in the rural slums of South Africa today relate above all to the terms and to the degree of their economic 'integration' into the principal metropolitan labour markets, and of their political 'integration' as black South Africans within a single state. There is much uncertainty over the outcomes of such struggles, partly because of confusion and contradiction within the state and partly because of the scale and momentum of popular resistance. Onverwacht/Botshabelo is analyzed here as a case study of confusion and contradiction within the state. KwaNdebele is analyzed as a case study of protracted and partially successful popular struggle against the imposition of Bantustan 'independence'.

---

[15] Cobbett, 'A Test Case', p. 27.

Displaced Urbanisation

In seeking to identify strategic lessons for the future in the experience of the inhabitants of the rural slums, it is vital to be clear about the criteria of 'urbanisation' which are deployed in the argument. In the past the term has been used to refer to the scale of the movement that has taken place into the 'prescribed' (urban) areas of 'white' South Africa, as a result of conflict between two opposing forces: the overwhelming pressure of poverty in the rural areas, on the one hand, and the remorseless effort of the state to push people back to the black reserves, on the other hand. The terms of the debate have shifted now, in response to the tidal wave of urbanisation displaced to the Bantustans. The term 'urbanised' is used now in the sense of daily access to or effective integration into or functional dependence on the urban labour market. But integration into and dependence on are very much matters of degree. A criterion of functional dependence on the urban labour market may be sensibly applied to incorporate the 'urbanised' population of the Bantustans in an analysis of contemporary trends in the political economy of apartheid. But it should not be used to imply either, on the one hand, that recognisably rural households beyond commuting range of the metropolitan areas are not primarily dependent on an urban wage for their livelihoods, through migrant household members; or, on the other hand, that people who live in the slums no longer aspire, ultimately, to recover a past livelihood on the land.

Onverwacht/Botshabelo

Onverwacht began as a 'place of refuge' for nearly 40,000 'illegal squatters' living at Kromdraai within Thaba 'Nchu who were repeatedly harassed by Bophuthatswana police after 'independence' in 1977.[16] They were all removed to Onverwacht in the second half of 1979 and Kromdraai was razed to the ground. Onverwacht was also planned as a site for the relocation of 'surplus' population from Mangaung, the black residential area of Bloemfontein; and for the concentration of people removed from small town locations and white farms all over the Free State. The population has massively expanded from a figure of 64,000

---

[16] The history of forced relocation in the Orange Free State is reviewed in detail in Volume 3 of *Forced Removals in South Africa* (The Surplus People Project: Cape Town, 1983). See also C. Murray, 'Struggle from the margins: rural slums in the Orange Free State', in F. Cooper (ed.), *Struggle for the City: migrant labor, capital and the state in urban Africa* (Sage: Beverly Hills, 1983).

by the end of 1979 to an unofficial estimate of 500,000 in 1985. By the end of 1984 the labour force domiciled in Botshabelo included some 23,000 daily commuters to Bloemfontein and 30,000 migrants to the Free State goldfields.[17] Initially the residents of Onverwacht complained bitterly of repeated harassment under the pass laws. Not only was it extremely difficult to find a job; it was also extremely difficult to get a work-seeker's permit - the *soekwerk* stamp - so that anyone who took the initiative of looking for work in Bloemfontein was immediately 'endorsed out' back to Onverwacht. This situation was later eased somewhat by an act of administrative discretion. From 1982 commuters from Onverwacht to Bloemfontein were given Section 10(1)(d) rights to compete on equal terms with urban 'insiders' who had Section 10(1)(a)(b)(c) rights.[18]

This is the basis of Cobbett's diagnosis of the 'integration' of Botshabelo within the regional labour market. But there must be two crucial qualifications, in my view, of this diagnosis. First, while it is true that the number of daily commuter buses between Onverwacht/ Botshabelo and Bloemfontein has steadily increased, partly in response to the administrative concession above, it must also be true that the number of commuters *relative* to the total population of the slum has declined. Unemployment has escalated much faster, in other words, than employment. Second, we must remember that the rural slums not only have a future but also a past. The overwhelming statistical fact about Onverwacht/Botshabelo and many other rural slums which have sprung up in the last ten to fifteen years is that they represent concentrations of ex-farm workers and their families, who have been decisively dis-integrated, so to speak, from the agricultural labour market. They carry with them, in their desperate search for urban employment, the enduring disadvantages of very little education, relative illiteracy and the non-transferability of limited skills.

Another obvious statistical feature of households in Botshabelo as in other rural slums is the extent to which family life is managed by women. The circumstances of one family may be briefly described.[19] In

---

17 Cobbett, 'A Test Case', p. 26.

18 Cobbett, 'A Test Case', p. 27.

19 A detailed case study of this household is presented in C. Murray, 'The political economy of forced relocation: a study of two households through time', in P. Spray & J. Suckling (eds.), *After Apartheid - renewing the South African economy* (James Currey: London, 1987).

October 1979 it was evicted with seventeen other families at 24 hours' notice from a white farm south of Tweespruit and dumped in Onverwacht without food, money or means of livelihood. In July 1986 the husband-father, a former tractor-driver, was effectively retired, having been unable to find any regular job. Two adult daughters with young children in the household were themselves domestic servants, respectively in Johannesburg and Bloemfontein. Another daughter remained at home where the only possibility of employment was in the local chicken farm where wages were appallingly low. Their mother, on whose broad shoulders rested the immediate responsibility for feeding and clothing this large household, entered the informal sector with vigour and desperation but initially with very low returns from long hours invested. She bought sheep on credit from the local butcher and then hawked the meat around Onverwacht. She graduated, in due course, to the most lucrative part of that sector: the concentrated weekend booze. But it is a risky business, and often violent and sordid as well.

This household encapsulates the structural disadvantages in the labour market experienced by ex-farm families and specifically by women. They have three options only: domestic service under conditions of extreme exploitation by white employers beyond the reach of daily commuting; residual employment at very low wages in a Bantustan or 'border' industry established to take advantage of an unlimited local supply of cheap labour; or an informal sector trade at home subject to strong competition and official harassment. A question mark should be placed, then, against the meaning of 'integration' in practice; and analysis of state strategy at the macro-level must be complemented by empirical study of the extent and the manner of that 'integration' in the experience of individual households.

It is this labour force which is described by the technocrats of state reformism, in their blandly enthusiastic advocacy of regional co-operation and regional development, as 'highly motivated and responsible'.[20] 'Highly motivated' in effect means extremely poor and desperate for any kind of employment; 'responsible' in effect means unorganised. Regional co-operation is recognised, however, as a 'delicate bloom'. This is also a coded phrase and acknowledges the fact

---

[20] Van Zeyl, 'IDPs on the Development Axis'. For a damning indictment of employment practices at the Botshabelo IDP, see W. Cobbett, 'Industrial decentralisation and exploitation: the case of Botshabelo', *South African Labour Bulletin 12*, 3 (March/April 1987), pp. 95-109.

that conflict between different agencies pervades the implementation of regional development. Bloemfontein IDP and Bloemdustria are administered by the Bloemfontein City Council and, prospectively, by the RSC. Botshabelo is on land owned by the South African Development Trust (SADT), the state agency responsible for purchasing land for black occupation under the terms of the Trust and Land Act 1936, and is administered by the Department of Development Aid, the rump of the old Department of Co-operation and Development. Selosesha IDP falls under the Bophuthatswana National Development Corporation (BNDC) and the Bophuthatswana government.

Such bureaucratic proliferation greatly compounds the difficulties of planning and implementing regional development initiatives. On 9 July 1986 it was announced that Botshabelo would become part of Qwaqwa, which represented a setback for the reformist technocrats since their strategy is based in part on the erosion of the political boundaries of the Bantustans. Despite official denials and strong opposition from within Botshabelo, its incorporation into Qwaqwa was judged in March 1987 to be 'imminent'. The logic of this can only be to push Qwaqwa into 'independence' alongside the TBVC states.[21] Meanwhile the political boundary between Thaba 'Nchu and 'South Africa' was reinforced by the official refusal of Bophuthatswana to allow dual citizenship. On 12 July 1986 big men from Mafikeng, the capital of Bophuthatswana, held a public meeting in Thaba 'Nchu and threatened the people that, if they applied for the new (allegedly uniform) South African identity documents which are replacing the hated *dompas*, but which remain a condition of employment in 'South Africa', they would forfeit all rights in Bophuthatswana, including citizenship and residence permits. If this is a serious threat, several hundred thousand commuters from Moretele-Odi to the Pretoria region and from Thaba 'Nchu to Bloemfontein face the appalling dilemma of whether to give up a job in 'white' south Africa or a place to live in Bophuthatswana. The people were confused and angry. 'Negotiations' are taking place, allegedly, to resolve this problem.

It is a story of confusion and contradiction at both economic and political levels. Regional development, the new reformism, is supposed to transcend the boundaries of Bantustans. But the prospective incorporation of Botshabelo into Qwaqwa and President Mangope's aggressive insistence on the exclusive integrity of citizenship of

---

21   *Weekly Mail*, 6 February 1987, 20 March 1987, 22 May 1987.

Bophuthatswana represent a 'hardening', not a 'softening', of the boundaries.

KwaNdebele

KwaNdebele is a belated afterthought in the grand design of 'separate development'. Until the mid-1970s there was no provision in land or administrative authority for the Ndebele people, scattered throughout the Transvaal on white farms and in different sections of Bophuthatswana and Lebowa. Representations from various Ndebele tribal chiefs led to the establishment of two regional authorities in 1974 and 1977. These arrangements incorporated three Ndebele groups living in the Moretele 1 district of Bophuthatswana, but excluded North Ndebele groups living in Lebowa, despite some agitation in the late 1970s from followers of one chief to secede from Lebowa and join the incipient South Ndebele Bantustan.[22] The (South) Ndebele territorial authority was constituted late in 1977. It became a legislative assembly in October 1979, consisting of 46 nominated members. Self-governing status was granted in 1981. The Chief Minister Simon Skosana (a former lorry driver with a Standard 4 pass) announced in 1982 that KwaNdebele would opt for 'independence' as soon as it had its own capital, industrial infrastructure and more land. Meanwhile it was reported that all the territory's liquor licences were held by government ministers and most new businesses were owned by them or by senior officials. Loans from the Corporation for Economic Development were apparently monopolised in the same way. Minister of the Interior Piet Ntuli, for example, who became the 'strongman' of the KwaNdebele

---

[22] The account of KwaNdebele presented below is drawn from the following sources: the annual *Survey* of the South African Institute of Race Relations, Johannesburg (SAIRR); Volume 5 of *Forced Removals in South Africa*; N. Haysom, *Apartheid's Private Army: the rise of right-wing vigilantes in South Africa* (Catholic Institute for International Relations: London, 1986), pp. 61-79; occasional Newsletters of the Transvaal Rural Action Committee, Johannesburg (TRAC); I. Obery for TRAC, 'Unusual Alliance Blocks KwaNdebele Independence', *Work in Progress*, No. 44 (September-October 1986), pp. 3-11; two papers presented at the conference of *The Review of African Political Economy* at the University of Liverpool, 26-28 September 1986: J. Yawitch for TRAC, 'The Anti-Independence Struggle in KwaNdebele', and TRAC, 'Resistance to Forced Removals in the Transvaal 1983-1986'; TRAC, *KwaNdebele - the Struggle against 'Independence'* (TRAC: Johannesburg, 1987); and various press reports (*Weekly Mail, Guardian*, etc.). I am indebted to all these sources. I have no experience of fieldwork in KwaNdebele.

government and the vigilante organisation Mbokhoto, had a supermarket at the capital Siyabuswa and a similar complex of shops and liquor outlets at Vlaklaagte, another of the new slums.[23]

In view of the paucity and inconsistency of the reports available, it is very difficult to reconstruct the process by which the land area identified as KwaNdebele has been expanded and partially consolidated at various stages over the last ten years. In 1976 KwaNdebele apparently consisted of about 75,000 hectares of land,[24] made up of 'black spots' scattered between Moretele 2 district of Bophuthatswana and Moutse 1, 2 and 3 districts of Lebowa, and a block of Trust farms to the south-west (see Map 4). These Trust farms now contain a series of sprawling slums which straddle the road between Cullinan and Groblersdal. New consolidation plans were announced in February 1983, which would increase KwaNdebele's size from 98,000 to 341,000 hectares. They embraced a large block of white farms in the Moloto region north of Cullinan and Bronkhorstspruit, part of the Ekandustria growth point and the Ekangala residential area, the Moutse districts (which had been excised from Lebowa in 1980), and 11 farms on the southern edge of Lebowa. Incorporation of the latter two areas was strongly resisted by the Moutse people themselves and by the Lebowa authorities; and the issue of Moutse in particular reached stalemate. Some white farmers protested that they would receive inadequate compensation and that the value of border farms would drop. Others anticipated that compulsory purchase would save them from drought-induced bankruptcy.[25]

It may seem that KwaNdebele's constitutional progress from bits and pieces of tribal authority in the mid-1970s to prospective 'independence' by the end of 1986 was an unseemly scramble. It may seem that its projected appropriation of fragments of Bophuthatswana and Lebowa was a blatant contradiction of the ideological rationale of 'separate development' and a cynical inducement to KwaNdebele's businessmen-thugs-politicians to take 'independence'. But a full sense of the absurdity and the sinister reality of KwaNdebele as an extreme case of displaced urbanisation emerges only by asking the question:

---

[23] This section is drawn mainly from the annual SAIRR *Surveys*. See also *Forced Removals in South Africa*, Vol. 5, pp. 47-59.

[24] T. Malan and P.S. Hattingh, *Black Homelands in South Africa* (Africa Institute of South Africa: Pretoria, 1976), p. 28.

[25] SAIRR, *Survey* 1983 (1984), pp. 324-326.

where have its inhabitants come from?

An estimated 90 per cent are recent immigrants, relocated since the late 1970s in a dozen slums stretching from Tweefontein and Gemsbokfontein in the south-west to Siyabuswa in the north-east. Probably not more than half of them are ethnically Ndebele. Even official estimates acknowledged an increase of population from 51,000 in 1975 to 166,000 in 1980. In March 1983 a joint statement from Pretoria and the Chief Minister's office said that more than 111,000 people had settled in KwaNdebele over the previous 12 to 18 months. In 1982 a survey carried out by the Human Sciences Research Council found that 55.4 per cent of the immigrants had come from white farms in the Delmas, Witbank and Middelburg districts to the south; 29 per cent had come from Bophuthatswana; and 8.5 per cent had come from 'white' urban areas.[26] There were also removals from 'black spots' elsewhere in the region. No-one knows how many people live in KwaNdebele today. Unofficial estimates range up to half a million. Most of these people moved 'voluntarily' to KwaNdebele, in the sense that they were not forcibly relocated in government trucks, apparently because the KwaNdebele slums afford the nearest legal home base from which the industrial region of Pretoria-Rosslyn-Brits is accessible and where families can live together albeit under very difficult and exhausting conditions. The fragment of Bantustan that is physically closest to this industrial region is in fact the Moretele-Odi block of Bophuthatswana, but many of the refugees in KwaNdebele have been directly or indirectly expelled from there, as non-Tswana without legal rights, by a policy of aggressive Tswana nationalism in respect of the allocation of jobs, housing and services.

It was the formal incorporation of Moutse into KwaNdebele on 31 December 1985 that provoked a determined campaign of popular resistance throughout the first seven months of 1986. The Moutse districts have a population of roughly 120,000, predominantly Pedi (North Sotho), and their excision from Lebowa and incorporation into KwaNdebele flew in the face of official rhetoric about rationalising 'ethno-national' identities. More importantly, however, KwaNdebele's well-publicised plans to take 'independence' fuelled opposition from the Moutse people themselves, because 'independence' would mean the loss of South African citizenship. Resistance to incorporation was thus

---

[26] *Forced Removals in South Africa*, Vol. 5, pp. 54, 205; SAIRR, *Survey* 1983 (1984), pp. 344-345.

not merely a question of anxiety over the oppression of non-Ndebele people within KwaNdebele. It was a question of refusal to endorse the loss of residual rights as black South Africans which follows the imposition of citizenship of an 'independent' Bantustan.[27]

On 1 January 1986 three attacks were launched by vigilantes armed with pangas and axes on several villages in Moutse 3. More than 380 men were abducted to Siyabuswa in KwaNdebele, where they were stripped and repeatedly sjambokked on the floor of the community hall which was awash with soapy water. Skosana and Ntuli were identified as directly involved in this. The vigilantes were members of an organisation called Mbokhoto, officially sponsored by the KwaNdebele government. Moutse people were thereafter repeatedly terrorised by South African police units, including KwaNdebele police, and by the Mbokhoto. At least forty people were killed, hundreds injured, many detained and assaulted. Some forced removals took place of both Sotho and Ndebele from Moutse to KwaNdebele.[28] Violence flared again in May 1986, sparked off by the death of a man from the Kwaggafontein slum. He had gone to the Mbokhoto headquarters to complain about the abduction of a number of schoolchildren including his daughter. His badly beaten body was later dumped outside his home. A riot followed his funeral. On 12 May a mass meeting was held to demand that 'independence' (scheduled for 11 December 1986) be scrapped and the Mbokhoto disbanded. On 14 May large numbers of people gathered to hear the KwaNdebele government response to these demands. The 30,000 crowd was repeatedly teargassed by helicopter and the meeting broke up in confusion. This brought popular resistance to a head and cabinet ministers already protected behind a barbed wire stockade were forced to seek refuge elsewhere.[29]

These incidents also fuelled a power struggle between the commoners Skosana and Ntuli, heading the KwaNdebele government, and the most important 'traditional' political faction, loyal to the head of the Ndzundza royal house Chief David Mabhogo. One of his sons, Prince Cornelius Mahlangu, was Minister of Health in the KwaNdebele government until December 1986. Another, Prince James Mahlangu, was head of the Ndzundza tribal authority which controls 23 appointed

---

[27] TRAC *Newsletter* No. 10, Moutse (April 1986).

[28] TRAC *Newsletter* No. 10, Moutse (April 1986); Haysom, *Apartheid's Private Army*, pp. 71-79.

[29] *Weekly Mail*, 16 May 1986.

127

seats out of 72 seats in the legislative assembly. He declared his sympathy with the popular protest and subsequently co-ordinated legal action against Ntuli. This reflects the ambivalent political position of the Ndzundza royal house and the extent to which the excesses of Mbokhoto had promoted an unusual tactical alliance - between traditionally conservative leadership within the Bantustan and youth and community representatives opposed to 'independence'. This alliance also loosely embraced some white farmers in the region who resent the incorporation of their land into the Bantustan proposed in the 1983 consolidation plans.[30]

Following the imposition of a general state of emergency on 12 June 1986, even more stringent security measures were imposed in KwaNdebele, banning reporting and forbidding non-residents from entering the territory. The entire public service went on indefinite strike on 15 July in protest against 'independence' and the arbitrary violence of Mbokhoto. The schools were boycotted from the nominal return date of 14 July. Nine youths who had fled to the Vlaklaagte slum in KwaNdebele from Mamelodi outside Pretoria, where their homes had been petrol-bombed, were massacred by men posing as ANC representatives who were probably Mbokhoto vigilantes.[31] Meanwhile, the 'Comrades' carried out revenge attacks and burned and looted shops and other businesses owned by members of Mbokhoto. Some of the 'necklaces' were inevitably indiscriminate, and violence was also attributed to a hybrid category of 'Comtsotsis' (Comrade + Tsotsi), ordinary criminals posing as political activists. According to a local priest, about 160 people were killed between mid-May and late July: he estimated one third had been killed by the police and army, a third by the Mbokhoto and a third by the 'Comrades'.[32] On 30 July Piet Ntuli, prime businessman-thug-politician, was killed by a car bomb. News of his death induced a spontaneous public celebration.[33] Chief Minister Skosana was left isolated and vulnerable. The Mbokhoto was immediately disbanded and on 12 August the legislative assembly

---

[30] For details see Yawitch, 'The Anti-Independence Struggle', and Obery, 'Unusual Alliance'.

[31] *Weekly Mail*, 18 July 1986.

[32] *Weekly Mail*, 25 July 1986; *Guardian*, 28 July 1986.

[33] *Observer*, 3 August 1986.

called off 'independence'.[34]

In retrospect, it is clear that specific opposition to the incorporation of Moutse turned into generalised opposition to 'independence' throughout KwaNdebele as a result of the daily experience of harassment in the slums. It is still unclear whether the rejection of KwaNdebele 'independence' represents, on the one hand, a significant breakthrough in political mobilisation within the rural slums, or on the other hand a temporary setback only for the protagonists of the Bantustan strategy. The unfamiliar tactical alliance between conservative 'tribal' leaders committed to the politics of separate development and radical youth committed to a unitary democratic state is obviously marked by strain and tension. By mid-October 1986, the KwaNdebele government had embarked on another 'spree of arrests', and Pretoria had failed to break the political impasse between the ageing patriarch of the Ndzundza royal house and Chief Minister Skosana. The prospect of reviving the question of 'independence' appeared to be vitiated by the death of Skosana himself in November. But he was succeeded by a 'hardliner', George Mahlangu, not by the popular opposition leader Prince James Mahlangu. The threat of 'independence' was renewed in March 1987 through the repeated detention of members of the legislative assembly who had opposed it, and through a 'unanimous' vote in favour in May.[35]

Otherwise, political tensions in KwaNdebele have been concentrated on the issue of the incorporation of the Moutse districts into KwaNdebele and the incorporation of a block of land adjoining Moutse 1 - the farms Bloedfontein and Geweerfontein - into Bophuthatswana. A major legal challenge to the excision of Moutse from Lebowa and its incorporation into KwaNdebele was heard at the end of November 1986. The court rejected the arguments of the Moutse communities, but the decision remains subject to appeal. The arguments relate to the loss of representation in the Lebowa legislative assembly; the loss of North Sotho as an official language; the loss of the franchise for women (KwaNdebele does not allow women to vote); and the imposition on the majority North Sotho population of Moutse of an ethnic minority status within KwaNdebele which contradicts the official ideology of the

---

[34] *Guardian*, 4 August 1986, 13 August 1986; *Weekly Mail*, 8 August 1986, 15 August 1986.

[35] *Weekly Mail*, 9 October 1986, 17 October 1986, 21 November 1986, 28 November 1986, 20 March 1987, 8 May 1987, 15 May 1987, 22 May 1987, 12 June 1987; *Guardian*, 7 May 1987, 12 May 1987, 22 May 1987, 29 May 1987.

Bantustan strategy.[36]

Another focus of bitter conflict is the implications of the passage of recent legislation which allows the central state to extend the borders of the 'independent' Bantustans and thus arbitrarily to incorporate whole communities within them. Several communities in the western and central Transvaal - Leeuwfontein, Braklaagte, Machakaneng - are being incorporated into Bophuthatswana despite vigorous protest.[37] They are 'black spots' in 'white' South Africa with a long history of refusal to be relocated. A community of about 15,000 people within KwaNdebele, who occupy the farms Bloedfontein and Geweerfontein (see Map 4) is also to be incorporated into Bophuthatswana. They are predominantly of North Sotho origin and strongly oppose the prospect of direct subordination to the Bophuthatswana state, which has repeatedly harassed and intimidated non-Tswana ethnic minorities within Bophuthatswana. While the land was to be incorporated, the residents were to be moved to the area of the Rust de Winter dam (see Map 4). The government appears to have rescinded its threat to remove the people, but still insists that their land will go to Bophuthatswana. The people concerned are determined neither to move from the land which they have occupied for over sixty years, nor to accept administration by Bophuthatswana.[38]

All of these communities face the loss of their South African citizenship on their incorporation into Bophuthatswana. None of them will necessarily be physically removed as a result. This underlines the insidious quality of the new 'solution'. Instead of removing the people to the Bantustan, bring the Bantustan to the people. Eliminate more black South Africans by a stroke of the pen. Not only, then, have some boundaries been 'hardened' to deprive TBVC citizens of rights in 'South Africa'. The 'hardened' boundaries are also being extended to generate more aliens and thence to deprive more people of such rights.

Conclusion

These two case studies may be used to illustrate an observation and a question of general importance. The observation is that any assessment of the significance of 'orderly urbanisation' and related aspects of

---

[36] *Weekly Mail*, 28 November 1986, 5 December 1986.

[37] *Weekly Mail*, 12 September 1986; *Guardian*, 27 October 1986.

[38] TRAC *Newsletter* No. 12, Bloedfontein and Geweerfontein (February 1987).

'reform' of the apartheid state must be based mainly on their impact on the lives of the inhabitants of the rural slums. On the one hand, these people depend for their livelihood on access to the metropolitan labour markets. On the other hand, they are most vulnerable to the strategies of exclusion devised by the state relating to the shortage of housing, the competition for jobs and the loss of citizenship.

The question arises out of the observation. How do struggles of the kind that took place in KwaNdebele throughout 1986 relate to the broader struggle for a unitary democratic state in South Africa? To the outsider, life in KwaNdebele is characterised by two images of struggle. One image is the grinding exhaustion of the daily passage on the Putco buses between a string of distant slums in the central Transvaal and places of work in or beyond Pretoria. The other image is of popular resistance spreading like a fire in the veld. On the face of it, the two images are difficult to reconcile. The only way to reconcile them, and indeed to answer the question above, is through a detailed study of community politics which would illuminate the interaction over time of complex strands of experience: those of violent social dislocation, escalating structural unemployment and tightening subordination to repressive Bantustan administrations. The history of organisation of women and of the youth must be of prime importance in such analysis.

Another significant variable in such analysis must be the physical and political distance between the black townships in 'white' South Africa and the rural slums of the Bantustans. For the most part, lines of confrontation in Soweto and the townships of the Rand, of the Western Cape and around Port Elizabeth appear relatively clear-cut. These areas are routinely terrorised by South African and black municipal police, by the army and by assorted vigilantes; and they are irrevocably politicised against the apartheid state. They are not subject in any direct sense to the intermediate distortions of Bantustan politics. By contrast, non-Tswana commuters from the sprawling slums of the Winterveld in the Moretele-Odi block of Bophuthatswana to the north-west of Pretoria have experienced brutal harassment by the Bophuthatswana authorities for many years. Likewise, ugly and protracted conflict on the edges of KwaZulu around Durban, between Chief Buthelezi's Inkatha movement on the one hand and unions and other organisations affiliated to the United Democratic Front on the other hand, reflects the fact that black townships in 'white' South Africa and rural slums on the border of the Bantustan are here physically contiguous with one another and in close proximity to the metropolitan region of Durban-Pinetown-

Pietermaritzburg. There is a major struggle in this region for control of future political directions.[39] The situation in rural slums which are incorporated within Bantustans and physically isolated from the metropolitan areas is different again. Inevitably they are insulated, to some degree, from the volatile currents of immediate confrontation with the central state. They are characterised, rather, by contradictory insecurities, strange alliances and ambivalent commitments.

An example of what I mean by contradictory insecurities is the appalling dilemma of people in parts of Bophuthatswana who, having established their homes within the Bantustan as refugees from municipal harassment in 'white' South Africa, now face the prospect of losing their jobs because they are treated as foreigners in the country of their birth. Alternatively, they face losing the right to live in Bophuthatswana. An example of a strange alliance is the highly tenuous coalition thrown up in KwaNdebele which embraces white farmers threatened with expropriation of their land, youth and community leaders closely in touch with the politics of resistance at a national level, and local forces of populist and traditionalist opposition within the Bantustan. How far was the successful surge of revolt in KwaNdebele in 1986 an expression merely of immediate and widespread popular revulsion against the vigilante organisation Mbokhoto? How far was it an expression of a more fundamental antagonism to a form of political 'independence' which would inevitably intensify people's material insecurities? An example of ambivalent commitments, or of the 'ambiguities of dependence' in Shula Marks' telling phrase,[40] may be found in the same set of particular circumstances. To what extent is the populist opposition leader Prince James Mahlangu facing 'inwards', so to speak, with his eye on 'independence' for KwaNdebele under his leadership as opposed to that of Skosana or George Mahlangu? At what point will he alienate sections of his local constituency which are committed to the destruction of the political framework within which he worked until recently?

---

[39] For a valuable account of the further complexities of conflict in a vast community of 'illegal squatters' paying rent to African and Indian land-owners and caught up in state manipulation of the Group Areas Act and imminent transfer of land to KwaZulu, see H. Hughes, 'Violence in Inanda, August 1985', *Journal of Southern African Studies* 13, 3 (April 1987), pp. 331-354.

[40] S. Marks, *The Ambiguities of Dependence in South Africa: class, nationalism and the state in twentieth-century Natal* (Ravan Press: Johannesburg, 1986).

Such questions illustrate the relatively 'open' character of what are often intensely parochial conflicts in the rural slums. It is vital that they be effectively integrated with the larger political struggle against the apartheid state.

Further Reading

Cobbett, W., Glaser, D., Hindson, D. & Swilling, M., 'South Africa's Regional Political Economy: a critical analysis of reform strategy in the 1980's.' *South African Review III* (Ravan Press: Johannesburg, 1986)

Hindson, D. , 'Creating New Controls' *Work in Progress* 41 (April 1986).

—— 'Urbanisation and Influx Control' *Work in Progress* 40 (January 1986).

Marks, S., *The Ambiguities of Dependence in South Africa: class, nationalism and the state in twentieth-century Natal* (Ravan Press: Johannesburg, 1986)

Murray, Colin, 'Struggle from the margins: rural slums in the Orange Free State' in Cooper, F., *Struggle for the City: migrant labor, capital and the state in urban Africa* (Sage: Beverly Hills, 1983)

Platzky, L., Walker, C., *The Surplus People* (Ravan Press: Johannesburg, 1985)

South African Labour Bulletin 11, 8 (September/October 1986)

Surplus People Project *Forced Removals in South Africa* (Cape Town, 1983)

8. Agrarian Historiography & Agrarian Reconstruction

WILLIAM BEINART

My paper begins with a conversation in a hut in Herschel district in 1984. It then traverses a range of historical writings about South Africa's rural areas in the twentieth century, if in a highly selective way. And it ends with some questions about the future, such as what are the implications of introducing fully private and alienable rights to land in the homelands; and how can patterns of ownership and production on a 20,000 acre Karoo sheep farm be changed?

It is not possible for an historian to suggest any future agrarian programmes or solutions. Moreover, just as it has been a fundamental tenet of recent agrarian historiography that the patterns of production established in the South African countryside have been intricately intertwined with the particular nature of political dominance in the country, so any unravelling of them will be deeply affected by future - and sadly as yet unpredictable - political outcomes. This final section will thus be short and tentative. Nevertheless, agrarian reform is a crucial and still rather neglected issue. Many analyses of power and inequality in South Africa start by mentioning the division of land between whites and blacks: the figures of 87 per cent reserved for whites; and 13 per cent for blacks - though not entirely accurate for the century as a whole - are amongst the best-known South African statistics. But, not least because of the overwhelming importance of urban growth and urban political protest in the last decade, discussions of change on the land are seldom given the prominence that this often quoted statistic would seem to demand.

Conversations in Herschel

In 1984 I spent some time in Herschel district conducting interviews on a fascinating rural political movement which had developed there in the 1920s. Herschel is located quite near the centre of the country, in the north-eastern Cape. It has been reserved for African occupation since

---

For a guide to the sources referred to in this chapter, please see the 'Further Reading' listed at its end.

the mid-nineteenth century. Formerly part of the Cape Colony proper, then administered as part of the Ciskei, the district was incorporated into the Transkei in 1976 when that territory was assigned independent homeland status by the South African government. The transfer was part of a broader political deal involving 'consolidation'. The Environmental and Development Agency, a small organisation dedicated to rural development which grew out of a student Voluntary Service group in the 1970s, runs a project in the remote village in which I stayed. EDA strategy has been to train local organisers, help set up democratically elected co-operative committees, then withdraw - providing largely technical and financial help. At night a few of those involved in the EDA project used to visit for discussions about the history of the area and the problems of the co-operative. One was the local organiser, a young former migrant worker with technical skills and some English, who still visited Johannesburg regularly and kept in touch with political developments there. Another was a key co-operative member, an older man who had spent many years on the South African Railways before retiring to his home village to begin serious farming on his smallholding. Aside from Xhosa and Sotho, he spoke only basic Afrikaans, and was more involved in village affairs. Both were members of a fundamentalist Christian Church which had strong prohibitions on drinking and smoking and a deep commitment to the Bible, to hard work, and sharing.

One night, a discussion about the problems of the project turned to the future and the broader possibilities for agrarian change. The older man argued that he would like to see the transfer of all the land of Zastron, the white-owned Orange Free State farming district immediately to the north, to the black people of Herschel. The land at their disposal would then be more than doubled at a stroke. He conceived of an extension of smallholdings, under something like the existing system of communal tenure, to areas occupied by white farmers, although the people should co-operate with one another. The problem was, in his eyes, that there was not sufficient land for the kind of smallholding activities in which he and the other more well-established agriculturalists in the village were involved. The younger man disagreed. There was not, he argued, sufficient land in the whole of Zastron to satisfy the need even for smallholdings for all the people of Herschel - not to mention the agricultural workers already in Zastron district itself. And too many people in Herschel had left farming behind, methods were too inefficient. Certainly he felt that more land was needed for the black population. But, to paraphrase and define his objections, some method had to be found of keeping large farming units on white owned land intact, and some kind of co-operative system had to be developed if blacks were to be able to use new land productively. An extension of the old mix of small individually held plots and migrant labour was doomed to failure. But he felt that people would not agree to a system of private land tenure.

This conversation seemed to me fascinating and important. These various scenarios have been thrown up in academic and political debates through the years, especially in relation to neighbouring countries. But on previous fieldwork trips to homeland areas, I'd found discussions along these lines more muted and limited to local issues like the shortage of plots, agricultural improvement, privatisation of land, what should be done about the rehabilitation policy, and how to cope with the extension of plantations into the homelands. Here were two protagonists who would be immediately involved in any process of change, who seemed, unselfconsciously, to be representative, who had some sense of the future and of the broader political economy of agrarian reform. The older man expressed confidence in a peasant option as part of the solution in South Africa, but conceived of it in the context of a radically altered distribution of land. The question arises as to whether he *was* at all representative, and whether there are still the social roots and social demands for the kind of option he was exploring.

Agrarian historiography - the transition to capitalism and rural dislocation

Acquaintance with some of the new agrarian historiography of the 1970s, and with a range of contemporary studies of South Africa, might suggest that the older man was not representative and that there is little scope for the peasant option. Two of the major themes that emerged in the historiography were the transition to capitalism on white-owned farms and the decline of the peasantry in the reserves, both processes which seemed to a considerable extent worked out or imposed by the 1920s and 1930s. To simplify a complex body of research: labour tenancy arrangements still predominated on many farms, but disguised what was effectively wage labour as African tenants' access to land for their own use on their white employers' farms had been severely curtailed; and peasant production in the reserves had given way to mass labour migrancy. The Natives Land Act of 1913, which outlawed all but labour tenancy and wage labour on farms and provided for the strict division of black from white land has been seen as a crucial turning point. Solomon Plaatje's evocative record of the eviction of sharecroppers from farms immediately after the passing of the Land Act - a central theme in his *Native Life in South Africa* (1916) - has served as a reference point to what has been considered a fairly continuous part of the experience of Africans on the farms. Implicit though not always explicit in the academic work were the propositions that smallholder production, whether in the reserves or on the farms, had been so undermined by the 1920s and '30s that the peasantry as an economic and political class had become marginal; and that the nature of class-consciousness amongst the mass of Africans was irrevocably changing.

This picture of the early decades of the twentieth century must be placed against recent studies of dislocation in the rural areas documented in the Surplus People Project report, the papers of the Carnegie Conference on Poverty, and similar research efforts. The position in Herschel district provides a local example of more general processes. During the political turmoil that accompanied the transfer of Herschel to the Transkei in 1976, thousands left the district to move south to the Ciskei. They opposed the transition to independence in principle, and also felt that they would be discriminated against by the local political leaders who had accepted incorporation into the Transkei and had already benefited from the decentralisation of authority. Their move south, however, brought few benefits. Some landed up in notorious Ciskeian 'dumping grounds', where economic conditions were probably worse and land even more scarce; moreover, Sebe, who headed the Ciskeian Territorial Authority, accepted independence a few years later in 1979 and turned out to be, if anything, more authoritarian than the Transkeian government.

Any benefit for the great majority who stayed in Herschel, in the shape of vacated plots and perhaps marginally better services, was soon counterbalanced by a new influx of people: those made redundant by changing, more mechanised, patterns of production on white-owned farms and others pushed out of the cities. The state's relocation policies have deeply affected all the homelands. But partly because of the relatively greater bargaining power of the Transkeian government, the policy of forced removals into that homeland, did not - at least in the 1970s - have quite such drastic implications in numerical terms as in some other smaller homelands.

Moreover, it has long been Transkeian government policy to avoid, where possible, large resettlement sites - huge urban concentrations in the countryside - that have blighted areas like Onverwacht to the north of Herschel in the Orange Free State, or Winterveld on the southern borders of Bophuthatswana near Pretoria, or the tiny Sotho homeland QwaQwa, or KwaNdebele.[1] These now house sprawling towns of perhaps 200,000 to 600,000 people. Rather, families relocated to the Transkei have been absorbed into smaller villages and towns. These are not, by and large, the old villages or scattered settlements, marked in Herschel by clusters of stonebuilt houses in the shadow of mountain ridges protected against the prevailing winds. They are the relatively new concentrated village sites: a result of the rehabilitation policies pushed through by the government since the Second World War in the African reserve areas, which have transformed previous patterns of settlement and land use. In Herschel, the great majority of people are now in these settlements of from 1,000 to 5,000 - of which roughly 100 are scattered across the district interspersed by arable and grazing areas. Nevertheless, the population has been growing rapidly and families have only residential sites, not arable plots. And although grazing land is still in theory communal and open to all taxpayers, the great majority of families have nothing or very little in the way of stock. Almost every family is deeply dependent on income from sources other than agriculture. And this is in a homeland district which, while not the most favoured in South Africa, is certainly better off, in terms of remaining rural resources, than many others.

In sum, to move from the particular to the general, the social geography of rural South Africa has been significantly reshaped over the last few decades. The proportion of the African population settled within the homelands has now climbed again to over fifty per cent, thus reversing a flow away from the reserves which characterised the first sixty years of the twentieth century. (Around 1960, for example, somewhere between 35 and 40 per cent of the African population was settled within homeland boundaries.) But the equation of homeland population with rural population can no longer be made. The whole concept of rural becomes problematic in discussing the position of the great majority of people now settled within the homelands: because of changes in boundaries which have incorporated urban townships like

---

[1]   For these, see chapter 7 by Colin Murray.

Mdantsane (East London) or Umlazi (Durban) into homelands; because of the huge expansion of quasi-urban settlements like Onverwacht; and because of the declining overall proportion of income derived from the land. Moreover, even the most rural homeland areas have been reshaped by rehabilitation policies. Something over 60 per cent of the Transkei as a whole - and more elsewhere - has now been regrouped into villages. Thus a large number of African people - more, I think than the 3 million enumerated by the Surplus People Project (SPP) - whether formerly on white-owned farms, or in towns, or in the homelands themselves, have experienced some kind of dislocation, involving some level of compulsion, in the last few decades. By far the largest category of people relocated, about half the SPP total of 3 million, has been made up of those moved from privately owned rural land to the reserves. Experience of these over-arching processes has certainly varied, depending on a range of more local political and economic factors. Herschel is not the same as Onverwacht. But it has been argued that very many people even in districts like Herschel, where there is little in the way of large township concentration, are 'functionally urban' or effectively wage workers.

Some historiographical modifications

As a broad indication of the pattern and results of agrarian change in the twentieth century, this picture has much to commend it. However, recent historical work suggests that modifications should be made to the more general models. I would like to explore - without dwelling on particular pieces of work - just a few points which affect our understanding of these processes.

The emphasis in the earlier phase of radical historical scholarship on industrialisation and the formation of a working class is now being counterbalanced by a series of detailed studies on agrarian issues and rural political protest. There is now greater recognition that for South African blacks the predominant experience was still, in the first half of this century, a rural experience. The demographic evidence tells us so: in the 1921 census less than 20 per cent of the African population, including migrant workers, was enumerated in the towns and, despite the huge urban migration around the Second World War, this percentage had not yet doubled by 1960. It is also now possible to pinpoint some of the variations in the pattern of rural change. And one of the major themes that has emerged, admittedly largely in studies covering the period to the 1930s, is that the transition to capitalism on the land by this time was incomplete. I want to explore briefly, and largely in statistical terms, this notion of an incomplete transition. One point is absolutely clear. There has been a steady, perhaps even spectacular, if fluctuating, increase in output on the white-owned farms. As a proportion of the GDP, agricultural production declined from roughly 20 per cent around 1920 to under ten per cent now, although this trend was reversed briefly between 1945 and 1960. But the physical volume of output on farms increased three to four times between the 1910s - when systematic statistics were first collected - and 1960. It had almost doubled again by the end of the 1970s: throughout this period, but especially in recent decades, arable production has increased more rapidly than pastoral.

That this was accompanied by an increase in the proportion of agricultural wage labourers, including migrant workers in relation to tenants, and that terms for remaining labour tenants became very onerous, has not been disputed. But the evidence suggests that some scope remained for farm tenants to grow crops and keep stock for their own subsistence at least up to the 1950s. In the Western Cape wine, wheat and fruit zone; in the Natal and Transvaal plantations; in the midland Cape sheep zone, production has probably been, for most of this century, based on large scale capitalist enterprises employing wage labour. Elsewhere, the position was more complex. Agricultural census figures show that while maize production by tenants decreased relative to total production on farms, it continued to increase, erratically, in absolute terms from the 1920s to about 1960. The number of cattle held by tenants decreased, but by less than 20 per cent, over the same period. Tenants could grow very little in the way of cash crops but maize and cattle were, and still remain the two most important items of agricultural production by value in the country as a whole. (Tenant production was almost certainly underestimated.)

Despite the complex system of credit, co-operatives, controlled markets, and subsidies set in place in the inter-war years, many white farmers remained financially vulnerable. Agriculture could still, in the 1940s, be considered by a government commission as the sick organ of the South African economy. Not only did succeeding depressions and droughts weed out the weak, but some of those who hung on were, at times, still dependent on their tenants' output for some of their income. Mechanisation was surprisingly slow in the inter-war years. Legislative controls over tenancy and the movement of Africans, although giving wide powers to landowners and the state, were only partially enforced. We know from the University of the Witwatersrand oral history project that determined sharecroppers could still find contracts which allowed a measure of independence up to the 1950s in the Transvaal, even if they had to move regularly in order to do so. In South Africa as a whole, in the 1950s, it was estimated that one-fifth of the white owned farms were occupied solely by Africans. Even in the Orange Free State, often considered the heartland of highveld capitalist farming, little over half the farms were occupied by white owners and labourers alone in 1959; tenants of all kinds, including sharecroppers, lived on many of the others. Farms occupied by Africans were often 'labour farms' (that is settled by tenant families which had to supply migrant workers to the mines and farms) but those on them could also maintain some agricultural activity. In inland Natal, state attempts to abolish labour tenancy were an important issue of conflict in the 1960s. Farmers feared that if they offered only wage labour contracts, they would lose their labour supply. Overall, while the African population on white-owned farms decreased slowly as a proportion of the total African population, it continued to increase quite rapidly in absolute terms until the 1960s. The chilling stories of evictions after the Natives Land Act must be placed in this larger perspective.

Thus although the struggle for most of the land had been resolved by the 1920s and 1930s, it was still possible for tenants in a surprising range of districts to defend their position. A more universal and complete transition to wage labour has been a phenomenon of the last two or three decades. Farm ownership has become more concentrated: the number of units increased slowly between 1930 and 1960 then decreased rapidly in the next couple of decades from 105,000 to 70,000. (Company landownership has again become widespread.) It is in this period also that mechanisation became more widespread: a study of a maize farming district in the Transvaal suggests that the late 1960s to the early 1980s were the crucial years, particularly for mechanisation of labour intensive harvesting activities. The number of African farm workers fell by nearly 20 per cent between 1960 and 1980. As a consequence it has only been since about 1960 that the African population on privately owned farms has stabilised, perhaps even decreased in absolute terms; and has decreased from 30 to 20 per cent of the total African population. And it is in this period that the surplus people have been more systematically pushed out or externalised to the reserves or homelands.

Similar reservations have been expressed in relation to the decline of the remnant peasantry in the reserves. In some more favoured reserve districts, agricultural production and stock holding continued to expand with hiccoughs, to the 1930s. Certainly these areas supplied large numbers of migrant workers; but it was possible for some families to invest wages in productive assets and to re-organise family labour and systems of cultivation in a way which would minimise disruption. I don't think that anyone has argued that production in the reserves continued to increase in absolute, much less per capita, terms after the 1930s. However, it has been suggested that the value of reserve production declined more slowly than had been supposed. It was only after the 1950s that the value of per capita production in the reserves or homelands showed a very steep decline. Indeed, inspection of a long series of figures for the Transkei - admittedly a more favoured area - suggests that while per capita production has declined steeply in the last few decades, the total volume of crop production and quantity of cattle held has still not declined much, even compared with the peak figures of the 1920s and 1930s.

At one level, these sorts of figures indicate a frightening stagnation. In the 1920s, African smallholders on farms and in the reserves still produced around a quarter of the maize in the country, possibly more, and held over 50 per cent of the cattle. Fifty years later those figures were probably less than 5 per cent and 30 per cent respectively. But looked at from a different perspective, they show that somewhere amidst the swollen population of the Bantustans, amidst the poverty of areas that have suffered deeply from apartheid policy, there are families which have been able to cling onto sufficient land and resources to maintain some smallholding agricultural production.

Moreover, although there has been some concentration of resources in the hands of political and financial accumulators in the homelands - and areas for plantation and mechanised cultivation schemes have been carved out - land tenure is still communal in the sense that land cannot legally be bought and sold. Surveys showing a rapidly decreasing *proportion* of families in the homelands with plots or stock must be set against the evidence of rapid population growth. My impression is that compared with the 1920s and 1930s, a slightly larger number of producing units are producing a slightly smaller total output on slightly more land. This remnant smallholding group is largely composed of families deeply dependent on wages; obviously it is of much less significance in areas like Winterveld, Onverwacht, Qwaqwa and the

Ciskei. As a proportion of the total population of the homelands it is diminishing, but it is not insignificant, numerically or politically.

I have concentrated in this section on a broad statistical outline, and neglected what is perhaps the most interesting historiographical development: studies of rural political struggles. In general, it has become clear that tenants and agricultural labourers, and particularly communities in the reserves, were not quiescent. The picture of a deeply eroded tenantry, and underdeveloped, impoverished and stagnant reserves has tended to obscure the extent to which rural Africans remained actors even when the way that they were acted upon severely constrained their economic and political options. Both within South Africa and outside, there has been a shift in historical work from more structural approaches to the history of struggle - a development which has reflected, and perhaps interacted with, the heightened level of political mobilisation in the country.

Especially in the 1920s, but certainly up to the 1950s, organised rural struggles tended to be focused on the assertion of rights to rural resources. By the 1950s, rural popular protests had become more deeply infused with issues - not absent before - relating to freedom of movement (passes), wages and prices. The example of Zeerust in the Western Transvaal in the 1950s, where state imposition of passes on women was a major issue, is a case in point. But in Pondoland, scene of perhaps the most sustained rejection of government authority, a strong communalist commitment to the defence of local control over local resources, and of political arrangements which the mass of local people could influence, remained at the heart of the 1960 revolt.

Since the early 1960s, the decentralisation of control to the Bantustan authorities and the incorporation of chiefs into these structures, combined with more effective repressive measures, seem to have muted more open and organised expressions of rural political protest in the homelands. Nevertheless, intense local political struggles are seldom far from the surface. Let me cite just one example. In 1977, the Transkeian government attempted to impose a levy on cattle ownership in order to stimulate sales, increase efficiency in pastoral production, and raise revenue. The announcement was immediately followed by widespread rumours of resistance; the government had to back down and reduce the levy to a quarter of its original level and then rescind this particular form of taxation completely.

On the white farms, the overwhelming issue in the last couple of decades has been eviction, removals and relocation. The Surplus People

Project reports are suffused with portrayals of the harrowing nature of this experience, but they also show the state's capacity to disorganise opposition to it. Farm tenants and labourers, isolated by the nature of the enterprises on which they worked, could seldom sustain resistance - except where they were part of a broader community which straddled white and black-owned land. It has been around the 'black spots', privately owned farms outside the homelands, that some of the longest-drawn battles have been fought - at first often in isolation, but from the late 1970s increasingly with some media coverage and assistance from urban activists. Mgwali, in the Ciskei is one example; Driefontein in the Transvaal, where the community leader Saul Mkhize was shot dead by police in 1983, is another. For many of those removed, independent access to land has become an impossibility and their energies have been devoted to survival on the peripheries of the wage labour market. But the SPP reports are also rich in oral material which stresses the importance of memories of the land.

One last point about historiographical advances: feminist studies have emphasised the differential experience and consciousness of men and women in rural areas where the migrant labour system resulted in a heavy demographic preponderance of women. The early feminist historiography tended to stress the importance of patriarchal controls in the rural areas. In this analysis, African women had been kept on the land and assigned greater responsibility for agricultural production because of the remaining power of African men. However, interpretations are now shifting, not least because of the accumulation of local studies on women's involvement in political struggle within and beyond the domestic sphere. Women's struggles were not least about defending their position in the rural areas, and asserting their authority within the homesteads - a possibility which arose not least because of the absence of men. I think that this insight materially affects our understanding of the consciousness of the remnant peasantry in South Africa.

It may seem that I have, in a rather unbalanced way, set out to show that there still are nooks and crannies of South Africa where a measure of smallholder production is possible. Moreover, it may seem that by dating some of the transitions under discussion to a rather later period than has been generally suggested, I am trying to argue that land, and particularly access to land for smallholding production, remains an important issue, a quite central aspect of consciousness, for a significant proportion of the African population: much more than would be indicated by comparing the volume of African production to white production. In other words, despite the massive structural shifts that have taken place in South Africa in this century, and particularly since the Second World War, those indefinable classes suspended somewhere between wage-labourer, tenant and small-scale producer remain a significant social force. In some respects this would be an acceptable interpretation. But I hope also to have indicated, on the way, just how far the processes of change - the transition to capitalism on the farms and the decline of the peasantry in the reserves - have gone.

Recent developments

Before looking briefly at a few of the implications of this argument, some more recent developments should be mentioned. In the early 1980s much of South Africa suffered a severe drought. This had a devastating effect on some of the homelands - and the evidence I have given about stability in production does not include this period. Further declines in production and stock-holding might be expected, even if these prove to be temporary, as in earlier droughts. The droughts coincided with a levelling-off and perhaps even decline in real wages for many migrant workers following the increases in the 1970s. A number of studies have also shown that the scale of unemployment has increased greatly and that unemployment has now been more systematically externalised to the homelands. It is a combination of these forces, increased farm capitalisation, drought and industrial recession, coming to a head in the early 1980s, that has pushed so many people into large squatter villages near major centres of employment. This in turn has produced new and explosive points of conflict between and within African communities. The fighting between those identifying as Zulu and Mpondo just south of Durban early in 1986, in which more than 150 died - the largest death toll in any single incident in the last couple of years - is one grim example. The trauma of Crossroads, near Cape Town, is another.

But this period of drought, together with other factors, had also had a significant effect on the white owned farms. Maize farmers, already saddled with debt from the years of heavy investment in machinery, may have difficulty in sustaining the costs of mechanisation in view of the losses they suffered. Reports of bankruptcy amongst farmers have not been uncommon - 'South Africa's bankrupt millionaires' as one headline recently put it. My favourite story, heard in a northern Cape bar, is probably apocryphal: it tells of a Free State farmer who drove into Rouxville in his Mercedes Benz, threw the keys of his farmhouse onto the magistrate's desk, said 'You can take it all' (in Afrikaans), then headed off to Johannesburg. Reports suggest that the total debt of white farmers has multiplied in recent years. The squeeze on farm profits threatens land prices. A number of commentators have linked the rise of far-right parties amongst Afrikaners at least partly to such agrarian problems: they have tended to win most support in the rural districts of the Transvaal, not least the maize farming districts. And underlying the whole problem is the question of how far the state is prepared to underwrite the farm debt at a time when the economy as a whole is in recession, and also to maintain high domestic agricultural prices. The black mobilisations of the last couple of years have not primarily been about food prices, but inflation along with unemployment are part of the background to recent insurrection; political decisions also have to be made about subsidies on basic staples. Possible sanctions on agricultural exports, while they have not yet had much effect, create further uncertainties. The point is also that these problems might erode the capacity of more vulnerable individual white farmers or those in more marginal zones to stay on the land. The government is already engaged in funding settlement schemes for white farmers in the northern Transvaal, both for military/security and economic reasons.[2] Vacated land would not now, as it may have been thirty years ago, necessarily be available for reoccupation by African tenants. The extent of control especially in more sensitive military zones is greater. But I would not be surprised to hear about reoccupations - always the silent strategy of dispossessed tenants - if the state's political hold on the rural areas suffers as much as it has in urban areas.

Questions about the future

It is at this stage, the conclusion, that the talk must become even more exploratory and tentative. Let me invoke the conversation in Herschel again as a way in. It is quite clear that the great bulk of the country's food supply and all its income from agricultural exports is dependent on the white-owned capitalist farming sector - and the complex systems of policing, subsidy, technical aid, and marketing that go with it. Not

---

[2]   For this, see chapter 4 by Gavin Cawthra.

only are some of these areas the kernel of opposition to major political changes, but any government, of whatever kind, would find it extremely difficult to unravel or shift the system without a food and foreign exchange crisis of major proportions. In the short term, a land reform programme which aimed at breaking up the core large farm units would render the state and the urban working class very vulnerable. Large investments have been made in every facet of agricultural production on some of these farms, from dams and conservation works to fences, plantations and processing works, which would be expensive and wasteful to dismantle. Pastoral farms which depend on open veld grazing, like a 20,000 acre sheep farm in the Karoo, would be more easily dismantled but even here the arrangement of paddocks, dams and wool processing buildings might not make for easy redistribution. The Zimbabwean government, faced with a similar set of issues on a far smaller scale, has - and I think not only for the reasons of its own internal ideology - trod extremely cautiously. On this point, it is difficult to disagree with the younger protagonist in Herschel.

What is not so difficult to conceive is changes in ownership over these large productive units. There are various possibilities. The most obvious, which need not await any major political transformation, would involve opening private farmland to purchase on a non-racial basis; there is a precedent for this in Namibia. Within South Africa itself, discussion about de-zoning some suburbs from the strict racial divisions entrenched in Group Areas Act is, or at least was in 1985 and 1986, widespread and some small changes seemed possible. Though there has been a recent swing against de-zoning by the government, especially following the 1987 election, estate agents, property developers and speculators, as well as some white property owners are beginning to see selective relaxation of the Act as an important means of boosting depressed property prices and turnover.

The farming districts would present more difficult obstacles for such an initiative, in both political and financial terms. Any demand for farms would be constrained by their expense; blacks would have to be admitted fully into the system of financial subsidy and loans. The issues of possible sub-division, and the readmission of tenants, would also have to be confronted by any government which allowed a freer, non-racial land market to develop. However, the fact that company ownership of land has increased at the expense of individual landowners might imply that a non-racial land market would have relatively little effect on the size of the farming unit. Significant

147

involvement by blacks in rural land purchase would no doubt partly be through shares in existing or new companies. Such black landowners might not themselves be significantly involved in farming as owner-occupiers, and might come to share the ideas about appropriate forms of capitalist production on the land that are already widespread amongst company landholders.

This would of course be a very limited reformist development with little effect on the division of wealth and inequalities in the society, and it would lead initially to the incorporation of a small number of people into the landed classes. However, some attention should be given to this possibility, not least because it is the one of the few very limited agrarian reforms that could take place under the present government. Limited rural 'de-zoning' could have important implications as part of a state strategy to cement a supportive black capitalism; and access to a common land market might significantly shift the interests and identity of the African elite. Private farm land, so systematically denied to African accumulators both in and outside of the homelands for many years, might prove a particularly attractive investment for both social and financial reasons for the more successful black urban businessmen - as it has both in some other parts of Africa, and, in the past, for other upwardly mobile segments of the South African population.

One further implication that is worth considering is that even some black ownership of the land might open up more scope for Africans to advance into managerial roles on white owned or company farms. And already amongst the very largely black rural labour force reside a great many of the technical and agricultural skills required to run sophisticated farming enterprises, as well as some older tenant and smallholder skills. If agrarian reform were ever to be pushed further than a non-racial land market, African farmworkers would no doubt have many of the agricultural skills needed to keep large units going. But they have very largely been excluded from the other crucial spheres of large-scale agricultural production: of dealing with finance, management, marketing, and tax and subsidy systems. Any advance in this sphere would be valuable for the future. (Access to a common agricultural education system would also be important.) If a mixed economy on the land is contemplated, then such experience would be at a premium. If state farms or collectives become a possibility - again this transition is less drastic than it sounds because of the increasing company ownership of land - then those manning them will need a wide range of skills, the lack of which have been a significant obstacle in such enterprises elsewhere in the subcontinent.

Policies involving state farms and various forms of co-operatives or collectives have been tried in a number of nearby African countries; at least in terms of increasing agricultural production, they have not generally been a success. Their introduction would of course depend on very major political changes. However, such enterprises would mean that the technical advances and organisation of some large farms could theoretically be kept intact. There are also some significant differences between South Africa and other African countries which have experienced difficulties in establishing large scale state farms and co-operatives. In South Africa, agricultural workers generally have greater experience of large scale agricultural enterprises. The state has played a crucial role in many aspects of agricultural improvement, finance and marketing - the state apparatus is to a significant extent there if it ever could be harnessed to other ends. Within the homelands, particularly, some of the new plantation and mechanised cultivation schemes have been initiated by parastatal corporations or even directly by government departments. And not least important, there may be relatively few alternatives in South Africa for rural people who want to stay on the land. State farms and state controlled collectives have run into difficulty elsewhere not least because of opposition from peasants with a preference for, and capacity to maintain, smallholder production.

It may seem a purely 'academic' exercise to entertain notions of such radical agrarian reform given the present political context in South Africa; the political barriers are immense. But such possibilities are beginning to be discussed both in the rural areas and in opposition political movements. Two very general points seem worth making in regard to these issues. Given the immense social disruption experienced by many black rural communities in the last few decades, schemes and programmes which imply compulsion of any kind for such communities in the process of reordering social relationships, are difficult to contemplate. In this context, it is important to study strategies elsewhere which have created the context for agrarian collectives or producer co-operatives to be established, alongside other forms of production, without imposing them. Zimbabwean experiments since independence could again be a starting point. The second, linked, point has to do with the nature of the demand for such changes. Black rural communities in the farming districts have had little opportunity to express themselves. Recent national meetings, such as they have been, have largely been concerned with the immediately pressing problems of defending 'black spot' communities and labourers from eviction and relocation. Some homeland governments do allow for a measure of popular participation and expression but within strict limits. Trade Union organisation is notoriously difficult amongst agricultural workers and the efforts made in the 1920s and again in the 1940s and 1950s left little lasting legacy. However, there is some indication that organisation is again getting under way, and future thinking about agrarian change needs to include ideas of how rural people can make themselves heard.

If the core areas of the large farm sector are to remain intact, as the younger protagonist in Herschel argued, then the possibilities for greatly increasing the population of such units, even if they become in some way collectives or nationalised state enterprises, is limited. The task of a reform programme would be not least to develop the skills of, and provide some kind of shared ownership for, those already on such units. It would certainly not satisfy demand for smallholdings on the land. However, along with the older man in Herschel, I have suggested that there is likely to be a significant demand for smallholdings amongst at least sections of the homeland-based population. Its intensity might well depend on the degree to which any government was prepared to extend agricultural support programmes to such units. There may be considerable areas of land outside the present homeland boundaries which, for a variety of reasons - and not soil fertility or rainfall alone - are more marginal to the large farming sector and have not attracted heavy investment: areas bordering on homelands, areas in more mountainous zones where small scale pastoralism is possible, areas where transport infrastructure is less developed. In Zimbabwe and Kenya, it is not least such land which has provided the basis for the expansion of smallholder production outside the former Trustlands and reserves; the indications are that they can become highly productive zones. These areas in South Africa need to be identified urgently, and the possible forms of redistribution discussed. As in Zimbabwe, the central problem might be that of controlling reoccupations, so that the social relations of the homelands - subsistence production with migrant labour - are not merely reproduced in slightly larger areas. But the old colonial idea of 'master farmers' in newly settled lands is probably also doomed to failure. Much of the evidence relating to agrarian change and agrarian accumulation amongst smallholders suggests that farm income is seldom more than part of the total family income and that innovation often depends on income from other sources.

One crucial issue, which will fall within the purview of state policy whatever the future form of the South African state, is that of whether the present form of landholding in the homelands should be more comprehensively changed and privatised. The entrenchment of communal land tenure in the twentieth century may, as a number of scholars have argued, have underwritten the migrant labour system. But now, most of those workers who have to keep their families within homeland boundaries and migrate or commute long distances to work no longer have any agricultural plots. The South African state has in any case far less control over such issues in the homelands than it did. Thus one major constraint on privatising landownership in the homelands has been removed.

I am not, however, one of those who sees the entrenchment of communal tenure in the homelands during the twentieth century as merely an imposition by the central state, designed to squeeze as many people as possible into the areas, prevent urbanisation, and destroy surplus production. I think a good deal of the pressure to maintain communal tenure came from both the chiefs and the people of reserves themselves - defending their last bastion against total dispossession, and intent on preventing the emergence of accumulators within their districts. As both the older and younger man in Herschel suggested, there is still considerable popular feeling in the homelands in favour of widespread access to land. Nevertheless there are significant new pressures within the homelands for a fully private land market and the issue is being extensively discussed. Technical officers, both white and more recently black, have long seen private tenure as one means of increasing agricultural output and efficiency in the homelands. As ruling groups within the homelands translate bureaucratic and political authority into commercial and financial success - and control over land distribution becomes a less crucial part of political power in the homelands - they seem to be chaffing against the restrictions on land purchase. Surreptitious and creeping privatisation is happening and a few chiefs have large private farms within the homeland boundaries. But it is still very difficult to accumulate land.

Given the extent of unemployment that already exists, it would be difficult to advocate a fully private land market in the homelands. I do not think that advocacy of a non-racial land market outside the homelands should be inextricably linked to the full privatisation of land within the homelands - the one should certainly precede the other. At the same time, the problems of instituting co-operatives or collectives in such densely populated and overcrowded areas seem immense. Any change would certainly be deeply dependent on providing access to more congenial urban contexts for the many who might want to leave the homelands. Freedom of movement would be a crucial element in any broader rural reform. And it seems important that any strategies for agrarian reconstruction on the farms and in the homelands seek to allow as many options as possible. If the white owned farms are one possible focus for the forces against political change, the homelands are another.

Further Reading

Beinart, W.,   *The Political Economy of Pondoland* (Cambridge University Press, 1982).

Beinart, W., Delius, P., and Trapido, S. (eds.)   *Putting a Plough to the Ground* (Ravan: Johannesburg, 1986).

Bradford, H.,   'The African Industrial and Commercial Workers Union in the South African Countryside' Ph. D., University of the Witwatersrand (1985) to be published by Yale University Press.

Bundy, C.,   *The Rise and Fall of the South African Peasantry* (Heinemann: London, 1979).

Keegan, T.,   *Rural Transformations in Industrialising South Africa* (London, 1987).

Klerk, M. de,   'Seasons that will Never Return: the Impact of Farm Mechanisation on Employment, Incomes and Population Distribution in the Western Transvaal' *Journal of Southern African Studies* 11 (1984).

Morris, M.,   'State Intervention and the Agricultural Labour Supply Post-1948' in F. Wilson, A.

	Kooy and D. Hendrie (eds.) *Farm Labour in South Africa* (David Philip: Cape Town, 1977).
Nkadimeng, M., and Relly, G.,	'Kas Maine: The Story of a Black South African Agriculturalist' in B. Bozzoli (ed.) *Town and Countryside in the Transvaal* (Ravan: Johannesburg, 1983).
Platzky, L., Walker, C.,	*The Surplus People* (Ravan: Johannesburg, 1985).
Simkins, C.,	'Agricultural Production in the African Reserves of South Africa, 1918-1969' *Journal of Southern African Studies* 8 (1981).
Surplus People Project Report,	*Forced Removals in South Africa* (Cape Town and Pietermaritzburg, 1983), 5 volumes.

Papers presented to Second Carnegie Inquiry into Poverty and Development in Southern Africa, Southern African Labour and Development Research Unit, University of Cape Town, 1984.

9. Class, Race & Gender

ELAINE UNTERHALTER

Instances

In November 1985, four months after the first state of emergency was declared, in the Pretoria township of Mamelodi, 4,000 women marched to see their local mayor. Their demands included the withdrawal of police and troops from the streets, an end to the restrictions on funerals, lower rents and the resignation of unrepresentative councillors. They carried a banner which said: 'Please don't shoot us, we don't want to fight'. As the women approached the offices of the town council many people, women and men, old and young, joined them until their numbers had swelled to 50,000. Then the police attacked, firing into the crowd. Thirteen people were killed that day: the funeral of the Mamelodi marchers, attended by around 60,000 mourners was one of the biggest anti-apartheid funerals in the Transvaal in a year of militant funerals attended by tens of thousands. Winnie Mandela defied her banning orders to attend the funeral and, dressed in the colours of the outlawed African National Congress, spoke confidently of the approaching day of liberation.

In September 1986, during the second, and now apparently permanent, state of emergency, some members of the United Women's Congress in Cape Town were putting up posters illegally in Athlone one evening calling for the release of detainees. A police van drew up behind them and the officers ordered them to get into the van and come to the police station. The women began to mock the policemen, refusing to get into the van. A policeman tried to push one woman, she threw him to the ground behind the van, out of sight of his fellow officer who was having to deal with an increasingly angry crowd of women from the neighbourhood, who had come out onto the street when they saw what was happening. In the end the police, humiliated by the jibes of the women and the anger of the neighbourhood, drove off, leaving behind the women they had sought to arrest, who then

---

This chapter is dedicated to the memory of Judy Kimble who died in November 1986 and with whom I discussed many of these ideas.

went on with their flyposting.

Magopa was an African-owned farm in the Transvaal, termed a black spot; in terms of policy on Bantustan consolidation the people living on it were expropriated and moved by force into the Bantustan of Bophuthatswana. The community organised against the removal, refusing to leave Magopa, until a dawn raid by armed police in 1984 left them with no other option. For a year or more before, however, they had refused to recognise the legitimacy of demands that they go. One day police came to serve removal notices on women hoeing a field. The women drew a line in the earth with their hoes. 'You may not come closer to us than this line' they said. They refused to accept the notices. The police had to leave.

In May 1986 a woman was brutally raped in the African township of the Eastern Cape town of Port Alfred. The woman identified the rapist, who was arrested, but later released. The women of PAWO, Port Alfred Women's Organisation, were deeply angry. They organised a seven-day stay-away from work, supported by all the African women living in the township in protest at the release of the rapist, which they contrasted with the detention of school students from the town two days before.

These are just four out of hundreds of examples of women's organised resistance to the present phase of apartheid that have been reported in the press or recounted by observers. These examples highlight some of the features that seem common to the general growth in women's activism: organised campaigns, networks of neighbourhood support, local demands that imply demands of national liberation, and immense courage in the face of the brutal, armed power of the state.

Women's resistance to apartheid, however, is not new. Although many episodes in this history remain largely unknown, women organised campaigns against the imposition of passes early in the 20th century and again in the 1950s, mobilised in rural areas against the imposition of Bantu Authorities and cattle culling in the 1950s, and campaigned to protect their rights to brew beer in urban townships. Women joined in Gandhi's early passive resistance campaign at the end of the 19th century; women workers were militant trade unionists, leading some successful strikes from the 1930s up to the 1950s; large numbers of women joined the ANC during the 1950s and the ANC Women's League had branches countrywide; it was the major affiliate of the Federation of South African Women and formulated a coherent set of women's demands in the context of the demands for national liberation; these demands are set out in the Women's Charter, which still forms the detailed basis of the ANC's commitment to women's emancipation. This rich history would require at least a book to do it justice. It forms the backdrop to the present phase of women's resistance to apartheid and in many cases is an explicitly acknowledged inspiration to present-day struggles. It is these which I want to examine in some detail.

There are four questions I want to look at. First, who are the women activists; secondly, what has impelled women to such prominence in the general struggle against apartheid in the last five years; thirdly, in what ways has women's militancy changed the content of the struggles against national and class oppression; and fourthly, what are the consequences, in terms of gender, of widespread women's resistance to apartheid?

Organisations

The question of who the women activists are demands some breakdown of the forms of women's resistance. I think these can be arranged along a continuum of organisational forms. At one end are women's organisations with a formal membership structure, like UWCO in the Cape or FedTraw in the Transvaal which are affiliated to the UDF, and which concentrate both on raising particular issues of women's oppression and on campaigns for a non-racial democratic South Africa. Similar in outlook to these organisations are trade unions with a large female membership, like the newly-formed South African Domestic and Service Workers Union and the Commercial Catering and Allied Workers Union with 70% of its 40,000 paid up members women; both put demands for paid maternity leave high on the agenda in terms of collective bargaining. The two major black trade union groupings, COSATU and CUSA, both have policy on equal rights for women, and unions affiliated to these groups have sometimes taken collective action on what might be considered particular women's demands, for example opposing the sexual harassment of women workers. I would therefore place the mass of trade unions half way between the women's organisations and the second major organisational form, which I situate in the centre of this continuum. That is those organisations, many of them dominated by women, which do not pose questions explicitly about women's oppression, but which challenge apartheid and organise resistance to it. Here I place civic associations, communities opposing forced removals, religious groups, armed and unarmed units of the ANC, and those organisations with predominantly white membership like the Black Sash and the End Conscription Campaign. At the far end of the continuum are unorganised women, who support the aims of national liberation, but who might only now and then attend a funeral, participate in a consumer boycott, or join a march.

In looking at women militants I want to try to identify the membership of the different groupings at three points along the continuum: the women's organisations, the women in general anti-apartheid organisations, and the women supporters of particular demonstrations or community initiatives. However, I must stress that these are analytical categories and do not demarcate rigid divisons between women activists. In fact there is a high degree of mobility, particularly between the women's organisations and the civic associations, which have absorbed into leadership roles many women schooled in women's organisations. It is also likely that women militants, unable to sustain a high degree of activism and the attendant stresses of police harassment and detention over a long period, might lapse into the third category of supporter.

The women's organisations have brought together veterans of the 1950s and the Congress Alliance, like Albertina Sisulu and the late Dora Tamana with younger, educated, black women, many politicised through student politics, school boycotts, and the experience of forced removal. There are a small number of branches among white women, and a growing organisation in rural areas, particularly in the Cape and the Transvaal, but the mass membership of the organisations is black, working class women radicalised through poverty and what is deemed to be the illegality of their circumstances. For example UWCO, which has a branch structure, has smallish branches in the coloured areas of Cape Town, with a significant membership of professional women, and huge branches, up until mid-1986, in Crossroads, entirely made up of women workers, the majority of whom were domestic servants. Josette Cole points to the pressures on women in the Western Cape, deemed illegal in terms of influx control legislation and subject to repeated arrest, trial and imprisonment, as the major factor contributing to the growth of women's organisations in Crossroads, and a potential stumbling block in the attempt to build mass-based women's organisations amongst all women in the Western Cape, whether they had the right to remain or not.[1] FedTraw, in the Transvaal, has a small number of prominent professional black women members, with the bulk of the membership drawn from women workers, mainly in industry and service jobs, whose major concerns have been the struggle against increasing rents in a period of falling wage rates and the presence of brutal troops in the townships. The atrocities committed by the police and the military have also been of major concern to the white women members of FedTraw, at present still very few in number and almost exclusively English-speaking and middle class. Women in the rural branches of FedTraw appear to be mainly peasant women, living in Bantustans, many subsisting on the land only with the assistance of a wage from a migrant worker.

The membership of the middle group of women's organisations is harder to define. Many of the black women are in fact both members of women's organisations and activists in trade unions and civic associations. For example Lydia Kompe, a shop steward in the Metal and Allied Workers Union (MAWU) in the 1970s, later Transvaal Branch Secretary of the Transport and General Workers Union, is an important activist in FedTraw; Dorothy Nyembe, jailed for fifteen years for her work for MK, the armed wing of the ANC, was an important mobilising force in the growth of the Natal Organisation of Women (NOW) in the mid 1980s. Cheryl Carolus, an executive member of the United Women's Organisation in the Cape in the early 1980s, and then secretary of the UDF in the Western Cape, spoke in 1985 of the frustration often felt in the UWO as its women's branches disintegrated as women moved into the politics of the civic associations. Amanda Kwadi, an organiser for FedTraw in the mid-1980s, considers that the majority of the women members of the Transvaal civic associations are members of the women's organisations as well. However in particular community struggles virtually all the women of that community have mobilised to defend their community. An example of this is the Magopa women, whose action I described at the beginning of this chapter. They not only drove off the police bringing the removal notices, but also rebuilt the roads on the farm after one attempt had been made to hound the people off the land by bulldozing the roads and school. Another example is the women of Chesterville, a Durban

---

1   J. Cole, ' "When your life is bitter you do something": women and squatting in the Western Cape', in D. Kaplan (ed.) *South African Research Papers* (Department of Economic History, University of Cape Town, 1986).

township, with a long tradition of opposition to Bantustan government and Buthelezi's Inkatha. The members of the UDF-affiliated organisations of the township have been harassed, petrol-bombed and assassinated by Inkatha-supporting vigilantes. To protect the community, women have mounted all-night vigils; they sound the alert at any sign of an attack.

It is difficult to generalise about women in ANC units, since as yet very few women have been convicted for ANC activities. While white women in the ANC are apparently highly educated, English-speaking and urban-based, the black women come from diverse backgrounds, rural and urban, and are both well-educated students and workers with a minimum of education.

Women activists in the white organisations like the End Conscription Campaign and the Black Sash tend to be drawn from a very narrow band of white society: almost totally English-speaking professionals, or the wives of professionals, highly educated, and living in the largest cities. On very impressionistic evidence it appears that the women in these organisations have a higher degree of affluence and education than the white women in the FedTraw branches, although there is a tendency for white women activists to move in the opposite direction to their black counterparts. Many of them move from such organisations as the Black Sash into general women's organisations like FedTraw and UWCO, while many black women move from women's organisations into more general community ones.

The unorganised supporters of the national liberation struggle are, understandably, the hardest to identify. It seems that when a particular atrocity touches a community, like the massacre at Mamelodi or the police attack on Muslim activists in a Mosque in Cape Town in mid-1985, the women of that community will come out and show their outrage, but unless there are already functioning structures of an organisation in the area the women's anger might not be focused into future political activity. However, sometimes an atrocity might galvanise the formation of a women's organisation or affiliation to a campaigning group or trade union. For example, the police massacre at Uitenhage in March 1985 crystallised the formation of the Uitenhage Women's Organisation, which went on to establish links with other Cape women's organisations. Women in the Uitenhage Women's Organisation described this process:

> The hippos [police armoured cars] hide in dark corners and shoot our children. We cannot even send them out to the shops without

fear. The week after the massacre they drove through the streets just shooting at people in KwaNobuhle...We decided we had had enough. It was time the women united against the brutality our families face; to be a mouthpiece for women who suffer so much under apartheid; and to participate in the struggle as women. We started by holding house meetings but as the numbers grew we had to use church halls. We discuss the hardships we face, and the struggle to end those...[2]

To recap then: I suggest there are three main organisational forms to women's resistance. First, women organised in women's organisations affiliated to the UDF; then, women members of particular organisations opposed to apartheid like trade unions or civic associations, or communities facing a particular threat, or the Black Sash, and underground units of the ANC; and, lastly, largely unorganised supporters of anti-apartheid demonstrations. The mass of members of the women's organisations, the general organisations and the women supporters of particular events are working class women, living in urban areas or areas adjacent to large industrial complexes. Some professional women are active in the women's organisations and in the white women's organisations. In rural areas, although this may simply reflect our lack of information, it appears that women's resistance reflects community-wide resistance to some specific threat like forced removal or the atrocities carried out by the military or the police. FedTraw has, however, made big strides in the past two years in organising branches in rural areas in the Transvaal focused on a range of issues, and there is evidence of ANC activity in rural areas of Zululand, the Transkei and the northern Transvaal.

Triple oppression and resistance

The second question I want to look at is the reasons for the growth in women's organisation and the politically prominent role played by many women. This requires some survey of the conditions of the subordination of South African women. It is often said that black South African women are triply oppressed by race, class and gender. It is equally true that white women are oppressed by gender.

These are some of the features of that oppression: the pattern of racial domination in South Africa is well known, but that of black women probably less so. As part of the process of colonial domination

---

[2]   Quoted in 'Women's response to the massacres', *Anti-Apartheid Movement Women's Committee Newsletter* 20, (May/June 1985) p.10.

of South Africa in the 19th century, certain features of one particular African society were written down and codified as 'Native Law' and then applied to most of the African areas. This law stipulated that women under 'traditional' law could not own land and remained perpetual minors, unable to marry or enter into any contracts without the consent of a male relative. In many of the Bantustans today versions of this law are still current, as well as other supposedly 'traditional' practices like the flogging of women considered disobedient to their husbands. The racial division of South Africa and the attempts to direct labour to certain sectors of the economy, commonly referred to as the pass laws, had a particular effect on African women. Because men were recruited as migrant labourers as part of an attempt both to extract tax from African communities and at the same time maintain their so-called traditional structure, women remained in the reserves, later the Bantustans, carrying an increasingly heavy load of work and increasingly impoverished. Many women did migrate to cities and found work but they were often regarded with hostility, particularly their attempts to keep out of waged employment and to work in the informal sector. The apartheid philosophy of the mid-1960s equated the presence of African women in towns with the reproduction of an urban African labour force and concerted efforts were made from 1964 to refuse African women residence rights in the townships of South Africa. Hence the huge growth in the 'illegal' population of African women workers, the great difficulty women experience in holding on to a house rented from the administration board, and the high number of evictions of women tenants.

The class oppression of black women is evident from an examination of the South African labour force. Women are concentrated in the low-paid sectors of the economy like domestic service, agricultural work, the distributive trades, and shift work in industry. Large numbers of women living in the Bantustans work in decentralised industries, adjacent to the Bantustan borders, or actually inside the Bantustans, where there are no minimum wages, and often little scope for collective bargaining. The lack of adequate maternity benefit or maternity leave make for a high degree of insecurity in women's work and the unemployment rates among women tend to be higher than those among men. In the period of widespread labour tenancy on South African farms, up to the end of the 1970s, the wives and daughters of tenant farmers were compelled to work, virtually unpaid except for some food, as the domestic servants of the farm owners. The abolition of labour tenancy and the forced removal of hundreds of thousands of agricultural workers into the Bantustans has made the position of such women even more insecure. The only work available for them may be seasonal work, grossly underpaid for local farmers, or the option of 'illegal' migration to the industrialised centres. Many coloured women, working on the farms of the western Cape, were similarly paid in food, or even wine, the 'dop' system as it was known, and have been similarly marginalised with the mechanisation of farms and the growth of agri-business.

The gender oppression of black women is inherent in the examples I have given of race and class oppression, but can also be seen in the virtually complete absence of child-care provisions for working mothers, or the lack of gynaecological services in a country with the highest cervical cancer rate in the world: 35 per 100,000 women, and an estimated 20,000 deaths per year from backstreet abortions.

White women too suffer gender oppression. Although many work in professional, administrative or supervisory jobs and have a high standard of living, they too suffer from the lack of maternity benefits and the discrimination in employment: for example primary school teaching in white schools is almost exclusively the preserve of white women; there are a handful of male teachers, who are all, strangely enough, the principals. Up until two years ago no married woman could have a permanent contract as a school teacher. With the exception of one woman judge, three women MPs, and a handful of senior army officers with the responsibility for nursing and the training of women recruits, women are almost entirely invisible in the upper levels of the state. The South African press and television abounds with the nastiest sexist imagery, and it is extremely difficult for white women to break out of this type-casting and assert any kind of independence.

Aspects of this oppression usually constitute the sufficient conditions for resistance. If we look more closely at the different forms of women's militancy we can uncover what the necessary conditions for activism are. It seems to me that within the women's organisations it is because black women have experienced the full burden of that triple oppression that they become active. Early on in the history of Crossroads, the squatter settlement near Cape Town, the women, virtually all in vulnerable positions because they were illegals, set up local committees and self-help organisations. A significant number of women activists in women's organisations are women who head their households. Josette Cole found this was the case in Crossroads and women activists from the Transvaal have remarked on the same phenomenon, pointing to a membership with a significant proportion of widows.[3] Even the prominent professional women in these organisations like Albertina Sisulu have brought up children without a husband and had to support a family on a single wage. Migrant labour and the lack of housing are two of the chief reasons for the high incidence of female-headed households. A female-headed household is a household surviving on lower wages than those with two wage-earners, and these households have been particularly hardly hit by the rise in rents, sometimes of an order of 500% in ten years, and the rise in prices resulting from heavy increases in general sales tax. The web of restrictions on access to township housing is particularly weighted against women tenants. Despite township superintendents' ability to exercise discretion in this area, it has been commonplace in the townships of the Transvaal for the township police to arrive to evict a widow and her family, while her husband, in whose name the housing permit was issued, still lay in his coffin in the house, surrounded by mourners.

There has been a tremendous growth in the number of women in wage employment in the period 1960-1980. For example, 22% of African women aged 15-59 were in wage employment in 1960, compared to 32% in 1980; 32% of coloured women of the same age were in wage employment in 1960, 38% in 1980; 9% of Indian women of that age were waged workers in 1960, and 26% in 1980.[4] The growth in waged employment seems to have increased women's experience of oppression, because of the dangers and difficulties associated with work under the present regime. The same social trend seems to indicate a reason for women's activism in trade unions and the concern of unions to take up some women's demands. For example, the auto workers union negotiated an agreement with the BMW plant in Pretoria to open a creche for workers' children; there have been a number of strikes and union activities because of cases of sexual

---

[3] J. Cole, ' "When your life is bitter" ', pp. 53-4; A. Kwadi 'The form of women's organisation against apartheid: The example of FedTraw'. Unpublished seminar paper presented to the Women, Colonialism and Commonwealth seminar, Institute of Commonwealth Studies, London, Jan. 1987.

[4] G. Jaffe and C. Caine, 'The incorporation of African Women into the Industrial Workforce: Its implications for the Women's Question in South Africa' paper presented to conference *The South African Economy after apartheid*, Centre for Southern African Studies, University of York, Oct. 1986.

harassment of women workers. In 1983 a white worker at Unilever was sexually harassed by a manager; there was a one-day strike by the predominantly black workforce, who demanded that the man be fired; he was transferred to another plant.

The oppression women workers experience in their lives, the constant raids and attacks by the police for pass book offences, the lack of housing, which is likely to become the new focus for police control and harassment of urban residents in the wake of the repeal of the pass laws in 1986, the low wages and job insecurity, the rise in prices and absence of male relatives who can be of assistance, go a long way to explaining women's membership of the women's organisations. All these factors have been exacerbated by the presence of the military who have often used the particular regulations that cover township residents, like pass laws and rent obligations as a cover for house-to-house searches, road blocks and attacks on the people. The vicious actions of the military in the townships in the last two years in particular have had an important effect on white women, who have focused much of their campaigning on their opposition to their sons doing military service in the streets of the townships. Rural women too, it appears, have been galvanised into joining women's organisations by police and military attacks on their area.

But the nature of the organisations themselves, their ability to take effective action over issues that concern women, and consult at a grassroots level is the other factor that must be taken into account. The women's organisations' political perspective has been to see the women's needs as priority and to concentrate on meeting these needs. For example, the women's organisations stress the need to build up women's confidence, to give women skills in public speaking and running meetings; they arrange creches, often run by the comrades, the members of the youth congresses, for children so that mothers can attend meetings, and they have most recently concentrated on spreading first aid skills so that people injured by police and troops need not go to hospital, where they are likely to be detained, but can be nursed in the community. FedTraw has, in certain areas, run sewing and knitting circles so that women may make clothes for sale on a small scale; they also run literacy classes and teach effective ways of vegetable gardening in rural areas. However, the women's organisations, although they focus on women's needs and women's issues, are not at all separatist. They are closely linked through a myriad of joint actions with the civic associations and the UDF. Their political outlook stresses the need for united action against apartheid. A number of activists and commentators have stressed that there is little initial mobilisation around gender issues, but rather around more general issues like rent, troops in the townships and so on. However, gender issues are raised in the course of women's discussions amongst themselves. The Port Alfred women's action against rape is a good example of this.

In the second form of organisation where women's activities are evident, those community-based campaigns or single issue campaigns, it appears - and this must remain a hypothesis until someone can do a rigorous study - that the women militants, while suffering some of the burdens of triple oppression, do not suffer them all. They may have passes, houses, secure employment, or wage-earning sons and husbands. The horrors of apartheid are evident to them, they may suffer from many of them, but they are not, quite, at the sharp edge of the knife, until some particular event, like rises in rent or electricity costs, or the forced removal of their community, undercuts some of their hard-won security. For the black women in this group their political perspective is formed by the civic associations or the anti-removal committee. The stress is on the need to fight off the threat of forced removal and build up their community, as in Magopa, to drive out troops and police and corrupt councillors, as in the Vaal township civic associations, to improve the education in schools through parent-teacher-student associations, and to secure lower rents through the rent boycotts organised around street committees.

For the white women in this group their lack of personal economic hardship colours the form of action they take. Theirs is a moral and intellectual condemnation of apartheid and their activism is based on the skills they have acquired in the fields of, for example, law, journalism, social work, and teaching. The white and black members of the ANC units come from similar backgrounds to the others in this category but appear to act neither in response to an immediate community threat nor as an extension of their professional concern. Because the ANC is organised underground, its women members seem to draw on long traditions and disciplined networks in their activism.

The third form of resistance I identified, that of the largely unorganised women, seems by definition to be kindled by particular events like a death in detention or particular campaigns, like the consumer boycott or the rent boycott. It is the strength of local organisation in street committees and civic associations or women's organisations that translate this form of activism into long-term, disciplined resistance.

It therefore appears, in answer to the second question I posed, that it is the degree of women's experience of triple oppression that will condition the form of organisation in which they are active. The more insecure a woman's circumstances, the more likely she is, given a plethora of organisations in her area, to join a women's organisation; the more comfortable her circumstances the more likelihood of joining a single-issue campaign. The civic and community associations and trade unions straddle the middle ground, talking not for the most marginalised women, but for those experiencing both hardships and some relative comforts. The increasing brutality and hardship which are features of this phase of apartheid, coupled with the growth and spread of organisations, including women's organisations, have impelled women into a prominent position in terms of their resistance to apartheid.

Women's emancipation in national and social liberation

The third and fourth issues I want to look at raise questions about the results of women's activism. First, how much has this affected the content of the struggles against national and class oppression? As I mentioned at the beginning of this chapter it was the activities of the ANC Women's League and the Federation of South African Women in the 1950s that led to the drafting of statements of women's demands in The Women's Charter, adopted in 1954, and the women's demands for the Freedom Charter compiled in 1955. Both of these accept that there are both common demands for all South Africans suffering national oppression and special demands and needs for women, such as maternity leave and pay, maternity services, day nurseries, birth control clinics, full opportunities for work, equal pay for equal work, and equal rights with men in property, marriage and guardianship of children. The Freedom Charter outlines the common demands of the people, which are the essential precondition for a liberated South Africa: but the Freedom Charter makes only a few references to the special needs of women. While certain clauses of the Freedom Charter like those on equal pay for equal work, for example, speak directly to women, the detail of women's emancipation is set out in the Women's Charter.

From the time the ANC was banned in South Africa until the 1980s, there was a very strong tendency within the ANC to assert that national liberation entailed women's emancipation, but not to specify where such emancipation must be located or how it was to be achieved. For example, in an interview in *Sechaba* in March 1981, Mavis Nhlapo of the ANC Women's Secretariat said:

We do not actually pay much attention to these differences [between men and women] and these struggles, because we believe that in the main course of the struggle for national liberation, women will assert themselves and therefore will assume their rightful place in the struggle and in society.[5]

However, in 1985 the ANC president went to Nairobi at the time of the Decade for Women conference and made a strong commitment that the ANC would not consider the task of national liberation achieved until the emancipation of women too had been accomplished. This statement recognised that the first process, national liberation, did not necessarily entail the second, women's emancipation. In 1986 an editorial in VOW, the journal of the ANC Women's Section, gave some detailed content to this:

We have, as women, issues which directly affect us and around which we can mobilise and rally other women into active struggle for national and social emancipation. For example rent increases, the sky rocketing cost of living, low and discriminatory wages, lack of maternity benefits, sexual harassment at places of work and in schools and colleges ... discriminatory tax laws, pass laws, evictions from homes when husbands die, lack of creches and nursery schools [...] We must educate more women on these problems by organising meetings, workshops and seminars. We must have as many women as possible to speak out on their problems which are common to us all and that need united action to eliminate them.[6]

It seems to me that it is because of the organised resistance of women in the last five years, just as in the 1950s, that the liberation movement has recognised the importance of specifying the areas of women's oppression and taking action in these areas.

A similar development has been evident in the legal organisations in South Africa. There is an awareness in the UDF, for example, that if women are to exercise the rights demanded in the Freedom Charter - that the people shall govern - they must build up their confidence and organisational skills in a women's organisation, and if women are to be drawn into political mobilisation it must be around issues that concern them. Within the unions, both CUSA and COSATU have adopted

---

[5]   *Sechaba*, March 1981, pp.17-18.

[6]   *Voice of Women*, First Quarter, 1986, p.2.

resolutions detailing women's rights and the unions' commitment to fighting to achieve these. The National Education Crisis Committee (NECC) took policy decisions in March 1986 on a range of issues relating to education and national liberation. One of these resolutions was on the need for child-care provision for working mothers and adequate pre-school education for children. COSAS, the now banned school students' organisation, which launched some of the school boycotts in 1984 and 1985, included in one of its demands an end to the sexual harassment of women students. Clearly, women's demands are coming increasingly to the forefront as part of the demands to end national and class oppression and are not being subsumed into the generality of those demands. This seems a considerable achievement on the part of the women activists.

Resistance and the reformulation of gender

The last area I want to look at is the changing content of gender which women's resistance has brought about. Gender is not a biological difference between the sexes but is the social way that sexual difference is constructed. I want to consider firstly some visual material that has been produced by women's organisations, civic associations, the Black Sash, and the ANC. In the posters and the pamphlets produced by these groups there are three different kinds of image. First, there is an image common to all predominantly black groups of the defiant and militant woman. Posters show Dora Tamana, frail and with a walking stick, raising her fist in the amandla salute, and there is the much used photograph of a woman, standing surrounded by troops in their armoured cars, raising both her fists in anger and defiance. The second image, used by the ANC and now to be seen on material produced by the legal women's organisations, shows a woman carrying her baby on her back and a gun. This image implies a transformation of gender roles: women carry a gun, but they still maintain an identity as mother, both of future generations of children and of the revolution. Both these images imply women asserting themselves, standing up against their oppression. By contrast the logo of the Black Sash has no gender content, it is a book, and there seems an absence of concern on the part of these women activists with their own gender subordination, in contrast with their agitation on behalf of African women.

While many branches of the national liberation movement, in their visual material, stress the strong and militant woman, there is a subtheme to the gender content of women's resistance. That is the stress on motherhood. Albertina Sisulu, addressing one thousand people at the University of Cape Town in June 1986, at a meeting to mark 100 years of women at the university said:

> No self-respecting woman can stand aside and say she is not involved while police are hunting other mothers' children like wild dogs in the townships [...] A mother is a mother, black or white. Stand up and be counted with other women.[7]

In a similar vein at the funeral of Victoria Mxenge, a UDF activist assassinated by vigilantes in Durban, Sister Bernard Ncube, the president of FedTraw and a nun, addressed the crowd:

> The struggle of national liberation is not only a struggle of our menfolk [...] join us, mothers who are still sitting.[8]

The address to all women as mothers, stressing this as their common experience, even in the words of a nun who has not borne children, at one level appears to run counter to the visual images which stress not so much women's domestic role as their political activism. However, I believe that the call to all mothers, while on the one hand containing a conventional gender reference, implies not literal motherhood, but an appeal to mothers of a new nation; moreover, in the vernacular, the word for adult woman is the same as that for mother. I think these excerpts from speeches play on this dual sense of the word.

To conclude, briefly, women's activism against apartheid is at an unprecedented level at present. Much of it has been organised in response to the brutality of the regime. The high level of women's mobilisation has had an important impact on the form and demands of the national liberation movement. While it cannot be assumed that the emancipation of South African women will necessarily follow from the present insurrection, very important organisational and ideological underpinnings to that process have been created.

---

[7] *Argus*, 3 June 1986
[8] *Guardian*, 19 August 1985.

Further Reading

Beall, J. *et al.*   'Women in Struggle: Towards a transformation of roles? African Women in Durban, 1985-8' *South African Review* 4, (Ravan Press: Johannesburg, 1987).

Berger, I.,   'Sources of class consciousness: South African women in recent labour struggles' *International Journal of African Historical Studies* 16, 1, pp.49-66.

Bernstein, H.,   *For their triumphs and for their tears: Women in apartheid South Africa* (revised edition) (IDAF: London, 1983).

Barrett, J., Dawber, A. *et al*   *Vukani Makhosikazi: South African Women Speak* (CIIR: London, 1985)

Ginwala, F.,   'ANC Women: their strength in the struggle. Interview' *Work in Progress* 45, (1986) pp.10-14.

Joseph, H.,   *Side by Side* (Zed Press: London, 1986).

Suttner, R., and Keenan, J.,   *30 years of the Freedom Charter* (Ravan: Johannesburg, 1986).

Lawson, L.,   *Working Women: A portrait of South Africa's black women workers* (SACED/Ravan: Johannesburg, 1985).

Lipman, B.,   *We make Freedom* (Pandora Press: London, 1984).

Kimble, J., and Unterhalter, E.,   'We opened the road for you, you must go forward: ANC Women's struggles, 1912-1982' *Feminist Review* 12, (1982) pp.11-36.

Walker, C.,   *Women and Resistance in South Africa* (Onyx Press: London, 1982).

Yawitch, J.,   'Research Report: The incorporation of African Women into Wage Labour, 1950-1980' *South African Labour Bulletin* 9,3, (1983) pp.82-93.

10. Diseases
of Apartheid

SHULA MARKS & NEIL ANDERSSON

By any account South Africa is a very violent society. Over the past two years alone over 2,000 people have been killed, most of them by the security forces; some 30,000 were detained in the Second Emergency declared on June 12th 1986; and thousands more have been injured. The psychological impact of the military and police occupation of the black townships, and of detentions, solitary confinement, brutal interrogation and torture is less easy to quantify, but is at least as profound. This state violence is accompanied by a more silent violence, no less devastating, and certainly as pervasive and pernicious: the violence of socially generated and preventible disease.

It is widely recognised by sociologists of medicine that disease patterns cannot be dissociated from social, economic or political power, while health care systems form part and parcel of the totality of social and productive relations, and 'mirror' society's structure. Much disease is socially produced, while resource allocation for health needs is equally dependent on political and economic relations. Conflicts within the health system reflect the inherent conflicts of a stratified society. Cedric de Beer puts it well: '...health is not a meaningless misfortune that attacks individuals without reason or warning .... patterns of disease are related to class, standard of living and political power ..... Injustice and exploitation are as important as germs in causing disease and social justice is as powerful a medicine as any drug.'[1] Nowhere is this more evident than in South Africa.

Advances in the field of medicine are at the heart of a great deal of South African government propaganda. Pictures of smiling doctors (white) and nurses (black) and chubby babies adorn the glossy pictorials celebrating the 'independence' of its 'new black states' or Bantustans. In 1976 the Secretary for Health proudly claimed that 'after painstaking research all endemic diseases of Africa have been eradicated in South Africa'. The statement is misleading: parasitic and

---

[1] Cedric de Beer, *The South African Disease. Apartheid, Health and Health Services* (C.I.I.R.: London, 1986) pp. 78, 79.

vector-borne diseases are still prevalent in South Africa, and in some cases have been given a new lease of life through the policy of uprooting and 'resettlement', and in overcrowded urban squatter camps. If the boast is a half-truth, the propaganda pictures are grotesque. In 1979 a black child was believed to die every twenty minutes of malnutrition: and this was before the recent devastating drought began to take its toll. Since the late nineteenth century, the true killers in South Africa have not been the 'endemic diseases of Africa' but the diseases of uneven industrialisation.[2]

This is not, of course, to argue that pre-industrial South Africa was in some miraculous sense free of disease: the 'endemic' diseases of Africa were debilitating and probably limited population growth, as did periodic famine and epizootics. Nevertheless, the contemporary patterns of morbidity and mortality for the black population are probably closer to those of early industrial Britain than of precolonial Africa. Thus, while whites enjoy standards of living and die of the degenerative cancers and cardiovascular diseases typical of the developed Western countries, for blacks, malnutrition and the associated infections dominate the pattern of disease and account for more deaths at almost any age than any other single cause.

In the past few years, a small black urban elite is beginning to show an increasing incidence of the diseases associated with a 'western' lifestyle: hypertension, cardiovascular accidents, diabetes mellitus and peptic ulcers. Black female domestic servants now have the highest rate of hypertension in the country. This should not disguise the fact that for the vast majority of blacks disease is determined by the physical impoverishment which results from the policies of apartheid, and which have been exacerbated by the intense drought of the early 1980s and the current recession.

Disease patterns: historical background

These patterns are not new. South Africa's contemporary disease patterns and health care system are rooted in the social changes which began with the discovery of minerals in the last third of the nineteenth

---

[2] For a full discussion, see World Health Organisation, *Health and Apartheid* (Geneva, 1983), especially chapter 2; and S. Marks & Neil Andersson, 'Industrialisation, rural change and the 1944 National Health Services Commission', in S. Feierman & J. Janzen, *The Political Economy of health in Africa* (forthcoming).

century: diamonds in Kimberley in 1868, vast seams of gold at very deep levels underground on the Witwatersrand in 1886. The industrial and agrarian revolution which followed the development of the mining industry, the new concentrations of population on the mines and in the rapidly developing towns and the special hazards of the mining operations as well as growing impoverishment in the countryside were to have swift and grave implications for the physical well-being of workers, both black and white.

The initial toll of accident and disease in the mining industry was horrifying and lay behind much of the white working class militancy of these years. (Of the eighteen leaders in the 1907 white mine-workers strike in 1907, fourteen had died of Miners' Phthisis by the 1913 strike, and two more were known to be suffering from the disease.) The heightened militancy of the white working class and the undiminished mortality amongst 'tropical' Africans led the state to intervene more forcibly. A series of laws known as the Prior Laws provided some protection and compensation for white workers, and in 1913 the South African government eventually banned the recruitment of Africans from north of latitude 22° south.

From this time, conditions for Africans actually on the mines probably improved, although the accident-rate remained high, and is still amongst the highest in the world, even taking account of the difficult technology of deep-level mining. The richer mines, under pressure from the state, began to improve their medical services, to build up-to-date hospitals to deal especially with accidents and to train African medical orderlies. By the 1940s the Gold Producers' Committee of the Chamber of Mines could boast (as it continues to do) that it had the finest hospital and health service in Africa:

> The system of medical care of the mine Native labour force provides an example of an objective, which medical authorities agree should be the goal for every community, i.e. a good diet and a periodic examination for all members of the population, no matter in what work they are engaged. The mine Native labourers, from whatever source, undergo two or even three separate medical examinations to determine whether they are fit to work on the mines at all and to differentiate them for different forms of labour on the mines....Their daily diet is ample and well-balanced and the physical condition of

the great majority of Natives improves as a result of it.[3]

This evidence, produced by the Chamber of Mines in order to justify continuing the migrant labour system, ignored the wider repercussions of South African capitalist development on African health. For, if by the 1940s actual conditions on the mines had improved out of all recognition, it is clear that at the same time the health of the majority of blacks had been dramatically transformed as a direct and indirect result of the mineral discoveries.

Indeed, as George Gale, then Secretary for Health in the Union government, pointed out in a long and important memorandum to the same commission, the migrant labour system in mining, manufacturing and domestic service had 'far-reaching effects' upon African health both as individuals and collectively through the impoverishment of the rural areas. While he agreed that the invidiual mine labourer was 'hygienically housed, well fed and medically cared for while on the mine', he continued:

[...] the mine medical services protect the mine-worker only so long as he is on the mine. They do not extend to the rural area to which he returns when his health breaks down *owing to the conditions of migratory labour*. Obviously they cannot; but the point is that the mine medical services do not meet the really serious detrimental effects, quâ health, of the migratory system.

To begin with, the mines recruit only physically fit persons. Among those whom they reject are many who have become unfit through venereal disease, tuberculosis, and muscular-cum-articular 'rheumatism' - chronic degenerative diseases of which the principal initial cause is conditions of mine labour.... The migrant labourer returning with untreated or inadequately treated venereal disease may infect his wife (and other women) in the rural area....Gonorrhea in women is a principal cause of sterility. Syphilis in women causes miscarriages and still-births, and even when living children are born they are frequently congenital syphilitics. Sterility, miscarriages and the birth of sickly children are a frequent cause of unhappiness and even divorce...In many areas the incidence of syphilis among child-bearing women is 25 per cent or over...[4]

These remarks remain true today, in the late 1980s, when, as we shall see, the state boasts of its improved medical services for blacks in

---

[3] Evidence of the Gold Producers Committee, in Department of Native Affairs, U.G. 28-'48 *Report of the Native Laws Commission, 1946-8* (Fagan Commission: Pretoria, 1948), p. 35.

[4] *Ibid.*, pp. 38-39, italics in original.

urban areas and points to the apparently dramatic drop in black infant mortality; the statistics of mortality in the 'reserves' - now called Bantustans - are conveniently ignored as they are no longer considered part of the Republic.

Yet not all malnutrition, venereal disease or tuberculosis were simply the result of migrant labour to the mines. South Africa's dependence on mineral extraction and her position in the world economy meant that the effects of uneven development were also felt in the towns which developed in the wake of the mineral discoveries. The most spectacular growth was in the seaports and on the Rand, where industries were heavily dependent on the demands of the mines. Housing and sanitary conditions in the urban areas concerned Medical Officers of Health from the turn of the century, and the fear that infectious disease was no respecter of class or racial boundaries led public health officials to be the foremost advocates of urban segregation. As elsewhere, the 'metaphoric equation' of blacks with infectious disease, and the perception of urban social relations in terms of 'the imagery of infection and epidemic disease' provided a compelling rationale for major forms of social control, and in particular the segregation of African 'locations'.[5] There was, however, little amelioration in the conditions giving rise to poverty-based disease: the low-wage urban economy and the underdevelopment of the countryside.

In the first decades of the century unhealthy working and living conditions, long hours of work and inadequate nutrition made an increasing proportion of the new urban population, whether black or white, susceptible to infectious and nutritionally related diseases. Epidemic disease such as influenza, measles, typhoid fever and dysentery took a frightening toll. As late as 1938, a Nutrition Survey conducted by the Department of Public Health revealed that 47.6 per cent of white schoolboys in the Transvaal were malnourished.[6] The differential access of enfranchised whites to state resources ensured that their welfare problems were solved ahead of those of the disenfranchised black population. Poor whites were absorbed into the better-paid jobs in industry as South Africa's secondary industrialisation

---

[5]   M. Swanson, 'The sanitation syndrome: bubonic plague and urban native policy in the Cape colony, 1900-1909', *J. Afr. Hist.*, 18, 3 (1977).

[6]   The figures for white schoolboys elsewhere were Cape 31.5 per cent, Natal 16.4 per cent and Orange Free State 43.6 per cent. Department of Public Health, *Nutrition Survey*, 1938, cited in the *Report of the National Health Services Commission*, 1944.

took off in the second half of the 'forties, while welfare services and free hospitalisation were developed at the same time.

The toll of disease was always more formidable for blacks than for whites. And while there was some concern for the fact that, in the towns, disease would recognise no colour bar, so that some basic public health measures were necessary for all, concern with the reproduction of the workforce in the countryside was never strong enough to ensure more than the most cursory action. While malaria and typhus were a recurrent scourge in the rural areas then, as now, it was above all malnutrition, tuberculosis (TB) and venereal diseases (VD) that did most damage.

The interaction between disease in the mines and locations, the migrant labour system and the spread of ill-health, especially TB, in the countryside was complex. For it was not simply the return of the migrant from the unhealthy towns and mines which led to the alarming spread of disease in the inter-war period. The diseases were not automatically transferred to the rural areas. The accelerating spread of TB, malnutrition and venereal disease in the 'reserves' from the 1920s resulted from the interaction of the health hazards of the mining industry, the migrant labour system and the low wage urban economy with the simultaneous and connected impoverishment of the countryside.

From about the 1920s (though in some areas it had already begun in the mid-nineteenth century, while in others it was only to become manifest in the 1930s and '40s) people who had once been able to produce an adequate subsistence and a surplus for the colonial markets, were now having to purchase their food. Despite the 'betterment' schemes of the late 1930s, by the mid-1940s government reports were showing that the production of African staples such as maize and sorghum had declined in the reserves throughout the country.

Tuberculosis was the true barometer of poverty in both town and countryside. We do not, of course, have very conclusive evidence on the health of Africans in South Africa until after the mineral revolution. Nevertheless, it is clear from eye-witness accounts of the African population in the first half of the nineteenth century and from the recollections of Africans and mission doctors recorded in the early twentieth that outside of periods of warfare, epizootics and drought, malnutrition was rare and TB virtually unknown in precolonial African society.

It was only subsequent to the late nineteenth century mineral discoveries, the widespread annexation of African territories and the inception of the migrant labour system that diseases of poverty were noted on any scale. As the 1932 Report of the Tuberculosis Research Committee remarked in inimitably bland fashion, although the disease 'may be fairly well tolerated under natural or tribal conditions, [...] susceptibility is fraught with extreme danger when exposure to danger is accompanied by a sudden change in occupation, food, housing and mode of life'.[7] Thus, widespread TB was noticed earliest in those areas which were the first to feel the impact of land and cattle loss, and internal stratification: the Ciskei and Transkei.

Within ten years of the opening of the Kimberley diamond fields, medical men in the eastern Cape began to remark on the alarming increase in VD and TB and by 1895 the Medical Officer of Health for the Cape Colony was sufficiently concerned to agitate for an enquiry and some kind of action. Elsewhere the disease spread somewhat later, as the rural areas began to feel progressive impoverishment and underdevelopment as a result of the migrant labour system: by the mid-1940s it was estimated that 75 per cent of the Transkei population had been in contact with TB. By the early years of World War II it had reached unprecedented levels even amongst the white population.[8]

To many observers it was clear that far more would have to be done to resolve the crisis in health for both black and white which had developed by the late 'thirties. Not only were preventible diseases rife; it was also widely recognised that the public health system was totally unable to cope either with the deterioration in health conditions or with the increasing demand for health services. In response to this and to the political pressures on the state in the early war years, a National Health Services Commission was appointed in 1942. Its brief was 'to enquire into, report and advise upon the provision of an organised National Health Service in conformity with the modern conception of "health" [which was carefully defined in the report] which will ensure adequate mental, dental, nursing and hospital services for all sections of the

---

[7] South African Institute of Medical Research, *Tuberculosis in South African Natives with special reference to the disease amongst the Mine Labourers on the Witwatersrand* (Johannesburg, 1932), 21.

[8] U.G. 28 - '48, *Report of the Native Laws Commission*, 36, citing a later report for the SAIMR (Publication no XXX) by Dr. Peter Allen based on a series of tuberculin tests in the southern Transkei.

people of South Africa'.[9]

The Commission's recommendations were wide-ranging and involved the total reorganisation of South Africa's current health care system. Its principal objective was stated to be the establishment of a national health service which would reach all the people of South Africa, regardless of colour. The aim was to establish preventive health services rather than to perpetuate the high-technology, hospital-based curative system.

A number of the recommendations of the Commission were embodied in the National Health Act of 1946 which was piloted through Parliament by Gluckman. Even before the full report had been published at the end of 1944, however, the Smuts government showed its unwillingness to undertake the action necessary to achieve a centralised, publicly funded national health service, which would integrate preventive and curative care. The government's failure to implement key aspects of the Report gave the medical profession its opportunity to stiffen its resistance particularly to the preventive aspects of the report. Then, with the accession of the National Party to power in 1948, the climate became even less propitious for advances in the health field.

In retrospect, it is perhaps not surprising that the recommendations of the National Health Services commission were dropped after 1948. The central dictum of the Commission, that 'unless there were drastic reforms in the sphere of nutrition, housing, health education and recreation, the mere provision of more doctoring would not bring more health to the people of the country',[10] demanded a drastic restructuring of the social order which went well beyond the white consensus. Perhaps it also exceeded the capacity of the political economy, which was still so heavily dependent on the primary sectors of farming and mining. The general transformation of the position of the 'poor whites' as a result of South Africa's industrial expansion into secondary industry during and after World War II and the expansion of medical aid schemes made issues of state-funded welfare for whites of far less urgency than they had been in the 'thirties. From the Afrikaner nationalist point of view, black welfare should be paid for by capital

---

9   U.G. 30 - '44, *Report of the National Health Services Commission*, (Pretoria, 1944), 1.

10 *Report of the National Health Services Commission*, p. 28. They were quoting directly from the memorandum of the Medical Association of South Africa (MASA); see *Jnl. of MASA*, 13th July 1943.

rather than the state. Forced to take action to ensure the reproduction of the workforce and the protection of whites from epidemic disease, there was some expansion of urban hospitals and clinics for blacks (beyond those already provided by the mines) and a very considerable - but wholly insufficient - increase in the number of black nurses - though on a newly segregated basis.

Like the Chamber of Mines in the 1940s, the South African government has more recently taken refuge in the statistics of hospital expansion to answer its critics' allegation that apartheid lies at the root of much ill-health in South Africa. Moreover, apologists for the South African government and some members of the medical profession argue that deplorable as the country's health statistics are, they are simply the product of its processes of industrialisation and urbanisation and a reflection of its dual economy. The Chairman of the Executive Committee of the Society of Psychiatrists in South Africa, a man who prides himself on his liberal credentials, claimed in 1979 that the differences in morbidity and mortality and the unequal health care facilities in the Republic were the result of 'cultural and socioeconomic factors in a developing country which have nothing to do with politics'.[11]

The allegedly backward, stagnant rural economy and now, increasingly, population growth are held responsible for an African morbidity and mortality not dissimilar to those experienced in other parts of the Third World. In 1971 the Minister of Health commented:

> We get that kind of person who says the Government must provide more food and more balanced food and more pensions. But when there is a specific case of a widow with six children on her hands, what is the cause of her problem? ... It will get us nowhere to have the small number of whites ... exerting themselves to have their growth rates and production capacity absorbed by an abnormal increase in the number of people who are unproductive.[12]

Admittedly, the rhetoric has become more sophisticated since the early 1970s, but the underlying response has not: population control has become the most heavily funded aspect of South Africa's health service, in an attempt not so much to cope with underlying poverty, disease and misery as to maintain continued white political control.

---

[11] L.S. Gillis, Letter to the *Lancet*, 1, 767 (1978).

[12] Cited in B. Brown, 'Facing the black peril', *Journal of Southern African Studies*, 13, 2 (1987), p. 256.

Nor can South Africa's policies of apartheid and its economic development be dissociated in the way much of the contemporary rhetoric would have us believe. Although it is true, as we have seen, that South Africa's disease patterns *have* been transformed by its industrial revolution, and have in large measure resulted from it, this is not unrelated to apartheid: apartheid, like segregation before it, can be seen as the specific form in which industrialisation has taken place in South Africa, with the benefits accruing to whites - and the costs transferred to blacks.

Contemporary health patterns

While the contours of South Africa's epidemiology were set by the earlier years of industrialisation in a segregated state, the more specific policies of the apartheid state over the last forty years - influx control, forced removals and the uprooting of millions of people, the increased impoverishment of the Bantustans and political repression, all of them intrinsically related to South Africa's processes of 'modernisation' - have also made their own contribution to the country's patterns of disease. While not all ill-health in the Republic is the result of industrialisation or apartheid, the differential incidence of disease and mortality in South Africa is socially structured, and it is above all the policies of apartheid which over the past forty years have determined this.

Table 1. *Estimated Population of South Africa*

	1985		2000*
White	4.8M		5.3M
Coloured	2.8M		3.7M
Asian	.9M		1.1M
African	23.5M	(of which 6M in TBVC)	34.9M
	32.0M		45.0M

Table 2. *Estimated Percentages of the Population Residing in Urban and Rural Areas*

1985

	RSA		TBVC	
	Urban	Rural	Urban	Rural
White	89	11	-	-
Coloured	78	22	-	-
Asian	92	8	-	-
African	46	54	11	89

8.6% whites are over the age of 65, compared to about 3 per cent of the other population groups.

Table 3. *Estimated personal income, per capita, 1980*

	Per capita	Average annual growth
		(Per capita, 1975-80)
	Rands per annum	%
White	4,743	10.5
Coloured	1,013	11.5
Asian	1,453	13.4
African	503	12.3

Source: RF/1986: *Final Report of the Commission into Health Services* (Pretoria, 1986), p. 11.
* Projections by Prof. J.L. Sadie, cited in SAIRR, *A Survey of Race Relations in South Africa, 1981* p. 52.

The health of the majority of blacks is undermined by the social conditions which have provided prosperity for the approximately five million whites who control the productive resources of the country. Disease patterns follow income: and whites still earn nearly nine times more than Africans on average and about four times more than Coloureds and Asians - despite the rises for certain groups of black workers. Thus according to Merle Lipton, from 1970 - 82, real wages for Africans in manufacturing and construction rose by over 60 per cent, compared with 18 per cent for whites; on gold mines real wages for Africans quadrupled, while those for white miners rose by 3 per cent; on white farms, real wages for Africans doubled between 1968-9 and 1976. As a result the white share of personal income declined from over 70 to under 60 per cent, while the African share rose from 19 to 29 per cent.[13]

Substantial as these increases may appear, they should be set against the further deterioration of rural resources and rapidly increasing unemployment. In the 1970s, the ratio between the income of urban and rural employed Africans - 8:1 - was approaching that between white and black.[14]

At the same time, unemployment is at record levels, as the structural inequalities of the South African economy have been exacerbated by the current recession. Some estimates put it at about 40 per cent of the work force - more than 3 million out of a total workforce of between 7 and 8 million.

According to an estimate made by the University of South Africa's Bureau of Market Research, only 46 per cent of Sowetans between the ages of 20 and 64 earned a wage in 1985, compared with 67 per cent in 1970.[15] Earnings and unemployment in the rural areas are much more difficult to estimate. Even on the best possible figures, however, 81 per cent of households in the Bantustans live below the urban minimum living level, and 13 per cent receive no income at all. These are the most optimistic figures put forward by Charles Simkins, who maintains that there have been widespread improvements in rural incomes since 1960. The improvement - if such it was - seems to have been due almost entirely to the improved wages of migrants and to the growth of Bantustan bureaucracies. According to the Research and Strategic Division of the Development Bank of Southern Africa, the per capita gross domestic product of the Bantustan inhabitants had increased from R40 in 1970 to R46 in 1980. Not only did they accept that this increase was 'amongst the lowest in the world', they also admitted that poverty in the Bantustans was 'adopting proportions of great

---

13   M. Lipton, *Capitalism and Apartheid*, (Gower: Aldershot, 1985), pp. 65-66.

14   S. Greenberg, 'State against the market in South Africa: prelude to crisis', unpublished paper presented to the seminar on the societies of southern Africa, Institute of Commonwealth Studies, October, 1984.

15   *The Guardian*, 14 October 1986, cited in G. Dor, 'Recent developments in the political economy of health in South Africa', MA London, 1986, p. 34.

magnitude'.[16] There is no evidence to suggest that this has changed in the last seven years - and much to suggest that it has in fact become considerably worse.

As has frequently been pointed out, the infant mortality rate (i.e. the number of deaths of infants below the age of one year expressed as a rate per 1000 live births in any year) is regarded not only as an indicator of infant health, but also of that of its population as a whole and the socio-economic conditions under which they live. Despite the sophistication of the South African census data, however, there is still no national record of African live-births and deaths, and it is therefore impossible to estimate this with any accuracy or even to trace with any assurance of reliability changes that have taken place over the years. In 1944 the National Health Services Commission deplored the fact that 'the absence of reliable and complete health statistics makes rational, effective planning of health services very difficult'. Yet last year (1986) the Browne Commission of Inquiry into Health Services was still wringing its hands over South African statistical information as still 'generally inadequate in both quality and quantity'.[17]

Indeed as the census machinery has become more and more sophisticated, it has become more rather than less difficult to discern health trends: certain diseases like kwashiorkor for example are no longer notifiable, while people living in the so-called independent Bantustans (Transkei, Bophuthatswana, Ciskei and Venda) are excluded completely from the national figures on the basis that they are living in 'foreign countries'. Rates have to be collated from a variety of local sources of varying reliability; nevertheless, despite their limitations they 'serve to further highlight the differences between the race groups': in all the studies the rates are highest for Africans, lowest for whites.[18]

---

16   C. Simkins, 'What has been happening to income distribution and poverty in the Bantustans?', *Second Carnegie Inquiry*, (Cape Town, 1984), Paper 7. Simkins' figures are disputed by McGrath who maintains they give a false impression because of the unreliability of the statistics and the incorporation into the Bantustans of metropolitan areas with higher per capital incomes. See also *Race Relations Survey 1984*,(South African Institute of Race Relations), 38, pp. 568-569, for the Development Bank report.

17   RF67/1986 *Final Report of the Commission into Health Services* (Browne Commission) (Pretoria, 1986).

18   J. Botha & D. Bradshaw, 'African vital statistics - a black hole?', *South African Medical Journal (SAMJ)*, 67 (1985), pp. 977-981.

Thus a study of infant mortality rates over the period 1970-83 found that the infant mortality rate (IMR) at national level was 12.6 per 1000 for whites, 50.7 among Coloureds and 86 for urban Africans in 34 magisterial districts. The 1983 figure for urban Africans would increase to 102 per 1000 if Soweto were excluded, and further still if Cape Town were also omitted. In both these cities there has been a considerable improvement in infant mortality as a result of the establishment of maternity and neonatal clinics with very specific targets in the black urban areas. As we shall see, this partly reflects the state's response to increasing political militancy in the urban areas, and the demands of capital for a more stable workforce. If the black rural areas were to be included in the statistics the African rates would escalate further: in 1980 infant mortality in the Transkei was estimated at 130 per 1000. In areas like Qwaqwa or KwaNdebele it is likely to be considerably higher. Gastro-enteritis, chest infections and perinatal problems remain the most significant causes of death among black infants. White infant mortality - which had declined still further to 9.7 per 1000 in 1985 - is largely due to congenital defects.[19]

Black children over the age of one year are also at far greater risk of dying than their white counterparts, and the risk is again far higher in rural than urban areas. Thus, in 1975, black children (African, Coloured and Asian) were 2.6 times more likely to die from any cause than their white counterparts. In 1984, despite a considerable improvement (child mortality had dropped from 4.8 to 1.9 per thousand), these children were still nearly five times more at risk than their white counterparts.[20] Rapidly as things may have improved for urban blacks, for whites the improvement has been greater.

19 A.A.B. Hermann & C.H. Wyndham, 'Changes among whites, coloureds and urban blacks in the period 1970-1983', *SAMJ*, 68 (1985) p. 215; L.M. Irwig & R.F. Ingle, 'Childhood mortality rates, infant feeding and the use of health services in the rural Transkei', *SAMJ*, 66 (1984), pp. 608-613; Central Statistics Services, 'Deaths, 1985 - Whites, coloureds and Asians', *Statistical News release*, (Pretoria) 6 June 1986, p. 11.3.

20 *Annual Report for the Medical Officer of Health for the City of Cape Town* (Cape Town, 1984), p. 129, TABLE III.41.

Table 4. *Infant Mortality in Selected Urban Areas*

Rate per 1000 livebirths: 1981-1984

		WHITE	ASIAN	COLOURED	BLACK
Cape Town	1984	10		21	28
Durban	1984	20	18	17	49
Kimberley	1984*	15	46	73	94
Pietermaritzburg	1984	16	19	20	-
Kingwilliamstown	1981	9		25	103
Port Elizabeth	1984	12		45	64
Springs	1983	8		105	96
Pretoria	1981	15	16	32	43
Johannesburg	1983	12	19	21	26
Germiston	1981	10	29	69	32

* The calculations of infant mortality may differ from those presented in the official sources although based on the same numbers. This results from the adoption of atypical definitions by those authorities, some excluding children who died in the first week, some in the first month. The denominator presented here is live births.

Source: MoH Reports for different cities.

For rural African children the figures are stark. A recent review of death certificates revealed that nearly one half of all deaths (105/236) in Onverwacht-Botshabelo in the Orange Free State, which now has a population of about half a million, were under the age of 2 years. Approximately one half of these were attributed to malnutrition. In two other areas surveyed by the same author the proportion of child deaths under the age of two years was slightly lower, but still constituted above one third of all deaths. A cross-sectional study of the nutritional status of 658 children under the age of five carried out in one district of Gazankulu in 1984 established that 30 per cent were below the 97th percentile, where one would anticipate 3 per cent. In the one to two age group the figure was nearly 40 per cent.[21]

---

[21] M.L. Griffiths, 'Causes of death in a rural hospital in 1983', *SAMJ*, 68 (1985), p. 578; *SAMJ*, 65 (1984), pp. 364-367.

Part of the reason behind this continued increased risk to black children is that, for all the talk of reform, their social and living conditions have if anything deteriorated further over the past few years. As increased numbers of people have been pushed off the white farms and out of the towns and so-called 'black spots', the meagre 13 per cent of the land allocated to the 'Bantustans' has become even further eroded and impoverished. The populations of Qwaqwa and KwaNdebele for example have increased from about 20,000 to nearly half a million between the early 1970s and the mid-1980s. Water is inadequate and the vast majority of able-bodied men and an increasing number of women are absent as migrant workers. It is on their earnings that the lives of the Bantustan inhabitants depend. Despite government promises that the policy of removals has been abandoned, they have in fact continued. Together with increasing unemployment in the towns this has resulted in a crisis of unprecedented proportions in the Bantustans, which have become fertile ground not only for malnutrition, but also for epidemic and infectious diseases.

Thus, in the early 1980s, epidemics of cholera and typhoid raged in the Bantustans. Hundreds of people were known to have died from cholera alone, and probably more than 100,000 were affected. When the first cholera outbreak came to public attention, it was received with near hysteria by the press, which predicted that it would soon affect 'white' Durban, or even Johannesburg and Pretoria. By and large the South African government was less perturbed and successfully covered up the nature and incidence of the epidemics, especially once it was realised that cholera and typhoid, like the other diseases of poverty, could be safely confined to its 'surplus population' in the rural Bantustans. According to Dr. G. de Klerk, head of the Medical Association of South Africa, South Africa's health services were the best in the world; the spread of epidemics in South Africa could therefore be blamed on the breakdown of health services in the neighbouring black states.[22]

---

22   For a summary of the recent epidemics and an analysis of the way in which the South African state has handled epidemics in the past see Marks & Andersson, 'Typhus and social control in South Africa, 1917-1950' in Roy McLeod & Milton Lewis, *Disease, Medicine and Empire* (London, forthcoming); see also de Beer, *The South African Disease*, pp. 56-57; de Klerk is cited in de Beer, p. 60. See also 'Cholera in South Africa', *South African Outlook*, November 1981, p. 173; and A. Zwi, 'Cholera - a tropical disease?', in *Supplement to Work in Progress*, 16 February 1981.

Despite the fact that cholera, newly recognised as an epidemic disease in South Africa in 1980 and now endemic in at least five of the Bantustans, is more widespread than ever, it receives very little publicity. The figures have been few and far between and those which have been cited have been greeted with scepticism by the medical profession: many doctors put the number at five times the official figures wherever these have been quoted. Through a manipulation of the statistics and by the political sleight of hand which declares that the Bantustans are not part of South Africa, the extent of the epidemics could be minimised and responsibility sloughed off.

The issues were clearly stated by Professor Gerry Coovadia, then Associate Professor of Paediatrics and Child Health in the Natal Medical School when he said,

> Cholera is only a different shade on the canvas of ill-health. The cause of cholera is not to be found in biology, but in poverty. Inadequate and non-existent sanitation and the lack of piped clean water are the immediate causes of the spread of the disease. But the roots of cholera lie in an unequal distribution of resources - too much for some, very little or next to nothing for others. Many of us have been saying for years now that serious diseases which are preventible have been among black South Africans all the time.[23]

The cholera epidemic demonstrated graphically the failure of the state to provide sanitation and clean water supplies in the rural areas of South Africa. Yet the diseases of poverty have been successfully confined to the black and the poor.

Cholera also put the spotlight on other diseases and the lack of basic facilities in the rural areas. Thus, the number of typhoid cases notified has remained more or less constant over the years: between 3,000 and 4,000 cases in the erly 1980s.[24] Even one case of this disease in other developed countries is regarded as a public health failure. Yet it is commonly accepted that only about 10 per cent of all typhoid cases find their way into government records. These are alarming figures, for a disease which is supposed to be a thing of the 'past'. For blacks, typhoid is now as much a part of life as are mass removals. It is only when the disease encroaches on the 'white preserve' that it causes any stir.

Epidemics highlight the nature of power relations in society, just as heightened popular militancy serves to reveal social structures,

---

[23] *Sunday Times* (Johannesburg), 28 Feb. 1982.

[24] *Apartheid and Health*, p. 24.

processes and actors normally shrouded in darkness. The better-than-average reporting occasioned by the outbreak of 'abnormal' and frightening levels of disease often serves to illuminate the more routine and endemic killers: the epidemic may well be the tip of the iceberg which leads to a better understanding of the major killers. While the officially recognised epidemics may not be these 'major killers' - since bubonic plague and smallpox no longer destroy vast numbers and since the major killers like TB and malnutrition are seldom recognised as epidemics - their outbreaks nevertheless reveal the concerns of the state and the ruling class, both with their own safety and with the reproduction of the labour force.

Tuberculosis, like infant mortality, remains one of the most significant health indicators of the racially determined levels of poverty, in town and country. Today it has reached what can only be termed epidemic proportions. Whereas in the early years of this century, TB was taken from the mines to the countryside, today TB is endemic in the rural areas. There is a two-way traffic, although here again our figures for the rural areas are woefully inadequate. Thus even amongst Africans on the goldmines who are carefully screened on recruitment the incidence has ranged between 6 and 10 per thousand on different mines over the past five years, while overall there has been an increase in mortality from the disease.

Randall Packard, who has done the most extensive research on the history of TB in South Africa has argued that 'the rising tide of tuberculosis among black miners within the gold mines of South Africa' is to be attributed to longer contract lengths and the increased reliance of the mines on labour from the impoverished Bantustans where rates of TB are high. A considerable proportion of these cases are then reactivated on the mines.[25]

According to the South African National Tuberculosis Association, in the five years between 1977 and 1983 there has been a 22 per cent increase in TB notifications: from 50,850 in 1977 to 62,103 in 1983. These figures probably include the non-independent Bantustans, and exclude TBCV. By the end of 1986, the Director General of the Department of Health and Population Development reported that there were 'some 60,000 new cases identified annually. There are probably of

---

[25] R.M. Packard, 'Workplace, health and disease in sub-Saharan Africa', *Social Science and Medicine* (forthcoming, 1987).

the order of 100,000 cases under treatment each year.'[26]

In the absence of national statistics, evidence from individual cities must be relied on to provide a picture of the disease. In Cape Town in 1984, 7.25 per cent of all deaths among blacks were due to TB, compared with 1.75 per cent of coloured deaths, 1.6 per cent of Asian deaths and only 0.5 per cent of white deaths. No white child under two years of age died from TB in the decade 1975-84, whereas death rates among the other groups taken together have remained more or less constant over the same period (1 to 4 per 10,000 people).

From recorded notifications of TB in Cape Town, coloureds suffered 12.8 times higher risk of TB than whites in 1984, while blacks were 46.9 times more at risk. It should be stressed that whites are more likely to come in contact with the notification apparatus than coloureds or blacks, and that these figures take into account an increase of TB among whites of nearly 60 per cent over the previous five years. Looking at the age-specific TB notification rates, the picture is all the more startling: coloured children under the age of four in 1984 were 30 times more likely to contract TB than their white counterparts, while black children in the same age group demonstrated an incidence 205 times greater than whites. Nor is Cape Town an isolated case. The rates for incidence and mortality from Durban and Kimberley give equal cause for alarm.[27]

In 1984/5 the Department of Health and Welfare allocated R68m to combat TB, R47m of it for hospital services and R0.5m for preventive measures. The state has been cutting back on ethambutol and rifampicin, using cheaper but less effective drugs in an effort to cut costs, and in many areas mass screening for TB has been stopped. Some would argue that it had become pointless in any case, because there were inadequate resources for the necessary follow-up. Given the extent of the problem, which is also being experienced on an alarming scale by South Africa's economically dependent neighbours, it is clear that the preventive measures being taken are risible.[28]

Infant and child mortality, epidemic disease, TB - these are only the starkest indicators of the levels of morbidity and mortality in South

---

[26] SAIRR, *Survey*, (1984) pp. 721-722; and Dor, 'Recent Developments', p. 40; Pearson, Letter to the editor, *SAMJ*, 70 (1986) p. 773.

[27] In a study of hospital deaths in a rural area of the OFS, TB was the most common cause of death between the ages of 13-25 and 26-49 (Griffiths 'Causes of death').

[28] SAIRR, *Survey* 1984, p. 723; Dor, 'Recent developments', pp. 39-40.

Africa. In so brief an account these must suffice, although as the World Health Organisation monograph on Health and Apartheid makes clear, apartheid also affects the pattern of cardiovascular disease, has an impact on the incidence of occupational disease and accident rates and exacerbates a number of socially related diseases, such as venereally transmitted disease, alcoholism and mental illness. No one would argue that apartheid is responsible for all these ills; nevertheless the racial incidence of disease and allocation of health resources relate directly to the policies of the South African state, and its determination to maintain white domination.

Health services and health policy

As in the case of disease patterns, so South Africa's contemporary health system took its contemporary shape after the mineral discoveries in the late nineteenth century.[29] Until that time, medical services were undeveloped in the colonies, republics and African kingdoms which co-existed uneasily south of the Limpopo. Africans were largely dependent on the ministrations of traditional healers and the patent medicines brought by missionaries; in the Afrikaner South African Republic (Transvaal) there were fewer than thirty medical practitioners, trained mainly in Britain. The British colony of the Cape had the most established medical profession. The vast majority were private practitioners who had also trained in Britain and were registered with the British General Medical Council. The private medical practitioner has remained at the centre of personal health services for whites in the region to the present.

With the mineral discoveries, the new concentrations of population and the development of a migrant labour system drawing vast numbers of rural Africans into the urban areas led to the development of new methods of health control. The Cape was the first to set up a Public Health Department in 1897, although by then the Witwatersrand's Sanitary Committee had considerably elaborated its functions, in part as a result of the outbreak of smallpox on the Rand in 1893. It was only after the South African War (1899-1902) that the British administration in the conquered Boer Republics began to organise public health in the interior. By the first decade of the twentieth century most towns in

---

[29] For the history of South Africa's public health legislation until 1944, see UG no. 30-1944. Union of South Africa, *Report of the National Health Services Commission* (Pretoria: Government Printer, 1944), chapter V.

South Africa had municipal medical officers of health on the British model, as well as hospitals for infectious diseases, which were a municipal responsibility.

The Act of Union, which brought the four colonies and ex-republics together in a political union in 1910, did not attempt to unify the varied health services and measures in the region. The statutes of the old colonies became the statutes of the respective provinces, and all the provinces therefore inherited certain health responsibilities. It was not until 1919, when the first Public Health Act was passed in response to the influenza epidemic, that a Department of Public Health with its own Minister was established. It had general responsibility for non-personal health services in the four provinces, as well as for mental and most tuberculosis hospitals and for leper institutions, although the provinces and municipalities retained their earlier control over general and infectious hospitals respectively.

The 1919 Act also attempted to coordinate the public health legislation of the four provinces. Nevertheless, the three-tiered system remained and, according to the 1944 National Health Services Commission which tried unsuccessfully to rationalise it, 'from the very outset there was overlapping and confusion of responsibilities; each layer of public authority had some responsibility for public health, for hospitals and other health matters'. The then President of the South African Medical Association castigated it as a '..."crazy patchwork" of public medical services, determined not by scientific principle but by the accidents of constitutional development in South Africa'.[30]

Far from eliminating this 'crazy patchwork', today there are no less than thirteen different departments of health and welfare in South Africa, in addition to a variety of municipal and provincial authorities. The departments bear witness to the state's manipulation of health care for its own purposes of legitimising its Bantustan policies and, more recently, its attempted co-option of the Asian and Coloured communities. Thus in addition to the central Department of Health and Population Development (sic) headed by a white Minister in the tricameral parliament, we now have no fewer than twelve health ministers - one for each of the Bantustans, plus another one each for Coloureds and Asian 'Own Affairs' in terms of the 1983 constitution. Needless to say, all this has meant a proliferating bureaucracy and the

---

[30] Ibid., chapter V, para. 9, p. 18 and para. 23, p. 20, and chapter XIX, para. 49, p. 100.

creation in 1979 of an additional bureaucratic co-ordinating structure, the Regional Health Organisation for Southern Africa, to deal with the Bantustan health ministries. Nor is it surprising that the Browne report and other observers have viewed with concern the fragmentation of South Africa's health services and have called for their reintegration, particularly in view of the escalating costs.

The creation of this bewildering and wasteful array of health departments has not only been intended to lend credibility and legitimacy to the government's ethnic collaborators and provide jobs for the rural petty bourgeoisie; it has also enabled the state to slough off any responsibility for conditions in the rural areas, and to give the misleading impression that health in South Africa is improving, as we have already seen in the case of the figures for TB.

In all of this, the central state continues to control the health budget for the Bantustans, and uses this as a political lever to push them into accepting independence. For example, while Gazankulu (which refused to take 'independence') received R6.3 million for health in 1975 and only R7 million in 1981, Venda (which accepted independence) received consecutive increases of 40 per cent in 1979 and 92 per cent in 1980.[31]

The increasing cost of health care is a matter of some concern to the government; it has, accordingly, both tried to privatise urban health care and pleaded for more primary and preventive health services from local authorities. Yet less than 5 per cent (at best) of the health budget goes to preventive medicine. Since 1979, in common with most of the western capitalist countries, South Africa has pursued a variety of monetarist policies. Cuts in public expenditure have a direct effect on health in a number of ways: through cuts in housing, where it is now estimated there is a backlog of 400,000 houses; cuts in the salaries and numbers of the civil service; decreased subsidies on petrol, transport and food; and pressure on most departments, including health, to decrease expenditure through privatisation.

An increased tariff in state hospitals is one way of forcing people into the private sector; this holds the further attractions of being both largely unsegregated and speedier than the state sector. Over the past two or three years, even industry has begun to find it more cost-effective to enrol skilled workers in private medical-aid schemes. While doing nothing to resolve the ill-health of the majority of blacks, this

---

[31]   A. Zwi, 'Separate development in health', *Critical Health*, 10 (1984), pp. 33-39.

may have serious consequences for a future national health care system in South Africa.[32]

The repercussions of the recession on health care can be seen in the grotesquely overcrowded conditions in Johannesburg's black hospital Baragwaneth. Despite earlier promises, the state has not been able to build any new hospital facilities for Soweto. In 1985, furthermore, the Department of Health and Welfare forced Provincial Hospital Services to cut salaries, and associated personnel costs, by 8 per cent. The Cape Hospital Services have cut the annual bonuses and overtime pay of nurses, medical technologists and paramedics, and have increased their working week from 40 to 42 1/2 hours. Elsewhere there have been even more heroic measures; the Johannesburg Hospital has demanded that all staff work an additional half hour a day without extra pay, and has cut staff posts, drugs and the period of stay for patients.[33]

Not surprisingly, there have been several strikes among black nurses and health workers over the past few years, and the country is facing an acute nursing shortage among whites. In 1983, for example, 4,000 applications were received for nursing training; even though as many as 3,600 were accepted, there were still 3,500 vacancies. For African nurses the picture is very different: of over 31,000 applicants only 4,000 were accepted because of the lack of training facilities.[34]

There can be few countries where the rhetorical and ideological function of health care is so blatant. Thus over the past few years, all the discourse of the international primary and community health care debate has been adopted by the South African Department of Health, and the rhetoric of the Alma Ata declaration on community controlled primary health care pervades the sections on health in publicity on the Bantustans. By thrusting the responsibility onto the Bantustan authorities and even more by stressing the virtues of self-help and community medicine, the state evades its own obligation to provide an adequate health service. For all the stress on community health care, the total health budget of all the Bantustans is the same as the annual running costs of one of the large hospitals in Cape Town or Johannesburg.

---

[32] This draws heavily on Max Price, 'Health care beyond apartheid. Economic issues and the re-organisation of South Africa's health services', *Critical Health*, March 1987.

[33] Dor, 'Recent developments', pp. 28-30.

[34] SAIRR, *Survey 1984*, p. 714.

The privatisation of health and the new emphasis on improved health care for blacks in the towns, which as we have seen has begun to have some effect on the infant mortality statistics, have to be placed in the context more generally of South Africa's reformist strategy. From the late 1970s the state has faced multiple challenges coming from structural changes in the economy on the one hand, and from the increasing resistance and militancy of the underclasses, on the other. Many of the orthodoxies of Verwoerdian apartheid have had to be jettisoned in the face of the breakdown of influx control, as a result of massive unemployment and starvation in the reserves. At the same time the development of Afrikaner capital, with many of the same interests as monopoly capital in a more skilled (and that means better educated and healthier) and stabilised black workforce, has strengthened demands from English-speaking businessmen for welfare reforms which will leave their economic and political power intact.

The reform strategy has been characterised by an attempt to depoliticise change, and dress it up in the language of technocratic necessity;[35] by the increased power of the defence establishment; by the state's efforts to shift welfare responsibilities onto the private sector; and by an attempt to co-opt the black urban elite - the skilled workers and middle class - and to win them over to 'the free enterprise system' through 'welfare'. The last attempt has so far failed signally. Instead of buying off discontent it has served to politicize almost every sphere of everyday life.

Nevertheless, in the reformist strategy, much of it intended for overseas consumption, health has played and is playing a crucial role. Over the years the South African Department of Health has put out a number of glossy publications advertising its comprehensive and caring health service, although the latest, entitled *A New Dispensation: Health Plan for South Africa* (1986) is perhaps less glossy than earlier versions. It speaks in the new language of managerial technocracy:

> The new constitutional dispensation in the Republic of South Africa not only made it imperative for health services to be evaluated in terms of the provisions of the constitution but has also presented the opportunity for the optimal restructuring of health services and the development of a *National Health Plan* for the management thereof.

---

35 D. Posel, 'The language of domination, 1978-1983', in S. Marks & S. Trapido, *The Political Economy of Race, Class and Nationalism in Twentieth Century South Africa* (Longmans: London, 1987) pp. 419-444.

The plan is a logical and meaningful integration of essential perspectives regarding health, namely: A centralised policy for achieving national health goals and priorities; centralised responsibility for the provision of health services; decentralised implementation based on the National Plan for Health Service Facilities.

The Plan ensures a dynamic, co-ordinated and rationalised health service which can be managed in a cost-effective way to the benefit of all the peoples of South Africa.[36]

Under the 'new dispensation' there will be six levels of health service under the health plan, which 'will accommodate the provision of basic subsistence needs on the one hand and the provision of specialised tertiary care on the other, in a balanced way in line with the needs of the South African population'. This seems to mean that rural blacks will, with luck, get clean water - some day; in the meantime, highly paid surgeons will continue to do heart transplants for whites and perhaps some privileged blacks in the major cities.

Although the Health Plan recognises the decisive importance of clean water, adequate nutrition, sewage and waste removal and shelter for health, the Department of Health has no responsibility for their provision. Community health nursing and the community health centres, both of which are seen by the Browne Commission as 'pivotal' to the delivery of health services, also remain the responsibility of the provincial or local authorities. The Browne Report argues, further, that 'the community must learn to help and organise itself'; it advocates greater self-medication as an answer to the high cost of contemporary health care. This, like the state's heavy emphasis on population control, once more places the responsibility squarely on the shoulders of the victim:

As Cedric de Beer points out:

Over the last twenty or so years, especially amongst doctors working in poor rural areas, it has become increasingly obvious that 'social and economic conditions' have a major influence on people's health... Around the world, and in South Africa, these perceptions have led to ... the 'community medicine' approach to health care. This approach appears to move away from the classic, individualised, victim-blaming attitudes, towards a realisation of the need to understand health care in its social context. But the 'community medicine' approach has serious shortcomings which are in danger of giving new credibility to all the old myths and

---

[36] No date, no publisher; clearly RSA, 1986.

misconceptions ....

[It] regards itself as getting to the root of the problem. It sees that poverty causes disease, and the programmes devised are aimed at not just curing the sick, but at alleviating the conditions which make people sick in the first place. Unfortunately this approach ... remains trapped within the victim-blaming mode of thought. For example, the assumption that people need health education re-inforced the belief that illness arises out of ignorance. Further, the desire to use community development techniques to 'help people to solve their problems' rests on a belief that people are unable to solve their problems for themselves, and suggests that the problems are of their own making. In other words, the poor must be taught to deal with the problems caused by their poverty. But this line of argument ignores the truth that poverty itself is a symptom of a history of dispossession, exploitation and oppression.[37]

In South Africa there is a danger that what is planned is a dual health service: high-technology, privately-funded health care for whites and some urban blacks, and an inferior form of 'community care' for the majority of blacks. It is possible that the fragmented Bantu health departments will be brought under single control, as recommended by the Browne Commission; for the moment, the Regional Service Councils are seen as a way out of the contradictions of the Bantustans and their manifest inability to deliver the goods for the state, if only because of their rank corruption. At the same time, it would seem that the major state strategy will continue to be to increase the privatisation of the health services.

The debate about privatisation and a 'new dispensation in health' is a far cry from the battlegound in the townships of South Africa, where the Emergency has seriously interfered with the provision of medical care to those injured in the violence. In many areas it is clear that people are afraid of seeking help because of police intervention at clinics and hospitals. According to several accounts, seriously injured patients are often placed under police guard or even refused medical attention at health facilities in the townships. According to a Crossroads clinic report, several of their patients had been arrested in state hospitals, sometimes with the active connivance of certain health professionals, who 'put the interest of the police above that of the confidentiality of their patients by informing them of patients with

---

[37] Cedric de Beer, *The South African Disease*, pp. 73-74

gunshot wounds.'[38]

Yet the pressure on medical professionals to provide an unethical service for the state has provoked another reaction. A significant number of doctors, nurses and health facility administrators have systematically refused to collaborate, several providing clandestine traumatology services for the people injured in the unrest. Others have started community-based training schemes for voluntary health workers, to enable people with minor injuries to avoid attending state-run facilities and thereby risking arrest and harassment by the police. Still others, together with psychologists, psychiatrists and social workers have begun counselling services and counsellor training schemes to deal with the mental distress of detainees and torture victims. These could provide the basis of an alternative form of health care - for the people.

Further Reading

De Beer, Cedric,   *The South African Disease. Apartheid, Health and Health Services* (CIIR: London, 1986).

Marks, S. & Andersson, N.,   'Typhus and social control in South Africa, 1917-1950' in Roy McLeod & Milton Lewis, *Disease, Medicine and Empire* (London, forthcoming).

Price, Max,   'Health care beyond apartheid. Economic issues and the re-organisation of South Africa's health services', *Critical Health*, March 1987.

UG 30 - '44   *Report of the National Health Services Commission* (Government Printer, Pretoria, 1944).

World Health Organisation   *Health and Apartheid* (Geneva, 1983).

---

[38] See the forthcoming proceedings of the 1987 NAMDA (National Medical and Dental Association) Conference.

Zwi, A.,   'Separate development in health', *Critical Health*, 10 (1984).

11. Educational Resistance

HAROLD WOLPE

Introduction

Gross inequalities in the education of black and white people existed in the colonial period in South Africa and were reproduced, albeit in different forms, and extended once the South African state was established in 1910. Yet, only some years after the National Party assumed power in 1948 did black demands for education become an integral and major ingredient of the mass struggle against racial domination.

This is not to suggest, however, that since it was launched, the form, role and significance of the education struggle has remained unchanged. To the contrary, four phases (perhaps five if we include the decade between roughly 1957 and 1967 when little oppositional political activity occurred in and around the sphere of black education) can be identified in the period since the 1950s - each period being differentiated by the specific social forces which became the main actors, by the organisational forms and objectives of the struggle as well as by the varying strategies and tactics adopted. This diversity was a function of both the conditions within education and the broader economic and political situation within the country.

My object in this chapter is to discuss, in broad outline, the main features of the different phases of the struggle in order to identify the changing and important role of education in the confrontation between the national liberation movement and the apartheid regime, highlighting, in particular, the organisation of the struggle, in the contemporary period, around an as-yet underdeveloped notion of 'people's education'.

The periods with which I will be concerned may be identified as follows:

1) The opposition to the Bantu Education Act and its effects : 1953 to about 1957.

[2) 1957 to 1967, which I will not deal with.]

3) The Soweto uprisings and their aftermath : 1976 to about 1980.

4) 'Liberation first, education later' in the period of the early 1980s.

5) 'People's education for people's power' : 1985 to the present.

The opposition to the Bantu Education Act and its implementation

The first major struggle over education occurred in the early 1950s, in opposition to the proposed Bantu Education Act.

It is hardly necessary to recall that the stated purpose of the Act was to implement Christian National education in the sphere of African education and that this meant, in Verwoerd's notorious words:

> There is no place for him [the Native] in the European community above the level of certain forms of labour ... For this reason it is of no avail for him to receive a training which has as its aim absorption in the European community, where he cannot be absorbed. Until now he has been subjected to a school system which drew him away from his own community and misled him by showing him the green pastures of European society in which he was not allowed to graze.[1]

This view informed the provisions of the Act which empowered the government to establish 'Bantu Schools' and to ban any school or educational programme which did not conform to the conception of 'Bantu Education'. It then became a criminal offence to run schools and educational programmes which had not received state approval.

One response to this policy came from the churches which, through 5,000 state-aided mission schools, provided an important complement to state education for Africans. Rather than teach the imposed Bantu Education curriculum, many of these schools were closed down by the churches. Little opposition came from within the African schools themselves. On the one hand the teachers were weakly organised and, generally, politically quiescent. On the other hand there was virtually no student organisation within the schools due, at least in part, to the fact that of the 860,000 pupils, less than 40,000 were in classes above standard 4 scattered throughout the country.

In this situation, opposition to the proposed act was organised by the ANC, outside the schools, in the black communities. Through public meetings, demonstrations and united action with other organisations, the ANC tried to win broad support to prevent the Act from becoming law. When this failed, the ANC called for a boycott of the Bantu Education schools and attempted to provide alternative schools. Although many students observed the boycott at the behest of their parents, support for

---

[1]   Quoted in P. Kallaway, *Apartheid in Education.*

it was by no means unanimous. Furthermore, the alternative schools could not be sustained because of lack of resources and because the state used its powers under the Act to close these schools (or cultural clubs as they were called for the purposes of evading the law) and prosecute the teachers. As a result, organised opposition to Bantu Education petered out and the state was able to impose its control over the education of black people. Or apparently so.

The Soweto uprisings and aftermath.

An unexpected, and indeed for long an unremarked result of the restructuring of black education under the Bantu Education Act, was the enormous rise in the number of pupils attending the schools. The statistics show that in 1954 there were 860,000 African pupils in these schools; by 1968 the total was 2,397,152, of which 95% were in primary schools (70% in lower primary). By 1975 the total had reached 3,697,441; of these over 97% were in primary schools (74% in lower primary classes).

It may seem strange that this steep rise should have occurred during the period of extreme repression which followed the nation-wide unrest triggered by the killing of 69 peaceful demonstrators at Sharpeville in 1960. Perhaps the explanation lies in the fact that the repression provided the conditions of political stability which encouraged foreign investment, rapid economic expansion and a sharp rise in the demand for semi-skilled black labour in the industrial and tertiary sectors - that is, a demand for labour having at least a sufficient level of literacy for the purposes of this type of employment.

Be that as it may, the entire structure of Bantu Education was calculated to produce a black population which was not only poorly educated and subordinated, but which would also accept its subordination and low level of education as natural, as fitting for a racially inferior people. Hence, firstly, an extremely low level of state funding resulted in poorly trained and unqualified teachers, the virtual absence of laboratories, decrepit buildings and inadequate facilities. Secondly, syllabuses - which virtually excluded science subjects and mathematics - required the teaching of racist histories which proved the 'superiority' of the whites, devalued pre-colonial African societies, denigrated the role of black people in the construction of modern South Africa, and asserted the incapacity of black people to exercise political power and democratic rights.

Undoubtedly, Bantu Education has generally succeeded only too well in limiting the educational advancement of black people and in blocking the acquisition of basic skills - numeracy, literacy and so forth. But it should be noted that this 'success' seems to have boomeranged in the present changed economic conditions, for it has contributed to the persistent shortages of skilled labour.

Nevertheless, despite the ideological weight of its institutional structure, Bantu Education failed in its project to create a servile population. Towards the end of the 1960s the classrooms (particularly in the secondary schools) and the lecture theatres in the black universities became a more or less protected venue for the development and expression of an oppositional ideology. Indeed, given the virtual obliteration of the extra-parliamentary opposition and the pervasiveness of state terror, these were almost the only places, at that time, where such an opposition could develop. Black Consciousness emerged first as an ideological movement but then, in the early 1970s, Black Consciousness organisations, with some others, began to organise political actions in the schools and universities directed, in the first instance, against Bantu Education as an instrument of white domination. The schools seethed with activity. The record shows literally thousands of protests, strikes, sit-ins, demonstrations against the conditions of Bantu Education. Unemployment, and the deteriorating conditions of black education due to its massive and extremely rapid expansion without adequate resources, were the underlying factors.

These oppositional struggles erupted in the Soweto student uprisings of 1976; the revolt spread to many parts of the country as students came out in solidarity with Soweto. A period of extreme state violence followed. In 1976-7 the police shot and killed some 1,000 students and others, and arrested countless more as the state attempted to crush the student revolt.

The character and trajectory of the education struggles in 1976 and the following years contrast in a number of significant ways with the struggles of the 1950s.

First, in the 1950s, as I have already pointed out, the struggle against Bantu Education was initiated by non-student organisations outside the educational institutions; in the 1970s it was initiated inside the schools and universities by the students and their organisations. It is therefore important to note the demographic changes in the schools: as against the 1950s when African secondary school students numbered about 25,000, by 1975 there were over 318,000 such students. It was within this constituency and the black universities that major oppositional politics began to develop in the late 1960s.

Secondly, in the 1950s, once the Bantu Education Act was in place, the political struggles (demonstrations etc.) against the Act gave way to the campaign for a school boycott which was coupled to the attempt to establish alternative schools. The struggle for education became, to a considerable extent, focused on the task of setting up and maintaining independent schools.

In the 1970s - although from the beginning student actions took on a variety of forms: demonstrations, rallies, walk-outs, occupations and so forth - the major strategy of the struggle was, as in the 1950s, the boycott of the schools. But, in this Soweto period, the boycott became part and parcel of a strategy to politically mobilise the students to struggle against the state for the abolition of Bantu Education; the objective was not to defeat Bantu Education by setting up alternative schools. Given the boycott, political action had necessarily to take place outside the schools, in the townships and, indeed, in the streets of Johannesburg and Cape Town. Thus, although in the first stages of the Soweto revolt the students themselves were the actors and their demands remained centred more or less narrowly on education, the townships became the site of contestation.

Thirdly, while in the 1950s the 'community' (through the ANC) made the schools boycott part of its broader struggle, in the 1970s the students brought the communities into their own struggle, not merely by conducting their political activity in the townships, but more directly, by attempting to mobilise parents, workers and other members of the communities.

The broadening of the struggle into the communities reflected the understanding, which was soon brought home to the students, that Bantu Education could not be overturned unless apartheid itself was dismantled, and that this could not be achieved by the students acting alone without the involvement of workers, parents and community. But these groups were largely unorganised and quiescent, despite the revival of shop-floor struggles in the factories from 1973. Indeed, the failure of Bantu Education to produce a compliant and quiescent generation of youth was dramatised by the fact that it was their parents, subjected to the power of the state at their work and in their communities, who had become either fearful or incapable of acting, despite the continuing underground activities of the ANC and the Communist Party.

The story of the student-led community struggles, which included stay-at-homes and demonstrations, is complicated and cannot be told here. It is enough to stress that for a period, a relatively short period, the black youth - school and university students - occupied the centre stage and provided the vital stimulus which accelerated the regeneration of mass political opposition.

The leadership role of the students was not maintained for long. Paradoxically, this was because student intervention made a major contribution towards a restructuring of the political arena in South Africa. The resurgence of community organisations and politics, which followed the student-led actions, helped to resurrect the extra-parliamentary political terrain. This entailed, on the one hand, the ANC's reassertion of its leading role and, on the other, the revival of dormant organisations and the formation of new ones, culminating in 1983 in the United Democratic Front (UDF). All this was accompanied by the rise of the independent black trades unions, a significant section of which associated itself with the national liberation struggle. These developments shifted the centre of gravity away from the student movement. This is not to suggest either that the students' struggles lost their importance or that educational issues became detached from the broader opposition to apartheid. The effect was, however, twofold: first, other organisations, notably the ANC and, later, the UDF took over the leading role which had previously been exercised by the student organisations; secondly, the political activity of the student organisations became once more concentrated more or less exclusively on the student constituency, but not exclusively on educational issues.

'Liberation First, Education Later': the early 1980s

Various student organisations played important roles in the period from 1976 to 1980: the South African Students' Organisation in the universities and the South African Students' Movement in the schools were initially the most important; later the lead was taken by the Soweto Students' Representative Council which was formed in August 1976 and, after it was banned in 1978, by the Soweto Students' League. A number of student organisations came into existence at the turn of the decade; the most important of these was the Congress of South African Students (COSAS).

This organisation's focus on students, coupled with a conception of the linkages between educational and social transformation, can be seen from its statement of objectives. In brief, these included:

First, that students must be organised through democratically elected student representative councils (SRCs). Secondly, that students must serve the community: 'we are members of society before we are students' - and thereby demonstrate that students can play a 'progressive role in the broad democratic alliance'. Therefore, SRCs must relate the struggles in schools to the struggles in their communities. Thirdly, that in serving the community, students must recognise that they can play only a limited role in the overall struggle. That must be led by the working class; the duty of the students was to lend support to the trades union and community organisations.

COSAS organised the students in various actions, often in collaboration with non-student bodies from 1980 to 1983, but then the school boycott again began to assume increasing importance. In 1983 a school boycott was launched in the Pretoria area around demands for free textbooks, properly qualified teachers, the abolition of corporal punishment, the ending of sexual harassment and official recognition of the democratically elected SRCs.

As the boycott movement gathered momentum and spread over the country, the demand for democratically elected SRCs was pushed increasingly to the fore. Indeed, the struggle tended to shift from demands for the radical reform of the existing education system, to a contestation with the state over control of the school - as it were, for 'people's power' in education. The question, however, which arises is : was the boycott an appropriate strategy to achieve this objective?

In 1984 and 1985 the boycott strategy, which was pursued by COSAS and other organisations, gained very widespread support; at one point some 650,000 students and hundreds of schools were involved. The Department of Education and Training (DET) responded by closing many schools. Student activists were harassed, arrested and detained, particularly during the emergency in 1985; many were killed in demonstrations. COSAS was banned in August 1985. The South African Defence Force occupied numerous black townships and the school yards. The presence of the troops became a major focus of opposition.

By October 1985 schooling had been comprehensively disrupted, nowhere more so than in Soweto. Although the boycott remained the main form of student action, there were moves to re-open schools closed by the DET; there were also opposing strategies at work in relation to the examinations, with some students wishing to sit them and others maintaining the boycott.

Be that as it may, by 1985 the boycott had clearly succeeded in making the schools unworkable and ungovernable. In this sense the shift of the objectives of the struggle from reform to control reflected, in the sphere of education, the ANC's call to render South Africa ungovernable - although it is not clear that the boycott was a direct response to that policy. In any event, the slogan around which a more or less indefinite boycott became organised was: 'Liberation first, education later'. The boycott was no longer a tactic, it was a strategy.

What were the effects on the student movement and the education struggle of the boycott strategy? At least as the December 1985 National Consultative Conference on the Crisis in Education saw it, the positive mobilising effects of the boycott were offset by three negative consequences.

In the first place, the breakdown of the schooling system meant that large numbers of secondary school students (the major sector of the school population involved in the boycott) were being deprived of further schooling and, therefore, of even the limited opportunities offered by Bantu Education. For many parents this overshadowed any political gains of the boycott actions. But the collapse of the educational system also had potentially extremely negative consequences for the entire national liberation and trade union movement. A major role in the resurgence of trade union and mass struggles from the early 1970s had been played by a generation of young black people educated to secondary level, and higher, under Bantu Education; the educational deprivation of the present generation of secondary school students threatened to weaken their contribution to a movement which was becoming increasingly organised and complex in its functioning.

In the second place, by regarding the boycott as an end in itself the student organisations failed to understand its limitations. As one speaker put it at the Conference:

Another issue is that a boycott needs results. It needs to be successful. If a boycott drags on for months, so that some people start going back to school, students may feel disappointed and disillusioned.

The very success of the boycott in closing down the schools posed the question of 'What next?'. To this question the student movement apparently had no answer (other than 'liberation first') except to continue with the boycott. But its continuation meant that the students and their movement could not attempt to implement, in their own sphere, the call of the liberation movement to advance the establishment of structures of dual power discussed below. The students could not begin in practice to organise democratic control of the schools through the SRCs or through parents, teachers and students' governing bodies; from outside the schools they could only *demand* such bodies.

In the third place, while the previous two years had undoubtedly seen a great increase in the level of student mobilisation and their massive involvement in the boycotts, especially around the issue of democratic SRCs, nonetheless, the boycott did deprive students of a daily meeting place in which discussion and organisation could take place. The Education Crisis Conferences feared that the capacity to organise the students was reduced and their organisations began to lose coherence and even tended to disintegrate. Communications broke down between student and student on a mass level and between students and their leaders within organisations and, at times, between the leadership themselves. As the Conferences noted, all this led to a breakdown in communication between the students and their communities, resulting at times in a lack of community support for student campaigns and struggles. Communities were left uncertain as to the situation in the schools and the school boycotts. And thus with the banning of COSAS the students found themselves without a means of co-ordinating strategy. The result of this was their further isolation. The Conference concluded that the student organisations had not been able, despite the high level of student mobilisation, to 'take the gap that was opened to them and fill it with organisation'. It was this assessment of the situation which led to the intervention of the community organisations, and in particular, the Soweto Parents Crisis Committee, in the educational struggle.

'People's Education for People's Power'

The detailed history of the events leading to the National Consultative Conferences on the Crisis in Education in December 1985 and in March 1986 need not detain us here. What is important is that these gatherings, which founded the National Education Crisis Committee (NECC) early in 1986, were provoked by what many saw as the students' failure to exploit the conditions created by the boycott movement, so as to advance the educational struggle. Indeed, the continued adherence to the boycott stood in the way of advance. It was this issue which pre-occupied the Conferences.

The Crisis Conferences thus questioned and then rejected the slogan of 'liberation first, education later'; they then adopted, instead, the slogan 'people's education for people's power'. This implicitly criticised any opposition to Bantu Education which was purely negative in character and which, therefore, could neither project a fundamentally different educational system, nor consider how the struggle might be carried into certain of apartheid's institutions in order to begin their transformation even before the overthrow of the regime, indeed as part of the very process of overthrowing it. The adoption of this position is of great importance and must be understood in terms of the transformation of South African politics which began with the passing of the Tricameral Parliament Act and the stay-at-homes in October 1984.

By 1985, the key question had become reform or revolution. This signalled an enormous shift in the balance of power between the contending blocs by comparison, say, with the 1970s. Nonetheless, the situation was (and is) characterised by an unstable equilibrium in which the white power bloc, while holding state power, is unable to suppress the revolutionary opposition which, in turn, does not at present have the capacity to overthrow the regime and the system.

One of the essential features of this 'unstable equilibrium', and the one which has created the possibility of dislodging the regime and transforming society, was the strengthening and deepening of the mass democratic organisations in reaction to the 1985 Emergency. This gave birth, especially, to the construction of alternative structures of dual power at the level of street and block committees. In his Keynote address to the Second National Education Conference in March 1986, Zwalekhe Sisulu described this in the following words:

The slogan 'Forward to People's Power' .. expresses the growing trend for our people to move towards realising people's power **now** in the process of struggle, before actual liberation. By this we mean that people are beginning to exert control over their own lives in different ways. In some townships and schools people are beginning to govern themselves, despite being under racist rule.

[...] these advances were only possible because of the development of democratic organs, or committees, of people's power. Our people set up bodies which were controlled by, and accountable to, the masses of the people in each area. In such areas, the distinction between the people and their organisations disappeared. All the people young and old participated in committees from street level upwards.[2]

It was these developments which caused the crisis conferences to reject the slogan 'Liberation now, education later', with its merely negative opposition to Bantu Education, in favour of the positive, creative alternative 'People's education for people's power'. To quote Sisulu once again:

> It is no accident that the historic December Conference [i.e. the first national education conference] took place at a time when our people were taking the struggle for democracy to new heights. At a time when the struggle against apartheid was being transformed into a struggle for people's power. In line with this, students and parents were no longer only saying 'Away with apartheid, gutter education!' We were now also saying 'Forward with People's Education, education for Liberation'.

The boycott strategy, as has already been suggested, was incompatible with such an approach because it permitted only a struggle **against** Bantu Education, not **for** people's power in education. The contrast with the community struggles is instructive.

In the black townships, community opposition and resistance to apartheid, shown in their struggles against the local administrative institutions and the army and police forces, made possible the emergence of rudimentary forms of 'people's power' in the shape of street and block committees. In other words, the mass movement's ability to render the townships ungovernable created a situation in which alternative organs could begin to be put in place. However, the boycott movement which had, initially, played a vital role in increasing student mobilisation against the apartheid regime, made a parallel development in the schools virtually impossible. For the very constituency which might have pushed things forward was absent from the schools and thus unable to exert pressure at the institutional site of contestation. Thus, whereas the communities (unable to boycott their own townships) were able to move from defiance of state structures to begin to replace them with organs of people's power, the students were left with only their boycott, which put them outside the only 'place' where alternative structures could be built or alternative courses initiated.

---

[2]   NECC (1986), pp. 14-15.

The December conference agreed that the attempt to win control of the schools or to substitute new teaching programmes would be impossible if the boycott strategy were maintained. In one of its major resolutions it therefore decided that students should return to school, conditional upon certain demands being met by the DET. These included withdrawal of the SADF and SAP from schools, the release of detained students and teachers, the reinstatement of dismissed teachers, the unbanning of COSAS, recognition of democratically elected SRCs, and the lifting of the State of Emergency.

This decision implied that the long-term struggle for 'people's education' had to be coupled with immediate demands and the insertion of alternative teaching programmes. The return to the schools was to be understood, not as an acceptance of Bantu Education but, rather, as a recognition of the fact that the schools provided the fundamental terrain for the struggle towards people's power in education.

This position was reinforced in the resolution of the March 1986 conference which stated:

[...] believing that:

a) education struggles must increasingly involve parents, teachers and students and all democratic organisations

b) we will have to use new and creative tactics to advance education struggles

Conference therefore resolves that:

All children should return to school when the new term starts to:

i) demand the right to education and occupy schools which have been closed

ii) use the presence of students at school to assist in building and regrouping our student organisations

iii) implement alternative people's education programmes immediately.

These two Education Crisis Conferences did not merely echo earlier demands for control of education. They went further. The successive NECCs attempted actually to organise the struggle for democratic SRCs and for parents', teachers' and students' governing councils. Further, it coupled these with an insistence that the struggle be conducted in the schools. But it was the demand for an immediate implementation of 'alternative people's education programmes' which represented the radically new departure or emphasis.

In the struggles over education in the 1950s and 1970s described earlier, the aim was to end Bantu Education; what was to replace it was by no means clearly spelt out. What seemed often to be implied and what, in fact, was sometimes stated explicitly, was a demand that black education should be resourced on a par with white education and that the same education as whites received, of course freed of racism, should be made available to blacks. The formulation of the object of the education struggle in these terms seems to have been the inescapable consequence of the traditional critique of Bantu Education, which was based upon a comparison of its inadequacies and impoverishment with the supposed adequacies and riches of white education. White education was not itself subjected to a critique; its undemocratic organisation, its individualistic orientation, its internal inequalities, its elitism and its methods of teaching were never put in question. The underlying assumption was that white education would give black people access to the opportunities in the labour market and elsewhere which were, at present, the monopoly of the whites.

But even when this position was not adopted, the major thrust was a rejection of Bantu Education with little or nothing being said about alternative educational systems. Nor was this deficiency corrected when, in 1985, the students put forward the slogan of 'Freedom now, Education later'; although the starting point was a critique of Bantu Education, the question of what should replace it was to be postponed until liberation had been won. There was no room here for the struggles for education and for freedom to be combined within the schools.

The notion of 'people's education' began to be defined at the Education Crisis Conferences. A number of similar broad definitions were advanced: people's education is education which serves the people as a whole, which liberates, which puts people in command of their lives and which is determined by and accountable to the people. (Sisulu, Keynote speech). Or, in slightly different terms, an education which prepares people for total human liberation and for full participation in all social, political or cultural spheres of society, helps people to be creative, to develop a critical mind and to analyse. (Mkwatsha, Keynote speech, December 1985). The implication, as Sisulu, expressing a widely held view, put it was that 'people's education can only be finally won when we have won the struggle for people's power'.

But what the National Consultative Conference wanted to do in the context of the South African situation in 1985 was to define people's education less generally and, above all, **in a way which did not simply postpone its construction entirely until after liberation**. Indeed, for the NECC, people's education has a threefold character: it does define certain of the elements of a future education system, but at the same time, it projects them as objectives which can, to an important extent, be struggled for and realised in the present, thus putting in place the structures and practices which constitute the indispensable foundation for a future education system.

The Conference declared that people's education is education that:

i) enables the oppressed to understand the evils of the apartheid system and prepares them for participation in a nonracial, democratic system;

ii) eliminates capitalist norms of competition, individualism, and stunted intellectual development and one that encourages collective input and active participation by all, as well as stimulating critical thinking and analysis;

iii) eliminates illiteracy, ignorance and exploitation of any person by another;

iv) equips and trains all sectors of our people to participate actively and creatively in the struggle to attain people's power in order to establish a nonracial democratic South Africa;

v) allows students, parents, teachers and workers to be mobilised into appropriate organisational structures which enable them to enhance the struggle for people's power and to participate actively in the initiation and management of people's education in all its forms;

vi) enables workers to resist exploitation and oppression at their work place.

By formulating people's education in this way, the Conference laid the basis for the immediate construction of alternative educational programmes and structures which would co-exist with and begin to displace Bantu Education.

The Emergency declared in June 1986 clearly put enormous obstacles in the way of any attempt either to restructure the organs of control of the Bantu Education system or to teach alternative courses such as the new history syllabus recently prepared by the NECC. But the emergency powers are not, on their own, necessarily decisive; the presence or absence through boycotts of the students in the schools is equally important. The strictures on the struggle for education can only be eroded or evaded once the boycott ends.

The decision of the crisis conferences and policies pursued by the NECC to end the school boycotts and to organise the struggle around the programme of 'people's education for people's power' as against the boycott strategy and its slogan of 'liberation first, education later', raised in a very direct way the issue of the role of students and their organisations in the current phase of the struggle. There is room for compromise, but also conflict, here, both over questions of strategic priorities and organisational autonomy.

The national crisis conferences recognised both the obvious point that students and their organisations were crucial for raising alternative structures of education, and the more general point that educational struggle was central to national liberation.

The student organisations have long held the similar view, that the transformation of education is conceivable only as part of social transformation. They would doubtless agree with the position adopted by the crisis conferences or by the NECC when, for example, in March 1986 the National Education Conference noted the hardships caused to the communities by the rise in rents and of prices for other necessities, agreed that community and educational problems had the same source, and resolved:

> to urge all communities and democratic organisations to launch appropriate regional and/or national mass action campaigns, by considering all forms of rent, consumer and other boycott.[3]

However, such a broad view of the education struggle carries with it a conception of social forces and organisations outside education with which the struggle for people's education and power must jointly be waged. Thus the allies of the students are defined as the workers ('who are, in turn, the parents of our students'), parents, teachers, and the community and political leaders. Moreover, this alliance must be given force, according to the National Education Conference, by forging 'close links between students, worker and community organisations' and by co-ordinating action in the different areas.

The questions which arise concern the character of the alliance and the position of the student organisations within it. Although, as pointed out earlier, the student organisations lost their overall leading role quite soon after Soweto 1976, they retained a high degree of autonomy and a leading role within the struggle for education. It is clear that the formation of bodies like the Parents' Crisis Committee, the holding of the crisis conferences and particularly the constitution of the NECC were intended to redefine the relationship between student and other organisations: student autonomy would be reduced by incorporating

---

[3]   NECC (1986), p. 9.

them into broadly based co-ordinating organisations.

Although the NECC quickly achieved a central position in the education sphere, it is not yet completely clear how far it has been able to shape the character of the education struggle and win the adherence of students and their organisations since March 1986. In part this is because of the hampering effect of the Emergency and the difficulty in obtaining information due to the news blackout. Nevertheless, it seems possible to identify two stages.

From March to December 1986 the stay-away from the schools continued at a very high level, despite the call by the NECC and the student organisations associated with it to terminate the boycott. The boycott then virtually ended in January 1987. The South African National Students Congress, which associates itself with the NECC, was formed thereafter. In what way and to what extent this will lead to the resurgence of political struggle within the terrain defined by Bantu Education, but aimed at a radical restructuring of the control and content of education within the schools, is not yet clear. Indeed, a recent statement by Eric Molobi of the NECC puts this strategy in doubt, for he suggests that the struggle for people's education should be conducted by establishing 'people's schools':

> [...] the time has arrived for all freedom loving and democratic and progressive organisations, academics and students to initiate a national campaign of establishing schools. While demanding the re-opening of schools, we must go out there to use every church building, every garage, every empty room and available open space to establish people's schools to counter this traumatic, backward and reactionary policy of closing schools when education should be the right of every human being.

Whatever the direction, however, there are already signs of a new stage in the struggle for education.

Further Reading

Bundy, C.,   'Schools and Revolution' *New Society* Vol. 75 No 1202 1986, pp. 52-55.

Chisholm, L., and
Christie, P.,   'Restructuring in Education' *South African Review* 1 (1983).

Cooper, C., *et al*,   *Race Relations Survey* (Johnannesburg:

South African Institute of Race Relations, 1985).

Hyslop, J., 'Teachers and Trade Unions' *South African Labour Bulletin* 11, 6 (1986).

Kallaway, P., ed., *Apartheid and Education* (Ravan Press: Johannesburg, 1984).

NECC, *South Africa in Crisis: Report on the Second National Education Conference* (Distributed by CIIR: London, 1986).

12. Literature
& Apartheid

ELIZABETH GUNNER

I want to explore the ways in which writers have operated in a system which in a variety of ways has tried to shackle them, or to direct them along certain prescribed paths of expression. I also want to include in my definition of literature, potent forms of verbal art which may only occasionally, or never, appear as written literature; these may still provide a powerful comment on the experience of apartheid. Indeed in the South African context it is vital to redefine what constitutes 'literature'. Terry Eagleton has pointed out how notions of what 'literature' is have shifted in British society according to the taste of various periods, and he has argued for a broader definition of literature which challenges that expressed by the dominant ideology.[1] The South African situation, with its complex cultural strands, within which there exist radically different notions of the role of the artist, also demands a re-assessment of what constitutes 'literature'.

There has been much debate about the role of the writer and the artist in the current struggle, in journals such as the Johannesburg-based *Staffrider*. No single view prevails but there is a feeling at present that new demarcations have been drawn. The old reign of 'high culture and high literature', fostered by a looking to literary fashions across the seas, has gone for good. Current preoccupations centre on two issues. First, by what means can literature engage most effectively in the struggle for change? Secondly, there is a determination to forge a new aesthetic that acknowledges and exploits the dynamics of black culture, a culture that has both urban and rural roots, and which often vividly combines the historical and contemporary, as in Matsemela Manaka's play *eGoli* or in those of Maishe Maponya.[2] It is a culture that places great emphasis on the rhetoric of the spoken word and sees song and dance as important vehicles of contemporary artistic and political

---

[1] Terry Eagleton, *The Theory of Literature: An Introduction* (Blackwells: Oxford, 1983). See Introduction and Chapter 1.

[2] Matsemela Manaka, *eGoli: City of Gold* (Ravan: Johannesburg, 1981); Maishe Maponya, *The Hungry Earth* (Polyptoton: Johannesburg, 1981).

expression. Accepting these new demands means that written literature must be put within a new cultural continuum, so that it is seen as one of a number of forms of artistic expression that comment on and reflect contemporary experience in South Africa. It means that written literature itself may be forced to behave in new ways - closer to 'orature'; poetry may either be written but nonetheless frequently performed or it may be written in the knowledge that it will work best only when it is declaimed in a crowded room or hall, or by a graveside. Such poetry is often relatively safe from the censor because it travels as much by word of mouth as on the printed page.

In this new aesthetic the language question is also raised. Is English to be the queen of languages for the embattled poets and creative artists of the present and for those in the new society ahead? Or must there be some accommodation for the main African languages of Sotho, Xhosa and Zulu? Is there also a possibility that even Afrikaans, which is so often the language of oppression, may be taken hold of by the black majority and used as a vehicle of expression on *their* terms? At a People's Cultural Day held in February 1987 at the University of Witwatersrand, the popular black group from near Pretoria, The Soshanguve Black Tycoons, sang to a largely black audience of over two thousand people in three languages, Zulu, English and in one case, Afrikaans. The Afrikaans' song seemed to have been absorbed into the group's African idiom on their terms; it had been 'detribalised' and made into part of a new, composite cultural statement. But the songs the Black Tycoons sang were mainly courting and love songs, using the urban style known as *isicathamiya* and popularised by the nationally famous group The Ladysmith Black Mambazo. Significantly, perhaps, in the freedom songs, the songs of hope, despair and defiance rendered on the same occasion by a large Youth Group from Soshanguve, the languages used were Zulu and English - sometimes in the same song, as in the song which had one message, 'unity'. The words were simply,
HLANGANANI: COME TOGETHER PEOPLE OF AFRICA.
and it ended with the whole hall with its thousands of people clasping hands and swaying and singing the words. That composite expression of co-ordinated mass movement, of song and words, in this case ones which reflected a strongly felt political need, is itself characteristic of the new kind of African aesthetic which might emerge to form the basis of a new national culture.

In a recent article in the radical Afrikaans journal *Stet*, the poet Jeremy Cronin, author of the collection of poems titled *Inside* - written mainly while he was in prison - argues the case for a national culture. It must, he says, 'surely be primarily African in character, reflecting the aspirations and way of life of the majority of South Africa's inhabitants. It will also have to be primarily of the working class, for that is the only class capable through its numbers and its place in production of transforming our society in a democratic direction'. Cronin goes on to say that whites should lead the way for their own people: 'It is not a question of abandoning our roots, our own languages and cultures...but our cultures need to be developed and used to draw our people together in the struggle to eradicate apartheid and all forms of oppression and exploitation'.[3] You might say that there is nothing particularly surprising in what Jeremy Cronin is pleading for here. But it is worth emphasising that it is a poet writing, and one who has performed his poetry frequently at political gatherings in the Cape, primarily at United Democratic Front meetings. Indeed, it is often the poets and writers themselves who are in the forefront of the debate about the role of art in the struggle for change and who see the expression of their art as a legitimate part of that struggle.

If there are now signs of bold efforts to create a unified culture composed of different languages and cultural backgrounds, these must be seen in opposition to a history of determined balkanisation and fragmentation. The state has so many times seemed to understand only too well the power of rhetoric, either spoken or written, the power of art and cultural symbols in a political struggle, and has tried to repress them. One of the earliest of South African writers to create through his fiction a sense of a rich dialogue of peoples and cultures, and one who gave a sense of history being made primarily by the African inhabitants of the land, was Sol Plaatje. This remarkable man was the first Secretary of the South African Native Congress, formed in 1912, which later became the African National Congress. Although he wrote his novel, *Mhudi*, in English, he saw the value of his own language, Tswana, and published the earliest collection of Tswana proverbs. He also documented the upheaval and trauma caused by the enactment of one of the cornerstones of apartheid, the Natives Land Act of 1913. His novel *Mhudi* was written about 1917 but not published until 1930, when Lovedale Mission Press brought it out (in a somewhat censored

---

3   Jeremy Cronin, 'Towards a National Culture: Oedipus and Albino and Others', *Stet* 3, 2, (June 1985), pp.16-17.

form).[4] Set in the 1830s, the book was an epic tale of two Barolong lovers, Mhudi and Ra-Thaga, who made their way across the hinterland of the country from the dry western interior to the high country in the east, bordering on present-day Lesotho. There, in present-day Thaba-Nchu, they met up with the remnant of their people who had previously been scattered by the powerful Ndebele under Mzilikazi. The novel showed Barolong, Ndebele and Boers all seeking rights over the same vast hinterland; it showed Barolong and Ndebele people negotiating as equals or superiors with the Boers who crossed their paths. It showed them practising the art of government, with debate and democratic decisions, particularly in the case of the Barolong, whose leader was favourably contrasted with the more authoritarian figure of Mzilikazi. The novel also gave a strong sense of the importance of public oratory and public debate in the African societies portrayed. As part of the device of showing the societies from within, Plaatje included part of the praise poem of Mzilikazi, 'The Kicked One', the aggressive but finally tragic Ndebele leader.

This book may not have been widely read at the time of its publication in 1930, outside the then small circle of middle class black intelligentsia. The alternative image which it projected may therefore have been perceived by only a handful of black, and perhaps white, readers. Yet it drew a picture of a confident past and a history shared as equals between the country's different racial groups. It used history quite brilliantly, to create an image for the present and the future; it was an image that in its cultural egalitarianism and emphasis on a shared history flatly contradicted the ruling orthodoxy on racial hierarchy and segregation at that time. Also, in looking to the past as a source of wisdom and inspiration, *Mhudi* foreshadowed some of the preoccupations of the Black Consciousness writers and thinkers of the 'Seventies. It is in many ways a prophetic novel. As the German-Jewish critic Walter Benjamin reminds us, 'To articulate the past historically does not mean to recognise it "the way it was". It means to seize hold of a memory as it flashes up at a moment of danger'.[5] Plaatje was indeed seizing hold of a potent memory of the past at a moment of great danger, when the prospects for the African peoples of

---

4   Sol Plaatje, *Mhudi* ed. Stephen Gray, introd. Tim Couzens, (Heinemann African Writers Series: London, 1978); see also Brian Willan, *Sol Plaatje: South African Nationalist 1876-1932*, (Heinemann: London, 1984).

5   In Terry Eagleton, *On Walter Benjamin Or Towards a Revolutionary Criticism* (New Left Books: London, 1981), p.56.

his country - left out of the Act of Union in 1910, deprived of land rights in 1913 - were very bleak indeed. His novel provided a humane and courageous riposte to apartheid long before the term was officially invented.

If Sol Plaatje took images from the pre-colonial past to illuminate a moment of present danger, another writer R.R.R. Dhlomo, who published in both Zulu and English, turned his attention in his English writing to the industrial 'present'. He wrote in a style of melodramatic and macabre realism about the stark conditions of black miners on the Rand in the late nineteen-twenties and early 'thirties. His first stories were published in a renegade European journal - the first of many that were to follow - called *Sjambok*, published by the actor and author Stephen Black. Herbert Dhlomo, the brother of R.R.R., described the *Sjambok* as follows:

> The policy of the journal was to fight evil and corruption in the life of the community. It recognised neither class, colour, race nor rank. High and low, rich and poor, black and white meant nothing to this once famous, much feared journal. Wrong was its enemy, its red rag for attack; right its guiding principle and ideal.[6]

The critic Tim Couzens, biographer of Herbert Dhlomo, describes *Sjambok* as a kind of *Private Eye* of the time![7] R.R.R. Dhlomo's stories, often based on real events, were quite gory and full of pain and pathos. They depicted the brutalising effect of mine compound life on black miners, and exposed the tensions of authority, as white bosses operated sometimes through black go-betweens or sometimes directly with inept heavy-handedness, with the mass of ordinary men. A story like 'Juwawa', for instance, shows the revenge of a man who is hit by a white surveyor and turns to an *inyanga* or traditional doctor, for help. It appeared in *Sjambok* on 12 Sept 1930:

> In a sheltered spot at the foot of a towering waste-dump, Juwawa the boss-boy, one eye badly swollen and a large lump disfiguring his forehead, stood facing an aged blanketed figure, known in every Compound as 'Keleti, the Shangaan Witchdoctor'.
>
> The aged one, seated on a low boulder, was idly tossing the bones into a small circle traced in the dust before him. From the filthy folds of a piece of knotted linen which he had at last succeeded in untying, Juwawa now withdrew a gold 10s coin.

---

6   Herbert Dhlomo, *Inkundla yaBantu* (August 1946), reprinted in *English in Africa* Vol. 2, 1, (March 1975), p.9.

7   *English in Africa* Vol. 2, 1, (March 1975), p.3.

Dropping it into the circle where it lay glittering beside the bones he stood eagerly watching the wizard...A thin smile came fleeting to the lips of the wizard as he quietly contemplated the inflamed eye and quivering anger of the man before him.

Taking up his bones from their bed of dust, he held them tightly clenched in one hand, while the other covered his face. Slowly he started swaying, back and forth, side to side, and as he swayed he chanted softly. The purport of his chant was at first barely audible to Juwawa's straining ears, but as the voice grew louder, a look of cunning satisfaction crept into his face. Eagerly he strained forward, that no word might be lost; and when the old man suddenly broke off and with a sharp cry dashed the bones into the circle, examining their layout with aged, critical eyes, Juwawa stood breathlessly awaiting his verdict.

Completely satisfied - with his course of action now clearly settled in his mind, Juwawa turned and hastened back to the Compound.

As you can probably guess, the white surveyor was killed in a mining accident a few days later. Juwawa was suspected of being involved but nothing could be proved. He was dismissed and sent home. The story ends like this:

On his way to the Railway Station he sang; the atmosphere of his song, triumphant, and in the words a singular sentiment. 'Ya Keleti! Ya Keleti, that was good advice!' sang Juwawa, the savage.[8]

In this story Dhlomo outlines the limited options open to a mine worker such as Juwawa and shows his recourse to covert resistance, without condemning or condoning his actions.

In the mid nineteen-thirties, after his period of mine stories which exposed the seamy underbelly of industrial life, Dhlomo began to write in Zulu. He had presented an alternative image of the black worker - an image from the inside; now he turned his attention to something very different, an interpretation of the glorious Zulu past, for the benefit of Zulu speakers beleaguered in an inglorious and dispossessed present. In his four royal novels, particularly the first two, named after the early kings, *uShaka* and *uDingane*, he presented his readers with a fairly unsentimental image of the past, a past which somehow had to be seen in relation to the inauspicious present, where by the mid-thirties features such as the Pass Laws were an essential element in the life of

---

[8] 'Juwawa' in *The Sjambok* (22 August 1930), reprinted in *English in Africa* Vol.2, 1, (1975), pp.28-30.

every black man.[9]

Another Zulu writer who wrestled with the question of how to re-interpret the Zulu past and how to write in a society where his own people were becoming increasingly dispossessed and displaced was the poet, novelist and scholar, Benedict Wallet Vilakazi. His poetry showed his fascination with the English Romantic poets as well as with the *izimbongi* or praise poets of Zulu culture. Yet one of his finest poems, written when he had left Natal and was working in the nineteen-forties at the University of Witwatersrand, focused, as Dhlomo's English writing had done, on that symbol of capitalist progress, the mines. Like Dhlomo's, Vilakazi's eyes were fixed on the plight of the black mineworkers, as he tried to interpret the bleak present in the light of a very different and distinguished past, while also meditating on the future. This is a short-ish extract (in translation) from his long poem '*Ezinkomponi*' - 'On the Gold Mines':

> Rumble on, machines of the gold mines
> Thunder from first light to sun's sinking:
> Ah, stop plaguing me, I'll wake up.
> Rumble on, machines, and drown out
> The groans of the black working men
> Whose bodies ache with throbbing weals
> Struck by the thuds of the stifling air,
> On their limbs the stink of sweat and dirt:
> Sapped of the vigour of their loins...
>
> Not so loud there, you machines;
> Though whitemen may be without pity
> Must you too, made of iron, treat me thus?...
>
> Be careful, though I go unarmed today
> There was a time when from these worn-out arms
> Long-bladed spears were flung far and wide
> Whose whirling dimmed the whole earth;
> They shook the empire of the She Elephant *
> Thinned out Paul's ** boers - then I was struck down.
> Now I am forever dreaming, child of iron,

---

9   R.R.R. Dhlomo, *uDingane* (Shuter and Shooter: Pietermaritzburg, 1935); *uShaka* (Shuter and Shooter: Pietermaritzburg, 1936); *uMpande* (Shuter and Shooter: Pietermaritzburg, 1938); *uCetshwayo* (Shuter and Shooter: Pietermaritzburg, 1952); *Dinuzulu* (Shuter and Shooter: Pietermaritzburg, 1968).

That this earth of my forefathers once again
Will be restored to the rightful Black hands...[10]
* Queen Victoria   ** President Kruger

It is clear that although Vilakazi refers specifically to past Zulu victories he uses the references as emblems of a wider, confident African past. In his thoughts for the future, his reference to 'rightful Black hands' expresses a longing for a broader African repossession of the land and an inheritance that is far more than narrowly Zulu. His vision is both regional and national, and in an important way he is able to embrace both rural and urban sensibilities. This is rare among South African writers of any race.

B.W. Vilakazi died young, in 1947, at the age of 42, but even had he lived on into the 1950s he would probably not have interacted with the raucous, zany, prolific and frequently penetrating writers based on the Rand, and known, now, as the *Drum* generation, after the racy English-language black magazine for which many of them worked. The writer and critic Lewis Nkosi refers to this period of the 1950s as 'the Fabulous Decade'.[11] Nkosi, now Professor of English at the University of Zambia, was himself a *Drum* man in his youth. It was in this rich yet in many ways wasted period of literary creativity that the thread of exile began to show as a significant feature of South African creative life, an exile frequently forced on writers through political pressure. The Rand-based writers of this period whom I have in mind were Can Themba - king of them all in the eyes of many - Casey 'Kid' Motsisi, Bloke Modisane, Todd Matshikiza who wrote the score of the musical 'King Kong', Nat Nakasa, the young Henry Nxumalo, and Ezekiel Mphahlele, who worked on *Drum* for a time. This group of writers did not look to the past for emblems to illuminate the present. They fixed their eyes firmly on where they were. They were urban to their fingertips. They wrote about the crowded back-streets, side-streets, alleys, shanties and shebeens of places like Alexandra, and Sophiatown, the African area of Johannesburg that was soon to crumble under the bulldozers of separate development and the Group Areas Act.

---

[10]   B.W. Vilakazi, 'Ezinkomponi', in *Amal'ezulu*, (Witwatersrand University Press: Johannesburg, 1945), pp.41-45; in translation in Jack Cope and Uys Krige (eds.) *The Penguin Book of South African Verse* (Penguin: Harmondsworth, 1968), pp.300-305.

[11]   Lewis Nkosi, *Home and Exile* (Longman: London, 1965 rev. ed. 1985).

Some of Can Themba's pieces were fictional, such as his chilling piece about a husband's obsessive jealousy, called 'The Suit'. But many of his most memorable stories were accounts of everyday life for the thousands of black urban dwellers in sprawling urban and peri-urban Johannesburg. One such story, 'The Dube train', told of a typically crowded urban journey with a typical mixture of wit and disgust. The young thug or tsotsi on whom the story centres is a brutalised figure, but Themba in his understated, off-hand way, points out the deeper level of alienation that affects the responses of many in such a society. At one point, just before the crisis in the story that ends with the tsotsi being hurled 'clean through the paneless window' of the train, Themba relates how the tsotsi pursues a young woman whom he has been molesting:

The tsotsi followed, and as he passed me he reeled with the sway of the train.

To steady himself, he put a full paw in my face. It smelled sweaty-sour. Then he ploughed through the humanity of the train, after the girl. Men gave way shamelessly, but one woman would not take it. She burst into a spitfire tirade that whiplashed at the men.

'Lord, you call yourself men, you poltroons! You let a small ruffian insult you. Fancy, he grabs at a girl in front of you - might be your daughter - this thing with the manners of a pig! If there were real men here, they'd pull his pants off and give him such a leathering he'd never sit down for a week. But no, you let him do this here; tonight you'll let him do it in your homes. And all you do is whimper, "The children of today have never no respect!" Sies!'

The men winced. They said nothing, merely looked round at each other in shy embarrassment. But these barbed words had brought the little thug to a stop. He turned round, scowled at the woman, and with cold calculation cursed her anatomically, twisting his lips to give the word the full measure of its horror.

It was like the son of Ham finding a word for his awful discovery. It was like an impression that shuddered the throne of God Almighty. It was both a defilement and a defiance.[12]

The tsotsi is then, in fact, challenged and brutally dealt with. What perhaps disturbs the reader most is Themba's final comment: 'Odd that no-one expressed sympathy for the boy or man. They were just greedily

---

[12]   Can Themba, *The Will to Die* (Heinemann African Writers Series: London, 1972), pp.60-62. Both 'The Suit' and 'The Dube train' are included in the excellent collection of short shories edited by Mbulelo Mzamane, *Hungry Flames and other stories* (Longman African Classics, 1986).

relishing the thrilling episode of the morning'.[13] Themba was a cool, investigative journalist who in stories such as 'Kwashiorkor' exposed the horrors of child hunger, poverty and neglect in the middle of the golden city. Yet the *Drum* report that seems to have brought about the biggest clash with the authorities and, in particular, the Special Branch, was his series on white Christians' attitudes to a black man attending their services in the various denominations scattered through the white suburbs of Johannesburg. It was called 'Brothers in Christ - Mr Drum walks into colour-bar churches'.[14] Mr Drum (Can Themba!) receives a range of receptions as he tries out various churches, Baptist, Methodist, Seventh Day Adventist, Anglican, Roman Catholic, but the worst reception, and in a way the most humorously described is, predictably, from a Dutch Reformed Church. Here he is arrested after the service by a Major in the Special Branch, bundled into a car and asked if he is a member of the African National Congress. Themba replies,

'No'.
'Any other organisation?'
'No. Only "Drum".'

The Methodist Church has the last word in this report. As Mr Drum selects his pew and pages through his hymnbook,

A man walked over threateningly to me from the front pew - then he said, 'Glad to have you with us!' There was a big Christian brotherly smile on his face and the grip of his handshake was firm and sincere. They were trying to make something of people being 'brothers in Christ'. Their battle was a difficult one, but at least they had one thing on their side...the promise that man was fundamentally good.[15]

The writers of the Fabulous Decade were not political activists. They often took refuge in drink, and perhaps too often used the ironic or the comic mode. Can Themba was famous for his boozing capacity; Casey 'Kid' Motsisi set most of his sketches in the shebeens of Sophiatown and Alexandra; Bloke Modisane, in his autobiography, *Blame Me On History* seems to have been tipsy almost more often than he was

---

13 *Will to Die*, p.62.
14 *Will to Die*, pp.73-79. 'Kwashiorkor' is in *Will to Die*, pp.14-26.
15 *Will to Die*, pp.76,77.

sober.[16] Yet these writers gave a new sense of what black urban culture was. They defined it as having its own vibrancy, its own centre and its own identity. They wrote about it with the vigour of celebration and so in an important way they provided a counter image both to the racist view of the faceless black man, and to the one-dimensional if more compassionate liberal view of the black man as victim. As black writers in a world of white editors often constrained by financial interests, they lived dangerously on the tensions between vitality and despair, and they paid heavily for their dash and their bravado. Nkosi and Ezekiel Mphahlele have survived, but of the others, Todd Matshikiza went into exile in London where he wrote his autobiographical *Chocolates for my Wife* and died later in Zambia; Nat Nakasa left on a one-way ticket to America as the South African Government would only give him an exit permit, and he committed suicide not long after his arrival there. The young Henry Nxumalo who exposed the vicious system of black penal farm labour was murdered by thugs late one night in Sophiatown. Can Themba was banned, went into exile in Swaziland and died there. Only Casey 'Kid' Motsisi stayed on, writing for *Drum*, *The World* and the journal *The Classic* founded by Nat Nakasa. He died in 1977 and so for many years provided a much-valued link with that vital and spirited group of black urban commentators.

For some of the writers of the Black Consciousness era of the early and mid-seventies, figures such as Themba and Nakasa were vital early models. The writer and critic Njabulo Ndebele recalled in an interview I had with him in June 1984[17] that, as a boy from 1960 on, he had been an avid reader of his father's monthly copy of the creative journal *The Classic*. He went on to say that the writing of people like Nat Nakasa, Casey Motsisi, Can Themba and Lewis Nkosi had channelled his imagination 'towards our lives in South Africa. They gave me the sense that life around me was also a valid subject for literature'. That might seem an extraordinarily obvious thing to say, but in the context of the highly fragmented, constantly dislocated world of black South African life and writing, his remark shows the importance of links, and how fragile continuities within a specifically South African black, urban consciousness can nevertheless be built up.

---

16 Bloke Modisane, *Blame Me on History* (Thames and Hudson: London, 1964); Casey Motsisi, *Casey and Co.: Selected Writings of Casey 'Kid' Motsisi* ed. Mothobi Mutloatse, (Ravan: Johannesburg, 1978); Todd Matshikiza, *Chocolates for My Wife* (Hodder and Stoughton: London, 1961; David Philip: Cape Town, 1982).

17 Elizabeth Gunner, 'Time to Pluck the Apple', *New African* (July 1985), p.41.

The heady period of Black Consciousness of the early seventies which was to flower in blood in 1976, was marked in the first instance, though, by a resurgence of poetry rather than prose. It was in this era that the influence of other wider, older elements in black culture showed themselves - I am thinking of the emphasis on performed poetry mentioned at the beginning of this chapter. Much of the early poetry of the Black Consciousness period, for instance Oswald Mtshali's poems in *Sounds of a Cowhide Drum* (SCD),[18] was frequently performed to smaller or bigger groups in the townships. This in itself was a link with the aesthetics of traditional poetry. Also, unlike much western poetry, much traditional poetry is easily and naturally, political. As Tony Emmett has pointed out, 'There is no necessary break in continuity between traditional political poetry and modern politics; rather, oral literature and the interest in politics have proved remarkably adaptable to the twentieth century'.[19] Mtshali used stark images to capture the pain and degradation of black urban life in poems such as 'The Face of Hunger' (SCD p.39) and in the grisly poem 'An Abandoned Bundle', on a baby eaten by scavenging dogs while its mother

had melted into the rays of the rising sun
her face glittering with innocence
her heart as pure as untrampled dew. (SCD p.60)

He also wrote of rural poverty and dispossession in a poem such as 'Reapers in a Mealiefield' (SCD p.10) and so embraced rural consciousness into his picture of dispossession. He was criticised by Njabulo Ndebele for dwelling on the passive, victim image of the black experience, and for not going beyond this to assert, to challenge, and to celebrate a positive identity.[20] Yet there is in fact a strong note of celebration which captures the essence of black consciousness in some of Mtshali's poems. Coming as he does from the Vryheid area in Natal, an area steeped in the Zulu traditions of pre-colonial independence and cultural pride, he uses the cultural symbols from his past to comment on the present with relevance and urgency. These lines from the title poem celebrate a rich past-present identity and challenge his fellow

---

[18]   Oswald Mtshali, *Sounds of a Cowhide Drum* (Renoster: Johannesburg, 1971).

[19]   Tony Emmett, 'Oral, Political and Communal Aspects of Township Poetry in the Mid-Seventies', *English in Africa* Vol. 6, 1 (1979), p.72.

[20]   Njabulo Ndebele, 'Artistic and Political Mirage: Mtshali's *Sounds of a Cowhide Drum*' in M. Chapman (ed.) *Soweto Poetry* (McGraw-Hill: Johannesburg, 1982), pp.190-193.

Africans to redefine and conscientise themselves. The poem clearly relies in part on a tradition of spoken rhetoric from Zulu:

> Boom! Boom! Boom!
> I am the drum on your dormant soul,
> cut from the black hide of a sacrificial cow.
>
> I am the spirit of your ancestors
> habitant in hallowed huts
> eager to protect,
> forever vigilant.
>
> Let me tell you of your precious heritage
> of your glorious past trampled by the conqueror,
> destroyed by the zeal of a missionary...
>
> O! Hear me, Child!
> in the Zulu dance
> shaking their hearts into a frenzy.
>
> O! Hear me, Child!
> in the night vigils of black Zionists
> lifting their spirits into ecstasy.
>
> Boom! Boom! Boom!
> That is the sound of a cowhide drum -
> the voice of Mother Africa. (SCD p.68)

While poets such as Sipho Sepamla and Wally Serote have developed their own particular poetic idiom, this has been within the general trend towards a growing use of poetry to state the black experience and to challenge the structures of State power. Tony Emmett again points out that whereas older Black Consciousness poets like Sepamla worked in isolation, younger poets have tended to work in groups. And this, he says, points to the relevance of the community in black poetry. He reminds us of the real significance of these communities - and in this he echoes the voices of the 'Fifties writers, and contemporary writers such as Miriam Tlali:

> Townships like Sophiatown, Alexandra and Doornfontein sustain or sustained, not only physical but cultural and moral life in which the values of the white suburb become irrelevant. Unlike the white poet who writes within an individualistic tradition and who is usually a member of a highly individualistic community, the black poet is

often a member of a tightly knit community with distinctive mores, cultural norms and dialects. Riot, teargas, detentions, killings have all become an everyday reality in the townships and have found their way into the poetry.[21]

Whereas some writers such as Mothobi Mutloatse now urge a clean break with the old aesthetic values, others like Ndebele question this. He questions the long term usefulness of what he sees as the preoccupation with 'striking a blow for freedom'. This has led, he claims, to superficial writing, the creation of stereotypes, and this does not clarify 'the tragic human experiences of oppression'; it gives no real knowledge, only indictment.[22] His own Noma award-winning collection of stories, *Fools*, strikes no obvious accusatory stances but sinks the reader deep into the experience of the lives of his characters, the children, women, students, and grown men of the townships.[23] His stories celebrate, they define oppression and in a subtle, prophetic way they challenge the white moral authority to rule and hint at its demise. His works, as well as the vibrant and defiant poetry of the townships, are an important element in a new national culture that looks beyond apartheid. So too is the work of young women writers such as Gcina Mhlophe, who in her view of tradition deconstructs the oppressive attitudes of Xhosa patriarchy. Her story of a rape and kidnap which is sanctioned by custom is entitled, deceptively, 'Nokulunga's Wedding'.[24]

White artists, too, can look to a world beyond apartheid. The brave voice of Nadine Gordimer who, in her novel *Burger's Daughter* is able to encase real history and the real words of a banned man, the communist Bram Fischer, in the text of her narrative, must also surely form part of what could be called the new South African writing that challenges the present system at a very deep level.[25] Another challenge to the bland assurance of the state comes through the apocalyptic vision of J.M. Coetzee who, in his *Life and Times of Michael K*, sets out the

[21] Emmett, 'Oral, Political and Communal Aspects of Township Poetry', p.80.

[22] N. Ndebele, 'A Review of Turkish Tales and Some Thoughts on South African Fiction', *Staffrider* Vol.6, 1 (1984), p.44.

[23] Njabulo S Ndebele, *Fools and other stories* (Ravan: Johannesburg, 1983).

[24] Gcina Mhlophe, 'Nokulunga's Wedding' in Susan Brown, Isobel Hofmeyr and Susan Rosenberg (eds.) *Lip: from South African Women* (Ravan: Johannesburg, 1983), pp.82-86.

[25] Nadine Gordimer, *Burger's Daughter* (Jonathan Cape: London, 1979; Penguin: Harmondsworth, 1981).

limbo world of a country deep in civil war.[26]

Finally, one of the newest and perhaps most important elements in the present rich and distinctively South African spectrum of literature and culture is the contribution from the trade unions, representing the oldest and largest working class in the whole of Africa. The workers' play 'The Long March', devised by striking union members from the Sarmcol factory at Howick (a subsidiary of the British Tyre and Rubber Company), shows through a combination of Brechtian techniques, dance, mime and much humour, the story of their eighteen-month strike over the issue of union recognition. Most of the dialogue and the songs are in Zulu. Praise poets who are union members frequently perform to packed COSATU union meetings; they exploit the old forms, yet bring the content right up to the present, and the union choirs exploit a variety of vocal idioms to comment on the state of their country. One such song, with which I shall end, dwells on the need for exile by some in the current struggle. It thus keys into a deep seam of the experience of writers and activists, and of some who, like Alex La Guma, were both. But its theme is typically defiant and, in that, it both characterises the mood of the present and highlights a leitmotif of much that has been sung and written in the past:

Zithulele Mama	Be quiet Mother
Noma sengifile mina	Even if I die
Ngiyobengifele lona	I will be dying for
Izwe lakithi	Our country
Izwe leSouth Afrika.	The country of South Africa.

Zithulele Mama	Be quiet Mother
Noma sengifile mina	Even if I die
Ngiyobengi lwela lona	I will be fighting for
Izwe lakithi	Our country
Izwe leSouth Afrika	The country of South Africa.[27]

[26] J.M. Coetzee, *Life and Times of Michael K* (Secker and Warburg: London, 1983; Penguin: Harmondsworth, 1985).

[27] 'Zithulele Mama' on 'FOSATU Worker Choirs' cassette, Shifty Records, L4 Shift 6; see also Alec Pongweni, *Songs that Won the Liberation War* (College Press: Harare, 1982), p.35, where the 'same' song text appears as a Ndebele liberation song entitled 'Siyabashiya Abazali'.

Further Reading

Alvarez-Pereyre, J.,   *The Poetry of Commitment in South Africa* (Heinemann Educational: London, 1984).

Benjamin, Walter,   'The Storyteller: Reflections on the Works of Nikolai Leskov' in: Benjamin, W., *Illuminations: Essays and Reflections* ed. Arendt, Hannah, (Jonathan Cape: London, 1970).

Breytenbach, Breyten,   *The True Confessions of an Albino Terrorist* (Faber and Faber: London, 1984).

Clingman, Steven,   *The Novels of Nadine Gordimer: History from the Inside* (Allen and Unwin: London, 1986).

Coplan, David,   *In Township Tonight: Black City Music and Theatre* (Longman: London, 1985).

February, V.A.,   *Mind Your Colour: The 'Coloured' Stereotype in South African Literature* (Kegan Paul: London, 1981).

Gray, Stephen, (ed.)   *The Penguin Book of Southern African Short Stories* (Allen Lane: London, 1985).

Heywood, Christopher, (ed.) *Aspects of South African Literature* (Heinemann Educational: London, 1976).

Jordan, A.C.,   *Towards and African Literature: the emergence of literary form in Xhosa* (University Of California Press: Berkeley, 1973).

Kavanagh, R.,   *Theatre and Cultural Struggle in South Africa* (Zed: London, 1985).

Mofolo, Thomas,   *Chaka* trans. from the Sotho by Kunene, D.P. (Heinemann African Writers Series: London, 1981).

Mootry, Maria,   'Literature and Resistance in South Africa: Two Zulu Poets', *African Literature Today* 6, (1970), pp. 112-119.

Ntuli, D.B.Z.,   *The Poetry of B.W. Vilakazi* (Van Schaik: Pretoria, 1984).

Vilakazi, B.W.,   'The Conception and Development of Poetry in Zulu' *Bantu Studies* XII, (1983), pp. 105-134.

Walder, Denis,   *Athol Fugard* (Macmillan: London, 1984).

White, Landeg, and Couzens, Tim, (eds.)   *Literature and Society in South Africa* (Longmans: London, 1984).

Index

Index

Ndebele, Njabula (writer), 227, 228, 230
Ndebele people, 123-9
Ndzundza (Ndebele royal house), 7, 127-9, 132
'Necklace' killings, 128
Ngubane, Harriet (anthropologist), 49
Nhlapo, Mavis (ANC official), 167
Nkomati Agreement (1984), 73, 90
Nkosi, Lewis (journalist and literary critic), 4, 224, 227
Ntuli, Piet (KwaNdebele politician), 124, 127, 128
Nxumalo, Henry (writer), 224, 227
Nyembe, Dorothy (woman activist), 158

O'Dowd, Michael (economist), 19, 28
Onverwacht-Botshabelo (rural slum), 111-14, 118, 119, 120-3, 138-9, 142, 186
Orange Free State, 16, 111-14, 120-2, 135, 138, 141
Ovamboland, 70-1
Oxford History of South Africa, 19, 47-8

Packard, Randall (historian), 189
Parliament
        ineffective, 66; Tricameral, 28, 67, 209
Pass laws, 9, 28, 54, 55, 58, 120, 123, 143, 155, 181
        repealed, 7, 27, 110, 116, 164; restrict political organisation, 157-8; and women,
        121-2, 161, 164; *see also* Apartheid, Housing policy, Section 10 rights,
        Segregation
Peasants
        ambitions, 8, 120, 135-6, 144-5, 149-50, 151; impoverishment, 136-9, 177, 179;
        political struggles, 8, 143-5, 146, 150, 155; survival, 136, 139-45
Pedi people, 126
Plaatje, Solomon (author and politician), 137, 219-21
Pondoland, 143
Population, 115-16, 181-2
        control, 180; geographical trends, 138-9
Port Alfred Women's Organisation (PAWO), 155, 165
Port Elizabeth, 131
Poverty
        black, 4, 42, 45, 105, 115, 157; Carnegie conference on, 137; and disease, 173,
        176, 177, 182-4, 187-8; white, 54, 125, 140, 145-6, 176-7, 179
Pretoria, 117, 118, 138, 163
Prior Laws, 174
Propaganda, 66-7, 93, 172-3, 194; *see also* Misinformation

Qobosa, Percy (editor), 36
Questions, about:
        academic boycott, 11-12, 49-50; agrarian future, 134-6, 146-52; apartheid and
        economic growth, 53; capitalist reform, 62-3, 146-9; disease, 172-3; nationalism,
        7-9, 130-2, 217-19; past and future, 1, 2-4, 13-32, 91-3, 130-2, 146-52, 168-9,
        191-8, 208-15, 223-4; sanctions, 6, 63, 78-80, 86-93, 102-7, 146; the state and its
        legitimacy, 1, 4, 6, 10, 33-51, 52, 103; reform and revolution, 5, 9-10, 21, 69-70,
        100-2, 107, 146-52, 209-15, 218-19; women's emancipation, 166-9
Qwaqwa, 105, 114, 122-3, 138, 142, 187

Radcliffe-Brown school of anthropology, 48
Railways